Metternich and
the German Question

Metternich. *(Courtesy Bild-Archiv der Österreichischen Nationalbibliotek, Wien)*

Metternich and the German Question

States' Rights and Federal Duties, 1820–1834

Robert D. Billinger, Jr.

DELAWARE

Newark: University of Delaware Press
London and Toronto: Associated University Presses

Associated University Presses
440 Forsgate Drive
Cranbury, NJ 08512

Associated University Presses
25 Sicilian Avenue
London WC1A 2QH, England

Associated University Presses
P.O. Box 39, Clarkson Pstl. Stn.
Mississauga, Ontario,
L5J 3X9 Canada

The paper used in this publication meets the requirements of the American National Standard for Permanence of Paper for Printed Library Materials Z39.48-1984.

Library of Congress Cataloging-in-Publication Data

Billinger, Robert D., 1944–
    Metternich and the German question : states' rights and federal duties, 1820–1834 / Robert D. Billinger, Jr.
        p.   cm.
    Includes bibliographical references and index.
    ISBN 0-87413-407-2 (alk. paper)
    1. Austria—Foreign relations—1815–1848.   2. Metternich, Clemens Wenzel Lothar, Fürst von, 1773–1859.   3. Deutscher Bund (1815–1866)—History.   I. Title.
DB81.B55   1991
943'.073—dc20
                                              90-50002
                                              CIP

PRINTED IN THE UNITED STATES OF AMERICA

For Chris, Greta, Eric, and Uncle Billy.

Contents

Abbreviations

BFG	Anton Chroust, ed., *Gesandtschaftsberichte aus München 1814–1848*. Abteilung I: *Die Berichte der französischen Gesandten* (6 vols.; Schriftenreihe zur bayerischen Landesgeschichte, vols. 18, 19, 21–24; Munich: C. H. Beck, 1935–1937).
BGLA	Badisches Generallandesarchiv, Karlsruhe
BGSA	Bayerisches Hauptstaatsarchiv, Abteilung II: Geheimes Staatsarchiv, Munich
BOG	Anton Chroust, ed., *Gesandtschaftsberichte aus München 1814–1848*. Abteilung II: *Die Berichte der österreichischen Gesandten* (4 vols.: Schriftenreihe zur bayerischen Landesgeschichte, vols. 33, 36–38; Munich: C. H. Beck, 1939–1942).
BPG	Anton Chroust, ed., *Gesandtschaftsberichte aus München 1814–1848*. Abteilung III: *Die Berichte der preussischen Gesandten* (5 vols.; Schriftenreihe zur bayerischen Landesgeschichte, vols. 39–43; Munich: C. H. Beck, 1949–1951).
GSA PKB	Geheimes Staatsarchiv Preussischer Kulturbesitz, Berlin
HHSA	Österreichisches Staatsarchiv, Abteilung: Haus-, Hof- und Staatsarchiv, Vienna
NP	Clemens Lothar Wenzel Fürst von Metternich-Winneburg, *Aus Metternichs nachgelassenen Papieren*, ed., Prince Richard von Metternich (8 vols.; Vienna: W. Braumüller, 1880–1884).
PDB	German Confederation, *Protokolle der deutschen Bundesversammlung, 1815–1866.*
WHSA	Württembergisches Hauptstaatsarchiv, Stuttgart
ZSA	Zentrale Staatsarchiv, Merseburg

Preface

Fascination with Metternich, although perennial, has had varying motivations. Each generation has evolved a new image of the Austrian statesman to suit the needs of current politics as well as to reflect the state of historical research. To nineteenth-century German liberals and nationalists—not always the same people—Metternich was the archfiend of reactionary conservatism, the suppressor of the noble spirit of liberalism, and the delayer of the inevitable unification of Germany under Prussia.[1] Between the world wars, Metternich became a clearheaded ideologue, whose principles of conservatism were both warranted and appropriate for the creation of a *Grossdeutschland* (Greater Germany).[2] After the Second World War, Metternich became the unheeded prophet of doom who had unsuccessfully warned against the dangers of demagogues both liberal and national.[3] More recently, in an age of international ideological tensions between communism and democracy, Metternich has emerged as the pragmatic defender of Austrian interests.[4] It is the politics of the period of the interpreter that seems most important in directing both the research and the findings. So it is, of course, with all historical writing—and rightly so. Although the historian searches for the truth, it is a truth that must be both documentable and useful in current contexts—and of course, in that order.

This study, like those before it, reflects present-day interests. In this case, the present day is one in which German central Europe is again searching for an understanding of national identity and a means for its more perfect political realization. Once again the question—the famous "German Question"—concerns what a unified Germany should consist of, how it should be created, and what kind of politics would be suitable for such an entity. Such concerns have revived an interest in the German Confederation, both among professional historians and amateur writers, that is both new and stimulating.[5]

But no study of the German Confederation as "model" or object of past experience can be complete without a reevaluation of the German policies of the Austrian foreign minister who was

11

both the author of that body and its strongest defender. Initial work on the subject has been done in the valuable research on Clemens von Metternich's German policy by Enno Kraehe. His two-volume work takes the study of Metternich's policies on Germany from 1809 to 1815: the struggle against Napoleon and the Vienna Congress.[6] A projected third volume will deal with Metternich's struggle with Tsar Alexander, a major actor in both international and German affairs of the early 1820s.

The focus of my own study will be on the period between the Vienna Conferences of 1820 and those of 1834. These fifteen years saw two of Metternich's attempts to consolidate the political structure of the German Confederation. Through the Vienna Final Act of 1820 and the Sixty Articles of 1834, Metternich tried to give the German princes a proper appreciation of the unique balance of states' rights and federal duties that the confederation offered. Thus he attempted to make the Confederation a school of nationalism for the German princes, a school that taught a pacific, federalistic brand of German nationalism that was Metternich's own creation.[7] This period also saw the emergence of two new threats to Metternich's effort to solve the German Question. There were the rise of the Prussian Zollverein—with its aura of Prussian progressivism—and a renewed revolutionary threat from France. In France, the July Revolution sparked both an aggressive French nationalism and revolutionary emulation in neighboring European states. Meanwhile, Prussian progressivism complicated the problem by threatening either a war with revolutionary France or acquiesence to French ideas of popular sovereignty.[8]

Three themes emerge in a study of Metternich's approach to the German Question during this period of rising French and Prussian threats of the 1820s and 1830s. They are also the theses of this study. One is that Metternich's response to both French and Prussian dangers was the assertion and consolidation of a conservative, monarchic federal unity within the German Confederation. His quest was for German unity, not unification.[9] It was a unity, of course, that was designed to thwart European revolutions and wars and to protect the Austrian interest in avoiding the mastery of Germany by any other power—whether France or Prussia. A second theme and thesis is that Metternich sought not dominance over Germany, but the prevention of that dominance by any other power. It was his honest feeling that Austrian monarchic federalism was in the best interest of both European security and the safety of the German states. He feared that the day that another power's ideology excluded Austrian influence from Germany would be the day of the downfall of the German princes and the end of European peace. This is particularly obvious in his relationship with Prussia, Austria's rival for German leadership, but also her absolutely necessary ally.[10] A major goal of Metternich's German policy was to maintain Austro-Prussian cooperation at all costs. Finally, a third theme and thesis is that Metternich's "control of Germany" was never anywhere near what his popular reputation might imply.[11] The South German states, particularly Württemberg and Bavaria, remained—like Prussia—proudly independent monarchies with their own ideas of sovereign majesty, and their own views of both the shape and content of German nationalism. It will thus be with a particular focus on the South German states—Bavaria, Württemberg, and Baden—that this study will proceed.

That Metternich had any success in dealing with the rulers of these states lies in the fact that his own ideas for a solution to the German Question in the 1820s and 1830s were basically in consonance with their own. German unity against internal revolution or French invasion was best served through the federalism of the German Confederation. Federalism was also the best defense against the dominance in Germany of either of the great German powers, Austria or Prussia. The South German monarchs agreed with Metternich that the exclusion of Austria from Germany would be the end of the power of the individual German princes. They did not, however, readily agree on the proper balance between states' rights and federal duties. That story is the one to be unfolded here.

That I am able to attempt the tale is in large part the result of a Fulbright Fellowship to Vienna that introduced me to the archives in 1969–70 and confirmed my love and fascination for the land and people of Austria. Thanks to the friendly assistance of the personnel at the Haus-, Hof-, und Staatsarchiv in Vienna, the Generallandesarchiv in Karlsruhe, the Geheimes Staatsarchiv in Munich, the Hauptstaatarchiv in Stuttgart, the Geheimes Staatsarchiv in Berlin, and the Zentrale Staatsarchiv in Merseburg, my interest and research have continued in the years since. Those interests have also been sharpened by the example and encouragement of scholars such as Enno Kraehe, who first aroused my interest in Metternich, and fellow travelers of the Consortium on Revolutionary Europe circuit Roy Austensen, Wolf Gruner, Arthur Haas, Loyd Lee, Alan Reinerman, Karl Roider, and Ken Rock. Naturally the tolerance and support of teaching colleagues at Wingate College, editors, and friends have made life with *Metternich and the German Question* both possible and enjoyable along the way for myself and my family. It is particularly to my wife, however, that I owe an immense debt of gratitude and love for the encouragement to stop stalling and write up what I had. Here, therefore, it is.

Metternich and
the German Question

GERMAN CONFEDERATION
CA.1830

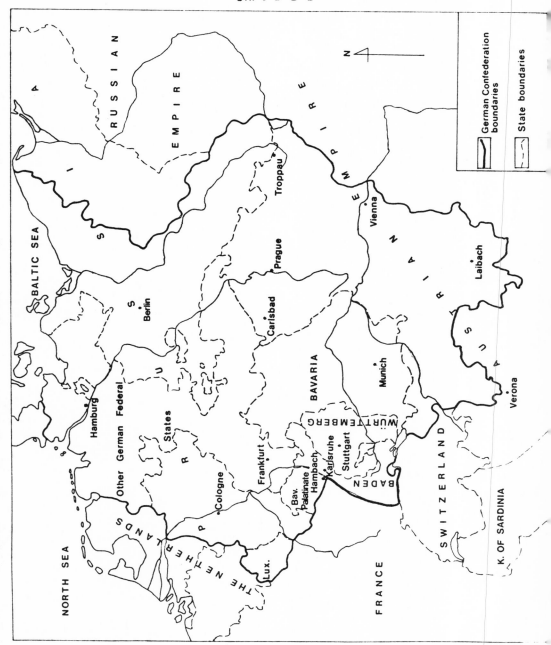

Map by Wladyslaw Jareck

1

Federal Duties and the Metternich System, 1815–1824

Metternich's answer to the German Question emerged clearly in the period between 1815 and 1824. It was that the states of Germany that survived the Napoleonic years should be integrated into a confederation and form, as such, the very keystone of the Vienna Settlement. The German Confederation that was born at the Congress of Vienna in 1815 was specifically designed by Metternich so that its key attraction to the thirty-nine German states that were the survivors of twenty-six years of war and revolution would be that it protected their states' rights and sovereignty. By so doing, it would distract them from their old habits of seeking protection from powerful non-German neighbors. It would end their status as the pawns of the pre-Revolutionary, Revolutionary, and Napoleonic periods, and makeweights that endangered the balance of power in Europe.

For the Austrian foreign minister, Germany in the form of the German Confederation was henceforth to be the keystone of European stability and the chief shield of the Austrian emperor. In exchange for protecting the sovereignty of the German princes, Metternich would ask only that they uphold their federal duties. Those duties he proceeded to reveal to them in the period between 1815 and 1824, as he felt Austrian interests threatened first by Great Power meddling and then by revolutionary tendencies within Germany as throughout Europe. In this period, Metternich first began the tactic that would both confuse and frustrate contemporaries and later historians. He would magnify the German princes' fears of revolution so that they would accept Austrian-inspired federal duties that would both limit outside meddling within the Confederation and stabilize that body against revolutionary imbalances within. Metternich's successes in this regard included the passage and the renewal of the famous Carlsbad Decrees in 1819 and 1824, and the signature of the Vienna Final Act of 1820.

As will be seen in this chapter, acceptance by the German sovereigns of the federal duties implicit in these documents did not come easily. At this point in the life of the newly devised Confederation, the German princes still looked to Great Powers other than Austria to support their preconceived notions of states' rights. The success of Metternich's efforts in these years, therefore, was dependent upon the success of the Metternich System in Europe as a whole. As we shall see, the success of Metternich's answer to the German Question between 1815 and 1824 was dependent upon the Austrian's mastery of the Concert of Europe system. That mastery was manifest in Metternich's diplomacy at the Great Power Congresses of Aix-la-Chapelle, Troppau, Laibach, and Verona. But as Metternich's mastery of the Concert of Europe waned after 1824, so too did the willingness of the German states to accept federal duties at the expense of their states' rights.

The German Confederation was a new centripetal force in central Europe. In the years before the Confederation, the aim of each of the German rulers was simply to preserve his sovereignty as best he could by a variety of German and foreign alliances designed to either please individual Great Powers or to withstand their wrath. The solution that Metternich offered to this German problem of fragmentation and insecurity was not a remodeled Reich, but a confederation of German princes and free cities dedicated to the preservation of the security of the individual German states.[1] It was a solution that Metternich came to as a result of his experience and observations during the Napoleonic years. Then, as thereafter, his chief concern was to see to it that the Habsburg Monarchy would survive. Germany interested him chiefly in so far as Austria could achieve a central European defense community as a barrier against France and Russia and as the keystone of the continental equilibrium.[2] That is not to say that Metternich was not interested in the German Question from a German perspective; he was after all a German imperial prince with a feeling, however vague at times, for a common German fatherland. However, such considerations were only a part of his Great Power politics. Imperial Count Clemens von Metternich-Winneburg had given up any hope for the restoration of the Reich shortly after the establishment of the Confederation of Rhine (the Rheinbund) by Napoleon in 1806.[3] Metternich, like his rival Napoleon, recognized that the Rheinbund states—particularly the newly expanded, but still fragile Kingdoms of Bavaria and

Württemberg and the Grand Duchy of Baden—were important new players in European diplomacy.[4]

With the decline and collapse of Napoleonic power—a decline that the Austrian foreign minister sought to moderate so as to balance the increasing influence of Tsar Alexander—Metternich based his solution to the German Question on his belief that to treat the Rheinbund as conquered territory would only unbalance Great Power influence in central Europe. For the sake of stability the sovereignty of the Rheinbund princes had to be assured and their fears of removal assuaged. As Austrian, Prussian, and Russian troops moved westward toward France in 1813, Metternich ensured the cooperation of the South German rulers, chief beneficiaries of the Rheinbund years, by assuring them their continuing rule and power. He did not alienate them as did Tsar Alexander and Prince Karl von Hardenberg of Prussia. Alexander and his German adviser, Baron Heinrich vom Stein, had visions of a new German Empire dominated by Prussia and Austria and protected by Russia. It would have been a Germany in which the former Rheinbund rulers would have had to share their reduced power with diets made up of popularly elected representatives and members of the old imperial nobility.[5] The latter had lost their political sovereignty during the period of the Rheinbund, when as "mediatized nobles" their domains had been placed under the sovereignty of such rulers as the Kings of Bavaria and Württemberg and the Grand Duke of Baden. Stein's proposals, seconded by Tsar Alexander, would have resurrected the powers of the imperial nobility in a restored Reich at the expense of the former Rheinbund princes. Likewise, the dualistic and absolutistic ideas of the Prussian foreign minister, Prince Karl August von Hardenberg, would have been no better for the German princes of the middle-sized states. Although protected from the inroads of a nobility-dominated parliamentary government envisioned by Stein and the Tsar, the Rheinbund monarchs would have found themselves squeezed back to their pre-Napoleonic powerlessness by the exaggerated dualism of Austria and Prussia. Some of them might even be "mediatized," consigned to holding merely seignorial and feudal, not sovereign, rights.[6]

Because of his diplomacy during the final battles against Napoleon and during the Vienna Congress, Metternich laid the foundations for a federation of German monarchs which, by protecting the sovereignty of the German princes, would make those princes and their states the bulwark that would protect

European, and thus Austrian, peace and stability. As a trusted and revered monarch among fellow German monarchs, the Austrian emperor, Francis I, could exert the influence necessary to protect Austria and Germany from the potentially disruptive influence of the two powerful and ambitious flanking powers, France and Russia. He could also limit and harness the energy of his old rival, the king of Prussia, for the preservation of the status quo in both Germany and Europe. The policy by which Metternich hoped to maintain this answer to the German and thus European Question can best be described as one of conservative monarchic federalism in Germany as a part of his larger Concert of Europe system. It was conservative in the sense that it called for neither innovation nor restoration. He saw as equally dangerous ideas of popular sovereignty, Prussian expansion, or a return to a pre-Napoleonic Germany with its myriad of minor princelings. Through this policy, essentially institutionalizing the status quo, Metternich both confused and disillusioned contemporaries and later historians. By establishing a confederation of the existing sovereign German states and rejecting a more unified German state with overtones of popular sovereignty, he alienated nineteenth-century liberals and their latter-day progeny. By rejecting a return to the old Reich, he gave up his own birthright and became a traitor to his own class. But by accepting and working with the status quo created by Napoleon's Rheinbund and enlarging it into the German Confederation, Metternich harnessed the instincts for self-preservation of the princes of the former Confederation of the Rhine to the new German Bund, a bulwark for peace and stability in central Europe. That was the heart of Metternich's German policy and his answer to the German Question throughout his tenure as Austrian foreign minister.

The obstacles to the effectiveness of Metternich's German policy were many. During the first decade of the Confederation's existence, Metternich faced the centrifugal force of South German particularism with its excessive defensiveness of monarchic sovereignty against any perceived threats from the Confederation. Complicating the problem was the intrusive influence of Tsar Alexander and his representatives in Germany. The Russians, through the marital relations of the imperial family with the ruling families of South Germany and through the encouragement of constitutionalism between 1817 and 1818, fostered the sovereign conceits of the former Rheinbund princes to the point of destabilizing the Confederation. Further complications were added through the hegemonial desires of a variety of Prussian ministers. Although their plans for Prussian dominance were thwarted in 1815, they continually sought means of wresting from Austria the moral leadership of Germany through economic, military, and constitutional projects that could not fail to alter the balance in central Europe. Finally, of course, there were the liberal and nationalist popular currents that remained from the Wars of Liberation.

How Metternich proposed to deal with these problems became evident in the decade after the founding of the Confederation. He proposed to use the fears of liberal and nationalist popular currents to create a monarchic unity on the part of the German sovereigns that would lead them to seek their salvation within the framework of the German Confederation rather than in the innovative but fragmentizing plans of fellow constitutional German states, Russia, or Prussia. Although Metternich's prime interest was in preserving the balance of power in Germany and thus in Europe, he saw this balance most endangered by concessions that states might make to the liberal and nationalist spirit of the age. The danger was then twofold. First there was the danger to the balance of power among the states of Europe; second there was the danger that concessions to revolutionary ideals would only set destructive forces at work. These forces could be either revolutionary or reactionary; either or both would be bad. The end result would be renewal of the instability of the period just passed.

The views that Metternich expressed to his emperor in the summer of 1819 justify this interpretation and help to explain both the cause and intent behind the famous Carlsbad Decrees. They, of course, were the federal legislative acts that enjoined cooperation among the German governments to suppress the increasingly virulent liberal and nationalistic spirit of German university students and the press. But Metternich had goals that went beyond repressing students and newspaper editors. He told Emperor Francis that he was concerned that the German Confederation, Austria's chief defense against the material and moral dangers that threatened from both West and East, was in grave danger. It was endangered by the nationalist agitation in Prussia, the representative constitutions in South Germany, and the advocacy of both nationalism and republicanism by the German press. Under the circumstances, the introduction of a democratic constitution in Prussia would result, he felt, "in the complete overthrow of all existing institutions." Metternich was determined, therefore, to put the German Confederation on a safer footing and ensure its existence. If worst came to worst, however, and revolutionary changes continued in Germany, he was prepared to recommend that Austria separate herself from the Confederation.[7]

As was his custom, Metternich used instances of minor revolutionary dangers to convince others of the existence of greater threats. Also he tried to secure the leverage that came from support by the Great Eastern Powers, Russia and Prussia. The origin of the Carlsbad Decrees is an illustration of this strategy. Intending to stabilize the Confederation by institutionalizing restraint to political change, he made use of student unrest to secure the leverage he sought. The assassination of August von Kotzebue, a secret agent of the Russian tsar, opened the way. When Kotzebue was killed in March, 1819, by a young German revolutionary, Karl Sand, Metternich saw the possibility of manipulating the resulting outrage and fear of both the tsar and the German princes to achieve his ends.[8]

Tsar Alexander, with his urge to be the mentor of Europe after his liberation of the continent from Napoleon, had sought influence in Germany by encouraging the independence of the South German princes.[9] To the dismay of the Austrians, Alexander's agents had encouraged the introduction of constitutional government within the individual states. In pursuit of integrating their newly acquired territories and asserting their independence from Austrian and Prussian influence, Baden, Bavaria, and Württemberg entered the path of constitutional government. The Prussian government was debating a similar move. Now an opening to halt the reformers was at hand, and beyond that the possibility of seeing to it that further reforms were limited by federal constitutional restraints. But first Alexander had to be convinced, although Metternich felt sure that the assassination of his agent would give the tsar second thoughts about hindering federal action against political murderers. Still, Metternich took the precaution of explaining the need for federal action to the tsar through the good offices of both the British and Prussian governments.[10]

As Metternich consistently saw Prussia as Austria's indispensable ally in federal affairs, he took particular pains to win the Hohenzollern ruler for the action he planned. Late in July 1819, at private meetings with King Frederick William III at Teplitz, the Austrian foreign minister put into effect both his tactics of personal diplomacy and his strategy of Austro-Prussian cooperation.

He sought first to separate the king from those of his ministers, like Hardenberg, who advocated the proclamation of a representative constitution in Prussia.[11] Second, he asked for Prussian support to secure the agreement of the other states to federal measures necessary for their own protection. Because of his success in both areas, he was able in August at Carlsbad to win the approval of Germany's leading diplomats to measures designed to give the Federal Diet the power to ensure the repression of political agitation throughout Germany. These so-called Carlsbad Decrees, agreed upon by secret conference, were perfunctorily transformed into federal law by the heretofore neglected Diet at Frankfurt on 20 September 1819.[12]

For Metternich the great importance of the Carlsbad Decrees lay not in their repressive character and short-term effect on student and press subversives, but in the means they established for federal cooperation to thwart revolution.[13] The powers of the Confederation were broadened and strengthened. States were individually to increase press censorship and place state officials in their universities to provide surveillance of potential revolutionaries. More important, a federal investigating commission was created and an execution order stipulated that the Federal Diet, by majority vote, could send detachments of confederate troops to ensure that state governments would fulfill their new duties.[14]

On paper, at least, the sovereignty of the individual states was infringed upon and federal duties increased to ensure the enforcement of Austrian-inspired norms in the Confederation.[15] The particularist rulers of South Germany had only just proclaimed representative constitutions to gain the support of their people for the integration of their diverse territories, but no less to prevent federal infringement upon the powers of their sovereign states.[16] Moreover, they had been encouraged by the agents of the Russian tsar. His foreign minister, Count John Capodistria, sought increased Russian influence in central Europe by supporting German constitutionalism as the basis for an independent bloc of South German constitutional states.[17] But with the confidence of their Russian mentor, as well as their own, shaken by the excesses in the universities, the press, and the new South German diets, the South German princes sacrificed a portion of their pride and independence in the interest of monarchic survival.[18] Metternich bent the German Confederation to his own purposes.[19]

Before the Russians or South Germans could formulate any

articulate resistance to his initiatives, Metternich went on to further institutionalize his ideas on a settlement to the German Question.[20] He implemented plans formulated even before the conclusion of the Carlsbad Conferences to rectify, as he said, the application of Article Thirteen of the Federal Act—the one regarding the institution of state constitutions.[21] Through secret German diplomatic conferences in Vienna in late 1819 and early 1820, he attained agreement to a strictly monarchic delineation of the Federal Constitution in the form of the Vienna Final Act. For security's sake, he also showered Tsar Alexander with communications describing his efforts to protect the monarchic principle and asserting the unanimous and positive reception of his ideas by the Vienna conferees.[22]

Metternich had learned at Carlsbad that he could never persuade the Bavarian and Württemberg governments to revoke their representative constitutions. In Vienna, however, he was able to get them to agree to articles that bound every German prince to retain effective control of his sovereign powers.[23] He also persuaded them to agree to a provision for federal interference in internal state affairs. Although they normally rejected any idea of such interference, the South Germans finally agreed that such action was permissible upon state request or in cases of internal revolt when an official request was impossible.[24] The opposition of the delegates from Bavaria and Württemberg deterred Metternich from developing the proposals of the disillusioned Baden government. Baden was willing for the Confederation to subject all existing constitutions, especially its own, to a wholesale reactionary revision.[25] Metternich was not deterred, however, from a major expansion of federal responsibilities by last minute footdragging by Württemberg. King William at first refused to sanction the results of the meetings as increments to the Federal Act without action by the plenum of the Federal Diet and the prior approval of all the European powers. That is, he wished to thwart a possible increase in federal power at the expense of his sovereignty by calling on Article VI of the Federal Act. Its provisions noted that changes in the Federal Act required a two-third vote of the plenum of the Federal Diet, in which each of the member states received at least one vote and the larger states up to four.[26] Württemberg also wanted to invoke the aid of the European powers who, as signers of the Act of the Congress of Vienna in 1815, of which the Federal Act was a part, could be seen as co-guarantors of that constitution. Joint Austro-Prussian pressure was necessary to force William to back down from this obvious appeal to his Russian brother-in-law.[27] Metternich insisted that the decisions of the conference were final and not even subject to review by the Federal Diet. That body unanimously and perfunctorily proclaimed its acceptance of the Vienna Final Act on 8 June 1820. Metternich bragged to his emperor that a word spoken by Austria was an unbreakable law for Germany.[28]

The period between 1820 and 1823 has been described as a time of "Metternich's diplomacy at its zenith."[29] It is so described because Metternich seemed to be able to manipulate the European powers during this period so that the interests of Austria were protected against revolutionary change, the balance of power in Europe was preserved, and all was done in the name of European peace and stability. At Troppau and Laibach in 1820 and 1821, Metternich succeeded in gaining Prussian and Russian cooperation and the moral support of France for Austrian action against revolutionary uprisings in Naples and Piedmont, all while avoiding the actual military intervention of these powers. Likewise at Verona in 1822, he restrained Tsar Alexander from military intervention in Spain and aligned France with the Eastern Powers by approving French action to suppress a Spanish revolution.[30] These triumphs for the Metternich "system" were, like Metternich's efforts through the Carlsbad and Vienna Conferences of 1819 and 1820, all part of his effort to preserve for Austria the peace and stability of Europe. In each case, Metternich was less fearful of revolution in general than in specific revolutionary actions that would either endanger Austrian territory or stimulate action by other European powers, whether revolutionary or counter-revolutionary, that would upset the European balance of power.[31]

But things are never settled finally in the world of diplomacy. Neither Metternich's success on the broader European scene nor in Germany was a foregone conclusion. In fact, Austrian concerns beyond Germany during the 1820s led to a questioning of her influence in Germany. In 1819 and 1820, under the shadow of revolutionary threats, the princes of Germany submitted— some reluctantly—to Austrian-led conservative federalism. As these threats receded during the 1820s and Austria became more involved in affairs outside the Confederation, the German states attempted to reassert their independence and particularism.[32] Federal unity, under Austrian direction, was never achieved to the degree to which Metternich hoped, his adversaries feared, and liberal historians have bemoaned. Particularism reigned. The

individual German states sought their own advantage and protected their own sovereignty with little reference to Austria and
the putative demands of the reformed German Confederation.
Metternich would feel forced again to try to duplicate his success
at Carlsbad in 1819 by the renewal of the Carlsbad Decrees in
1824. The unity of the German Confederation continually had to
be asserted against the particularism of the German princes.
Federal duties needed to take precedence over states' rights.

During the first half of the decade of the twenties, the most
important proponents of the particularist creed and a Third German—neither Austrian nor Prussian—answer to the German
Question were King William I of Württemberg and his representative at the Federal Diet, Baron Karl August von
Wangenheim. Even without the often-sought support of his
brother-in-law, Tsar Alexander, King William persisted in defy-
ing Austrian direction as had his delegate at the Vienna Conference in 1820. The King's thoughts were set forth in the famous
Manuskript aus Süddeutschland that aroused concern in Vienna
and Berlin in the fall of 1820. The booklet was written by a
Stuttgart publicist, Friedrich Ludwig Lindner, but, as was
quickly guessed by German statesmen, it was based upon ideas
given to Lindner by King William.[33]

The *Manuskript* expressed the heart of trialism, Third Germany's alternative to both the Austrian and Prussian answers to
the German Question. In place of an Austrian-directed confederation or a Germany united under Prussian dominance the
Manuskript issued a call for a Germany without the two great
German powers. It was a provocative alternative to Metternich's
proposed solution to the German Question and a cry of warning
against the "dictatorship of Austria and Prussia at Frankfurt."
Austria and Prussia were described as European powers with
non-German populations and interests, which should not be
allowed to dominate German affairs. Rather, a new Germany,
made up of a confederation of middle-sized states and enlarged
through the absorption of the small ones, could alone create the
independent Germany necessary for European equilibrium. The
"truly progressive" South German kingdoms should lead this
"Third Germany." They alone, through their constitutional ex-
periments, had come to an understanding with the spirit of the
century and were to be considered fit leaders for a "pure" German union. There it was! A Rheinbund alternative—although
without France—to challenge the Austro-Prussian dualism of the
existing Confederation!

Baron von Wangenheim's ideas were similar in motivation to those of his king, but they were more dangerous because they were more realizable. They did not call for dismantling the existing German Confederation. As Württemberg's representative at the Federal Diet from 1817 to 1823, Wangenheim was the most outspoken advocate of a confederation of the smaller states— under South German leadership—within the Confederation (a *Bund im Bund*). This inner confederation was to use representative constitutionalism as the unifying force among the smaller German states in their defense against Great Power—particularly Prussian and Austrian—bullying.[34] Wangenheim believed that only such a constitutional *Bund im Bund* could protect constitutional government and promote freedom of commerce in Germany. Only constitutionalism and freedom of trade introduced by the German sovereigns, he felt, could preserve the German states from revolution and amalgamation into a united German republic.[35] Such ideas, increasingly held by "reform conservatives" as the decade progressed, were anathema to Metternich.[36] He considered holders of such views bearers of dangerous ideologies and members of a "party" that aimed at overthrowing the existing order.[37]

Wangenheim and King William irritated Metternich through their opposition to federal projects proposed or backed by Austria. Wangenheim organized his South German colleagues to thwart Austro-Prussian initiatives regarding the reform of the German military constitution, the creation of federal fortresses, tariff reforms, and federal police measures.[38] Also, the regime in Stuttgart continued, despite the Carlsbad Decrees, to allow the uncensored publication of writings such as the *Manuskript aus Süddeutschland*. Württemberg's trialism went so far as to lead to opposition to the principle of intervention proclaimed by Austria, Prussia, and Russia at Troppau in November 1820 in response to the revolutions in Spain and Naples of that year.[39] The foreign minister of Württemberg, Count Heinrich von Wintzingerode, tried secretly to create an independent South German alliance with Baden and Bavaria to oppose the Troppau announcement. And when a revolution broke out in Piedmont in 1821, he sought to persuade the South German states to form an independent and neutral South German confederation. According to his plan, a neutrality league would come into effect if a war of principles broke out between Austria and France over the question of constitutionalism in Italy. The idea of a neutral league of constitutional German states was born.[40] It would arise perennially to threaten Metternich's German policy in years of international crisis. And it would be more threatening in 1830 and 1840, when there would be hints of Prussian interest in the plan.[41]

It is all too easy, with hindsight, to discount German trialism. Admittedly no third German solution to the German Question was successful in the nineteenth century. But as an option in the minds of contemporaries, it had a reality that should not be discounted. It especially should not be discounted as a factor in German politics of the 1820s. The early twenties were a time of uncertainty for the German Question because of international developments beyond German borders. Revolutions in Italy diverted Austrian attention beyond Germany and fostered threats to German federal unity, because South Germans feared Austrian interpretations of "federal duty" might involve them in non-German questions. Meanwhile, revolution from further away posed additional questions for South Germans and offered disquieting thoughts to Metternich. The Greek rebellion that began in April 1821 threatened Austrian relations with Russia, and Great Power disunity only encouraged South German questioning of Austrian manipulation of the German Confederation.

The Greek revolt stirred up old Russo-Turkish antagonisms, and Metternich feared a Russo-Turkish war could encourage revolutionary activity in Europe at the same time that it led to an expansion of Russian influence in the Balkans. He thus felt forced to support Turkish rule in Greece.[42] This made Austria a pariah in the eyes of the tsar and the philhellenic kings of Bavaria and Württemberg. Even the more conservative Prussian government made no effort to quiet pro-Greek feeling.[43]

As Russia and Turkey moved to the brink of war in 1822, Metternich became aware of the effect of this development on Russian relations with Germany. Similar to the days of Tsar Alexander's support of South German constitutionalism before the murder of Kotzebue, Russian agents were giving encouragement to South German particularism in an effort to win diplomatic support against Austria.[44] At the height of the international crisis, Metternich could not control his Germany of the Carlsbad Decrees. Even the Federal Diet at Frankfurt oppossed his will: a small group of diplomats under the direction of the envoy from Württemberg, Karl von Wangenheim, frustrated federal action by strict insistence on legal technicalities.[45] In March of 1822, this group even declared publically for the dissolution of the Mainz Central Investigating Commission, the federal institution created by the Carlsbad Decrees to root out radicalism in Germany.[46]

According to Metternich's minister in Munich, the Bavarian government was responding favorably to closer relations with St. Petersburg.[47] In fact, King Max Joseph was also expressing an interest in better relations with France. On 5 April 1822, Marquis Louis de La Moussaye, the French minister in Munich, reported that the Bavarian monarch said that the Austrian "system" built up at the conferences of Vienna, Carlsbad, Troppau, and Laibach was about to fall apart. The pacification of the Near East was the only way Metternich could still save it.[48] Without Russian cooperation, the Austrian system of international agreements for the maintenance of the European status quo was at an end and the German Question was again open for new solutions.

But despite the comments of the Bavarian king, Munich and Karlsruhe were hedging their bets by avoiding the open alienation of Austria. Unlike Württemberg, they avoided humiliation when Metternich secured the coup of Great Power unity at the Congress of Verona in November 1822. Metternich again proved his persuasiveness by convincing the tsar that all of Europe was threatened by a revolutionary brotherhood made up of the Greek Hetairia, the German Burschenschaften, and the Spanish communeros. The result was a circular dispatch that Russia, Prussia, and Austria sent to their envoys praising the unity of the three powers in their rejection of rebellion against established governments and calling on all states to cooperate against revolutionaries throughout Europe.[49] Equally important for Metternich's German policy was the tsar's retirement of Capodistria in August 1822, shortly before Verona. Karl Nesselrode, who replaced Capodistria as Alexander's chief advisor for foreign affairs, was a firm believer in cooperation with Austria and did not encourage South German independence as did his predecessor.[50]

The isolation and punishment of the King of Württemberg's trialism were at hand. The Eastern Powers stood as a block, and their renewed understanding temporarily reinforced Austrian influence in Germany. When in January 1823 King William circulated a dispatch against the arrogant assumption of European guardianship by the Great Powers—to be followed in February by similar pronouncements at the Federal Diet by Wangenheim—Württemberg took on opponents too powerful for a single secondary German state.[51]

Metternich's protests of slander to Stuttgart were followed by an appeal to the King's brother-in-law, the tsar. The Austrian appealed to Alexander to help protect the federal unity of Germany, which he pictured as endangered by Württemberg's outspoken opposition to its leading advocates. He found that the tsar had already expressed to King William the personal injury he felt inherent in the attack on the work of the Verona Congress and was reluctant to act further by withdrawing his minister from Stuttgart as Metternich proposed. He agreed, however, to act with Prussia and Austria not to separate Russia from her allies.[52]

In April 1823, when Austria and Prussia withdrew their diplomats from Stuttgart to protest Württemberg's repeated criticism of Great Power policy, Alexander supported this action by instructing his minister to prolong his vacation and not return to his post. The price for the end of Württemberg's diplomatic isolation was removal of Wangenheim from Frankfurt and the end of King William's Third German politics.[53] Despite the sympathy of the Bavarian government for Württemberg's cause—manifested by the pretentious presence of the Bavarian minister in Stuttgart and the suppression of any word of the Great Power coercion in the Bavarian press—the King of Württemberg, after some resistance, felt forced to meet Great Power demands.[54]

It should be noted, however, that Metternich and the Great Powers were not satisfied with Wangenheim's transfer alone. Their diplomats did not return to Stuttgart until King William atoned by joining the other German princes for a renewal of the Carlsbad Decrees on 16 August 1824.[55]

The departure of Wangenheim from the Federal Diet in July 1823 paved the way for the last major success of Metternich's Germany diplomacy in the 1820s—the renewal of the Carlsbad Decrees. The renewal was proof both of Metternich's diplomatic skill and the continuing need for that skill because of the tentativeness of the acceptance of the Austrian answer to the German Question.

The actual renewal of the Carlsbad Decrees had a strange history. The only provisions that actually needed renewal were the press censorship clauses that were due to expire in September 1824.[56] Since 1821, however, Metternich had continually despaired of the lax censorship in the South German states and felt that only some new federal action could bring these states to exert themselves to fulfill their duties to the Bund.[57] He was also sympathetic to the complaints of conservative South German ministers who feared the loss of control over their state diets. Thus he was receptive to the anti-constitutional expressions of

Baron Friedrich von Blittersdorff, who, in September 1822, was sent to Vienna by the government of Baden to sound out the Austrian ministers regarding such questions. Metternich's response was that he wished to talk personally with the foreign minister of Baden, Ludwig von Berstett, on his way to the upcoming conference of the Great Powers at Verona.[58] Metternich had plans for another Carlsbad-style maneuver that was to shore up monarchical government within the states of the German Confederation.

Following his familiar path of personal diplomacy, Metternich arranged for the Prussian foreign minister, Count Christian von Bernstorff, and himself to confer with the foreign ministers of Bavaria and Baden on the way to the Congress of Verona. Metternich thus coordinated the persuasive presence of the ministers of the two Great German Powers for separate conferences with Alois von Rechberg in Salzberg and with Berstett in Innsbruck. The result of these talks was an agreement for a meeting of a select group of German diplomats in Vienna in January 1823. These men included Christian von Bernstorff from Prussia, Georg von Zentner from Bavaria, Friedrich von Blittersdorff from Baden, and Leopold von Plessen from Mecklenburg.[59] Thereby, as in Carlsbad in the summer of 1819, Metternich hoped to prepare a whole series of reform proposals for easy formal passage by the Federal Diet. If he had his way, these would include provisions for the restriction of the publication of the protocols of the Federal Diet, a stricter enforcement of the federal press laws, and increased federal power to force the revision of state constitutions along more monarchic lines.[60]

But the Vienna ministerial meetings of 1823 were a bit premature and were thus one of Metternich's stratagems that failed. Zentner of Bavaria could not be persuaded to initiate federal measures that would restrict constitutional systems. Likewise, there was not yet agreement to restrict the publication of the protocols of the Federal Diet or to affirm the provisions of the federal press laws.[61] As for the idea of the federal revision of state constitutions along more conservative lines—with the end to public sessions of the diets—Zentner, the Bavarian delegate, found himself supported by Bernstorff of Prussia in the rejection of any such ideas. Metternich had not suitably prepared the groundwork for his initiative. Prussia and Bavaria hung back despite Metternich's efforts. The result was that Baden, the one South German state that would have readily agreed, felt constrained. Bavaria and Prussia rejected any proposal that would have the Confederation legislate internal state affairs. They insisted on the importance of states' rights over federal duties. Recognizing the importance of the problem, and despite a proposal from Baden that Metternich act to bring pressure on the reluctant German courts, the Austrian foreign minister decided that he would wait for a more auspicious moment.[62]

Meanwhile, however, Metternich did press piecemeal efforts for reform at the Federal Diet. In April 1823, he replaced the lethargic Austrian presidential envoy, Count Johann von Buol, with the more dynamic Baron Joachim von Münch-Bellinghausen, who pushed vigorously for some of the reforms that Metternich had spoken for at the Vienna meetings in January. Slowly the process of weakening the Federal Diet as a platform for criticism of Austrian politics was introduced. In July 1823, authors were forbidden to dedicate books to the Diet without its prior permission. In December deputies were prohibited from making use of "new federal teachings and theories" in debates. In February 1824, newspapers were no longer allowed to publish anything about the Federal Diet except excerpts from federal protocols. Finally in July two different protocols were ordained. One full set was to be distributed confidentially to the German courts; a second severely censored set was to be available for general distribution. Within four years the contents of the second set were so limited that their publication was ended altogether.[63]

Renewal of the Carlsbad Decrees and the institutionalization of the other federal reforms that Metternich desired did not come until 1824. The auspicious moment had then arrived. The unity of the Great Powers and the common conservativism of the South German governments brought changed diplomatic conditions. Metternich knew that Württemberg, having been coerced by the Great Powers in the spring of 1823, was reluctant to oppose alone any new federal measures.[64] He also knew that the governments of Baden and now even Bavaria were ready for action against their own liberals, although they insisted that they be "coerced" by the Great Powers. They did not want to risk the ire of their diets by helping to initiate reactionary federal measures—even ones that they now themselves desired.[65]

After taking the usual precaution of assuring both the tsar and the king of Prussia of the necessity for reform in Germany, Metternich was ready to begin again his diplomatic offensive to win the hesitant South German ministries.[66] In April 1824, he elaborated his plans for new German diplomatic conferences in June at his estate at Johannisberg on the Rhine. There, under the guise of visiting his vineyards, he planned to prepare a program for implementation at Frankfurt.[67]

As usual, careful personal diplomacy was involved in preparation for gaining assent to Austrian solutions. At the end of May, Metternich stopped at Tegernsee to meet with King Ludwig of Bavaria's most influential advisors: Prince Karl von Wrede, Count Alois von Rechberg, and Baron Georg Friedrich von Zentner.[68] Metternich was pleased to find even Zentner, the "father of the Bavarian constitution" and an opponent of the original Carlsbad Decrees, in a very conservative mood. Zentner, in fact, was willingly maneuverd into drawing up proposals for the renewal of the Decrees. He, like his colleagues, had been changed by internal Bavarian pressures. First, the Bavarian ministry had had trouble gaining the acceptance by the diet of a new state budget. Second, a conspiracy had recently been uncovered among members of a Bavarian regiment at Erlangen. The aim of the conspirators was the creation of a republican Germany with an elected emperor—hardly an attractive alternative to the Bund for Bavaria's monarchic particularists. The Bavarian ministers were troubled, and Metternich put their fears to his use. He decided, in fact, to organize the discussions at Johannisberg on the basis of Zentner's memorandum. This would make it more likely that the very pivotal Bavarian ministry would feel bound by its own conservative proposals and not participate in or organize an opposing South German bloc—as it was so often inclined to do.

With Bavarian agreement on the need for tough measures, Metternich's success with the other German particularists was as good as assured. Metternich had also strengthened his hand by arranging for the presence of two Russian diplomats to be present to add Russian weight to German reform proposals.[69] He encountered little dissent from the Zentner memorandum among the representatives from Prussia, Grand Ducal Hesse, Hanover, Electoral Hesse, Nassau, and Oldenburg who visited him at Johannisberg. Even the foreign minister of Württemberg indicated, by his agreeableness, a desire to regain the good graces of the Austrian minister.[70] The most enthusiastic delegate, however, was Baden's foreign minister, Berstett. As at the Vienna meetings the year before, it was his government that was most concerned to limit the influence of its diet on governmental affairs. Berstett now proposed a common set of rules of order for the diets of the German states. His aim was to make all but exceptional diet sessions closed to the public. Although Metternich's other visitors did not accept Berstett's extreme proposals, they did agree to work in the future toward a general rule concerning parliamentary publicity. This understanding, along with an agreement for the renewal of the Carlsbad Decrees, was to be the basis for action by the Federal Diet. Metternich hoped, optimistically, that the Johannisberg talks would be the beginning of additional conservative reforms by the Confederation.

Emperor Francis approved, with thanks, Metternich's efforts for the "maintenance of world order and repose."[72] On 16 August 1824, the members of the German Federal Diet unanimously approved the federal measures that signified continuing acceptance of Austrian solutions to the German Question. The provisional press law of 1819, set to expire after five-years on 20 September 1824, was made effective until they could agree upon definitive federal press law. The university law of 1819 was declared effective without renewal, and a new federal commission was to be appointed to study the need for increased university disciplinary measures. Finally, it was agreed that the constitutional states were to impose rules of order on their diets that would keep their sessions from becoming forums for attack on monarchic prerogatives.[73]

Metternich's friend, secretary, and ideological spokesman, Friedrich von Gentz, rejoiced that the "revolutionary system"—popular sovereignty—could no longer win the upper hand in Germany without the complete collapse of the German Confederation. Metternich declared that for the first time the German Confederation was completely meshed into the "system of the Great Powers."[74] He felt that he had finally made the German Confederation a strong link in the conservative chain that he had forged between the Great Powers at the congresses of Troppau, Laibach, and Verona.

Thus between 1815 and 1824, Metternich successfully articulated and institutionalized an answer to the German Question. That answer was that Austria, Prussia, and the parts of Germany that had survived the Napoleonic period as the Rheinbund would be linked defensively into a confederation of sovereign states. These states, their territorial and governmental status quo guaranteed by their confederates and thus without the need of outside support, would become the keystone of stability in central Europe. No more would the governments of these German states need to seek French, Russian, or even Prussian support for their survival. No more would they be the pawns of Austria's enemies, whether territorial or ideological. Defending their sovereignty was the key. Using their fears of Prussia and Russia, Metternich first brought the smaller German states into the alliance against Napoleon in 1813 by guarantees for their sovereignty. In 1815 he led them into the German Confederation by making that body the guarantor of that sovereignty. Similarly, between 1819 and 1824, he defended their sovereignty against a vociferous press, revolutionary university students, and obstinate diets. So doing, Metternich consolidated the German Confederation for the defense of the status quo against unsettling change whether domestic or foreign.

The path was not an easy one. Along the way Austria repeatedly confronted the suspicions of the South German particularists, encouraged by the reforming interests of Prussia-German nationalists and the omnipresent, but ill-defined interests of Tsar Alexander, who wished to be seen as Europe's savior and mentor. Metternich's German policy in these years was an integral part of his European policy, and his German successes were a result of the success of his larger European policy. That policy was to achieve and maintain peace in Europe by balancing and controlling the interests of the Great Powers by their mutual interest in security. The assistance of the Great Powers was then used to persuade the cooperation of the smaller states, likewise for the maintenance of the status quo. Metternich's achievement in formulating and instituting the federal duties of the members of the German Confederation between 1815 and 1824 came as the result of his ability to persuade both King Frederick William of Prussia and Tsar Alexander of Russia that they should support him in his quest for European security. It was their support for Metternich's European policy that checked the influence of those Great Powers in Germany. In Europe as a whole and in Germany in particular, the Austrian foreign minister used fear of revolution, not primarily to repress revolutionary ideology, but to achieve cooperation for the maintenance of the balance of power. That balance could be upset by the instability of individual states and the tendency of the larger states to use that instability for the expansion of their own power and influence. France had done so between 1793 and 1814. Metternich feared that both Russia or Prussia could do the same between 1813 and 1824. But as long as the members of the German Confederation accepted Austrian-inspired federal duties that would stabilize that body from within, there would be little opportunity for Great Power meddling. And as long as Russia and Prussia cooperated with Metter-nich's European system, the German princes had no alternative to Metternich's solution to the German Question.

The acceptance of Austrian-inspired federal duties by the German rulers was a result of their inability to find satisfactory alternatives. To many of the German princes, Austria was an interfering Great Power and a potential threat to their states' rights. But between 1815 and 1824 those rights were found to be inadequately supported by a defeated France and by a Russia half-heartedly supportive of constitutionalism. Nor did the indecisive and uncertain initiatives of the Prussian, Bavarian, and Württemberg governments offer satisfactory alternative answers to the German Question. Metternich's "system" remained the only feasible alternative. Between 1824 and 1830, however, changes on the broader European horizon would open the possibility of other options. As Metternich lost influence in Russia and France, he found that he lost influence in Berlin and the South German courts as well. The whole European Metternich System was so intertwined that the weakening of the system in one area meant its weakening elsewhere. Whereas the German rulers accepted federal duties under the influence of the Metternich System betwen 1815 and 1824, they asserted their states' rights because of the changing European balance between 1824 and 1830.

2

States' Rights and the European Balance, 1824–1830

The success of the Metternich System in Europe in general and in Germany in particular was clearly evident between 1815 and 1824. Using the desire of all the European governments for peace and stability in the decade after the Napoleonic Wars, the Austrian statesman managed to not only preserve the Quadruple Alliance but, after the Congress of Aix-la-Chapelle in 1818, add France as a member of the Concert of Europe. Not the least of his diplomatic success, however, had been achieved both in and for Germany. There he succeeded in convincing both the Great Powers and the German rulers of the need for a German confederation to be the keystone of the European peace settlement. The German Confederation that was founded during the Congress of Vienna in 1815 was to be a strictly defensive body in central Europe. Metternich persuaded the Great Powers that it would protect the sovereign rights of the German rulers, thereby tying them to an interest in the maintenance of the status quo. At the same time, he assured the German princes that their states' rights could best be maintained by cooperating in the fulfillment of those federal duties that protected the status quo in all of Germany. Thus in 1819 Metternich, with the acquiescence of the other Great Powers, maneuvered the German states into passing the Carlsbad Decrees that instituted federal regulations against the rabble-rousing outbursts of the press and of university students. Then in 1820 he achieved agreement to the Vienna Final Act, which enshrined the monarchic principle as the proper constitutional basis for Germany and authorized federal forces to come to the aid of endangered member states.

The Carlsbad Decrees and the Vienna Final Act, which spelled out the federal duties that Austria expected of her German confederates, solidified Germany in a common defense against internal revolution and at the same time made outside interference unnecessary. While Metternich used the cooperation of the Great Powers to unify Germany against revisions of the status quo in Germany, he also attempted to develop a Germany unified against Great Power interference. The Metternich System used Great Power cooperation to support the Austrian answer to the German Question and used the Austrian answer to the German Question to keep Great Power influence out of Germany.

All of this depended on Metternich's ability to maintain a continuing concensus among the governments of the Great Powers. Only then could the Austrians feel secure that their answer to the German Question would be accepted in Germany. But with the decline of the Concert of Europe, after the triumphs of Troppau, Laibach, and Verona, the German states began to seek other solutions to the German Question. Those solutions were offered particularly by Prussia and the South German states. First separately, and later together, these states sought, in the face of Austria's increasing international isolation between 1824 and 1830, to expand their independence and power through the creation of German tariff unions. These tariff unions, first the Prussian Zollverein, then the South German Union, and finally a combination of the two, created a new basis for an alternative answer to the German Question. That answer, one that might include a narrower definition of German territory and a new description of the proper form for German state constitutions, was hardly compatible with Austrian interests and Metternich's policy. In this chapter we shall see how first the declining fear of revolution among the German princes, then the international isolation of Austria, and finally the emergence of new alliances in Germany between Berlin, Munich, and Stuttgart made the continuing acceptance of Metternich's answer to the German Question anything but assured by the eve of the July Revolution in France in 1830. The period between 1824 and 1830 in Germany was characterized by a new assertion of states' rights over federal duties.

The best indication of the declining fear of revolution in Germany after 1824 was the ignoble end of the Mainz Commission. This federal commission, a product of the Carlsbad Decrees, had been given authority to conduct investigations and order the detention of suspects to determine the extent of the revolutionary network in Germany. The results of the investigations were to be made public to prove the existence and extent of the real revolutionary danger. But not until May 1822, however, did even a select committee of the Federal Diet see any results of the investigations. Hopes that the commission would uncover a vast conspiracy were not realized. In vain Metternich attempted to urge the members of the commission to renewed vigor when he called them to meet with him at Johannisberg in August 1826. They could only conclude that the secret activities of discontented Germans were of little consequence. Although the Mainz Commission presented a final report to a committee of the Federal Diet in December 1827, no presentation was made to the full Diet until March 1831. Not a word was officially made public.[1] So much for revolutionary dangers.

But it was the breakdown of the Quadruple Alliance in the late 1820s that decisively undermined Austrian-inspired federalism in Germany. Metternich's policy in the European crisis created by the Greek Revolution and the resulting Russo-Turkish friction robbed him of the Russian support he needed to keep Prussia, and thus the other German states, under the wing of the Habsburgs.[2] The Eastern Question, which had threatened Metternich's system in 1822, was not so easily handled after 1825. At the end of that year Russian policy with regard to the Greek Revolution escaped Austrian influence. The fears that Metternich had conjured up in Tsar Alexander's mind regarding the revolutionary consequences for Europe of a successful revolt in Greece died along with the Tsar on December 1. The new tsar, Nicholas, was less in awe of Metternich. He also had a traditional Russian revulsion against Turkish power and a desire to reassert Russian honor and influence in the Near East.[3]

Metternich's reluctance to force Turkey to concessions in Greece alienated Austria from Russia and from the other major European powers. This isolation soon became both apparent and real. The British, interested in an independent Greece but hoping to restrain Russian expansion, signed a protocol with the tsar in April 1826. It provided for their joint mediation and possible military intervention for the goal of making Greece an autonomous dependency of the Ottoman Empire. The French, desiring to take part in a possible redistribution of European territories, joined Russia and England a year later to form the Triple Alliance. Riding the tide, Prussia drifted further from Austria and toward the other Great Powers.[4] By the time the Russo-Turkish War broke out in April 1828, a combination of Austrian intrigues and blustering, aimed at breaking up the Triple Alliance and maintaining peace in the Near East, had brought Russian bitterness toward Austria to a high point. There was even talk of a

Franco-Russian war against Austria.[5] In the event of such a war it seemed probable that the German Confederation would dissolve. The French, who wanted a revision of the Treaties of 1815, hoped that Prussia and the South German states would side with them and Russia. A reordering of Europe might give France the left bank of the Rhine and Prussia acquisitions in central Germany.[6]

In an effort to prevent such a possibility—the collapse of both European peace and the German Confederation—Metternich tried to reassure the tsar of Austria's non-provocative intentions.[7] The Austrian felt that a large part of the Prussia military and civil bureaucracy wanted nothing more than a Russo-Austrian war so that Prussia could expand her influence throughout Germany. Although he knew the conservative and peaceful intentions of King Frederick William III and his foreign minister, Bernstorff, Metternich felt that if war came Prussia would side with Russia.[8]

The Prussian ministry was not the only one in Germany that felt that Austria had too long been the center of the political universe. As Austria was forced to concentrate her attention on Near Eastern affairs, a new spirit of independence appeared at the German courts.[9] Of the secondary states, Bavaria especially used the opportunity to follow policies that in other circumstances would have been resisted by Vienna.[10] King Ludwig, who ascended the Bavarian throne in 1825, was as ambitious and as anti-Austrian as the "ultra-Prussians" in Berlin. Like them, he was unrestrained by consideration for Austria and her system of federal unity. He considered himself a good German nationalist, but like Americans of the Southern States during the same period, felt that the essence of national patriotism lay in the protection of the sovereignty of the confederated states from which, and for which, the union had been created.[11] Under Ludwig's leadership, the Bavarian government, like the Prussian, introduced innovative policies that were aimed at consolidating state, not federal, power. In each case, this involved the creation and expansion of tariff unions behind which lay political as well as economic motives. Both Bavaria and Prussia each had their own solutions for the German Question. And part of those solutions were economic.

The German Question, it must be remembered, was tripartite: territorial, political, and economic. Part of the Question involved what territories to include within the political definition of Germany. Another part involved determining the form of government suitable for Germans. A third involved the form of economic connections that should be established between and among the Germans. The initiative taken by Prussia in 1818, by the creation of a common tariff union uniting all of its territories, was a decisive step toward a Prussian answer for this part of the Question.[12]

The Prussian Zollverein was an initiative that Metternich could not counter economically, because of his inability to influence Austrian economic policy.[13] The disastrous rise of the cost of German goods passing through the territories of the Prussian Zollverein was a topic of heated discussion at both the Carlsbad and Vienna conferences of 1819 and 1820. While Metternich was using these conferences to attempt to achieve concensus among the German governments on a political solution to the German Question, he was losing concensus on the economic issue. Because of its own internal economic interests, Austria resisted the efforts of Baden, Württemberg, and Hesse-Darmstadt to develop the idea of a single federally organized tariff union.[14]

The failure of Austrian leadership on the economic front opened the way for several competing more regional or *Kleindeutsch* alternatives. The first of these came from Württemberg. King William of Württemberg sought to use repeated economic meetings of the South German states in Darmstadt and Stuttgart between 1820 and 1825 to further his "Third German" or "trialistic" notions of a political union of the "pure" German states. Because of their large non-German populations and wider European interests, William considered neither Austria nor Prussia really pure German states. Fortunately for Austria, the unwillingness of the other South German states to give up their own immediate economic and political goals negated William's hope for a quick "Third German" economic and political solution. Baden, with considerable transit trade, held on to her demand for relatively free trade. Bavaria, with varied agricultural resources and growing industries, insisted upon retaining many import duties. Additionally, Baden agreed with Bavaria that any open profession of trialism would unnecessarily alienate Austria and Prussia.[15]

Bavarian fears of the disadvantageous political consequences of German economic alignments were diminished by the revival of the Eastern Question after 1825 and by changes in leadership both in Prussia and Bavaria. In July 1825, Friedrich von Motz became the new finance minister of Prussia. In October, King Ludwig became the ruler of Bavaria. These were men who were not afraid to use economic means that would limit Austrian influence in Germany to increase the political power of their own states.[16]

The political motivations behind the economic policies of Ludwig I and Frederich von Motz would lead to cooperation between the Prussian and Bavarian governments for the creation of a major new economic and political alignment in Germany in 1834. But their early individual and divergent attempts toward new economic-political alignments are worthy of brief reconsideration because they demonstrate the power of German particularism, the German characteristic that both threatened and assisted Metternich's repeated efforts to influence the solution to the German Question.

Ludwig of Bavaria, unlike his father, rejected Austrian solutions almost as readily as he disdained French ones. Constantly asserting his "Germanness," he at the same time removed his foreign minister, Rechberg, because of his Austrian leanings.[17] His hope was for Bavaria to reassert her influence in Germany and become the head of the purely German states.[18] As early as 1825, Austrian agents reported Bavarian attempts to win neighboring states for the creation of a South German trade union.[19] In 1826, Ludwig also suggested Bavarian-Prussian commercial talks that were rejected in Berlin by a still cautious Prussian ministry.[20] But while Bavaria's other neighbors were deterred by political considerations, including fear of expanded Bavarian power, King William of Württemberg was attracted. William, the old trialist, could not help but be receptive to Bavarian memoranda that pictured a Bavarian-Württemberg economic union as the nucleus of a pure Germany. Such political ideas, plus the desire to avoid higher Bavarian tariffs, motivated the government of Württemberg to sign a preliminary tariff convention with Bavaria on 12 April 1827.[21]

Meanwhile the tide of politics was turning in Berlin. Finance Minister Friedrich von Motz and Johann Eichhorn, still a ministerial assistant and later, after 1831, director of the German section of the foreign ministry, influenced Foreign Minister Bernstorff to seek Prussian political power through trade expansion. Grand Ducal Hesse was their first target.[22] There the efforts of the two South German kings to expand their tariff union had produced a counterproductive reaction. The upper Rhenish courts of Grand Ducal Hesse, Baden, and Nassau would have nothing to do with a system that was likely to foster Bavarian hegemony in South Germany. Their suspicion blocked the further expansion of the South German Tariff Union that Württemberg and Bavaria officially formed in January 1828. South German failure and the beginning of a new Prussian economic-political initiative was made definitive in February 1828, when Grand Ducal Hesse joined the Prussian Customs Union. The Darmstadt government had approached Berlin as early as 1825, but then the Prussian authorities were cool.[23] By 1827, with Motz fully in control of the finance ministry and in an altered European diplomatic context, Prussian policy had changed. With the support of the foreign ministry, the Prussian finance minister decided that political goals, not immediate economic ones, should be the determining factor in the expansion of the Zollverein. Grand Ducal Hesse was to be won from the Austrian camp, the German princes were to be shown that Prussia could be a desirable economic partner, and then possibly Electoral Hesse and Nassau would join the Zollverein and consolidate Prussian connections across all of northern Germany.[24]

Austrian observers were quick to point out the political motivations behind both the South German and Prussian-Hessian unions. Count Kaspar von Spiegel, the Austrian envoy in Munich, observed in his report of 27 February 1828 that the commercial union between Bavaria and Württemberg was far from being without political intention. In his view, it bore the marks of the trialistic notions of former days.[25] Metternich received similarly disconcerting views in regard to the Prussian-Hessian union. According to the Austrian president of the Federal Diet at Frankfurt, the new northern union was the work of a liberal, anti-Austrian faction within the Prussian government. In his view, Finance Minister Motz and Johann Eichhorn were using the Prussian tariff system to alter the structure of power in the German Confederation and to weaken Austrian influence.[26]

Metternich's own reaction was that "the course of the Prussian court in all German affairs has assumed in the last months a completely false direction, which I attribute to the agitation of a faction known only too well to me."[27] He was reluctant, however, to be open in opposition to Zollverein developments because of his desire to preserve Austria's relationship to Prussia at a time when Vienna was increasingly isolated from the Great Powers over the Eastern Question. As he told his envoy to Berlin, "I especially do not want our higher political relationship with the court of Prussia to be spoiled by a bit of true political rubbish."[28]

Metternich did, however, encourage his deputy at the Bund to work carefully to prevent the spread of both the Prussian and South German tariff unions. No more states were to be allowed to join either union. Doing so would endanger their independence—and thus their susceptibility to Austrian influence, the historian might add. At the same time, Metternich reasoned that the more tariff unions there were in Germany the less political importance any one of them would have. The emergence of a "neutral" third tariff union—which occurred in September 1828—was to be encouraged.[29] In all of this, Metternich stressed the need for care to avoid open opposition to the interests of Prussia. He did not want to endanger Austrian-Prussian collaboration in other German affairs.[30] However, he did warn the Prussian minister in Vienna, Baron Bogislaw von Maltzahn, that "as soon as these unions cease to be regarded from the purely administrative standpoint, and when they are based upon a political tendency, they are opposed to the fundamental laws of the Confederation."[31] Tensions mounted.[32]

At first, Ludwig of Bavaria was even more worried by the expansion of the Prussian Zollverein than was Metternich, and his worries spurred his efforts to expand the South German Tariff Union. He had ordered every effort to be made to keep Grand Ducal Hesse from ratifying its treaty with Prussia. He even called upon Austria and France to hinder such an expansion of Prussian influence.[33] It was Ludwig's ally, King William of Württemberg, who proposed a link-up with Prussian power rather than opposition to it. If Prussia was to push her tariff system toward the south, it was best to make the most out of the inevitable.[34] William expressed his willingness to cooperate with Bavaria to resist Prussian economic expansion, but he recommended that Ludwig offer Berlin negotiations for a tariff treaty instead. An inducement that William mentioned was that Ludwig might demand in return from Berlin a favorable mediation of a long-standing Baden-Bavarian territorial dispute. This so-called Sponheim Question involved Ludwig's idée fixe of regaining Bavaria's pre-Napoleonic territory on the right bank of the Rhine so as to rejoin the otherwise separated two portions of the kingdom of Bavaria. The geopolitical importance of such a change, which would have encircled Baden and Württemberg in the north and made Bavaria the dominant power in South Germany, was lost neither on Ludwig nor on the other German princes.[35] But in the spring and summer of 1828, Ludwig was as yet unwilling to seek a compromise with Prussia regarding Bavarian economic and territorial expansion. He was angered that the government in Berlin had hindered his own tariff union scheme and that Prussia's moral support for Baden prevented the fulfillment of his heartfelt territorial desires.

The advantages of acquiring the favor of Prussia—with her large measure of political, military, and economic influence—were forcefully propounded by Baron Johann Friedrich von Cotta. This influential private citizen, publisher of the liberal *Allgemeine Zeitung* and respected friend of the kings of Württemberg and Bavaria, gave the needed impulse for the opening of Prussian-South German tariff talks. Aware of the ambivalence of the South German kings toward an alliance with Prussia, Cotta took it upon himself to make preliminary soundings in Berlin. In September 1828, while attending a scientific congress in the Prussian capital, he spoke with Motz and other influential Prussian statesmen. Finding them interested in a north-south tariff agreement, Cotta had enough encouragement to secure approval from the South German kings to enter negotiations at Berlin.[36]

Cotta's personal observations regarding the military and political influence of a commercial alliance with Prussia intrigued the South German ministries. The foreign minister of Bavaria was convinced that any initial economic disadvantages of a union with Prussia would be outweighed by the political advantages gained. Similarly, although the foreign minister of Württemberg saw no economic advantage for his state in a new commercial union, he believed it was in Württemberg's best interest to establish intimate relations with a state as important as Prussia.[37]

Metternich was painfully aware of the political motives and implications behind the South German interest in a commercial treaty with Prussia. This was especially true when the Prussian and South German unions neared merger in the spring of 1829. The British ambassador in Vienna—probably because of his fear for his own nation's economic interests in Germany—was only one of those who warned Metternich that the motivating force behind a north-south trade treaty was the desire to form a counterweight to Austrian political influence in Germany.[38] Metternich agreed with that observation. He decried the animosity against Austria that was increasingly apparent in Munich and Stuttgart and asserted that the South Germans had no cause for bad feelings toward Austria. She did not oppose their economic interests, as they claimed. However, Austria did oppose South German plans for self-aggrandizement. Metternich contended that it was for such a purpose that they entered the current commercial treaties. Their design, Metternich said, was to form a powerful league against Austria.[39]

There are indications that, in the spring of 1829, the Austrian foreign minister did more than merely complain privately of Prussian and South German ambitions. There is evidence that he made unsuccessful attempts in both Berlin and Munich to involve Austria in the Prussian-South German negotiations. At one point, Motz seems to have offered Austria an agreement that he must have known she could not accept. Metternich found Emperor Francis' financial advisors unprepared to approve Austrian tariff reforms and reductions necessary for such an agreement. It was felt that such changes would prevent the government from raising and lowering tariffs as home industry required. The Austrian finance officials could only advise Metternich to work against the Prussian tariff system that Austria could not economically afford to join. Metternich was without home support, and he was too late to prevent a Prussian-South German treaty in 1829. From now on he could only try to weaken the political effects of the new treaty by an attempt to better Austrian trade relations with Bavaria.[40]

The treaty joining the Prussian and South German Customs Unions was signed on 27 May 1829, although it was not finally ratified by Bavaria until July 12. It was the fruit of complicated and often acrimonious negotiations that demonstrated the importance of political considerations involved in this nominally economic development.[41] The end result did not provide for the complete tariff union that Motz had desired. It did, however, create a comprehensive commercial treaty that was to go into effect on 1 January 1830. Its provisions allowed most products of native growth and manufacture to pass duty free from one union to the other. Other articles such as textiles and butter had their duties reduced by twenty-five percent. More important, the uniformity of customs administrations was to be developed and all efforts made to remove the remaining barriers to trade and commerce between the member states. The treaty also called for annual conferences for the support and expansion of these agreements.[42] The basis for a kleindeutsch (small Germany, without Austria) economic, and potentially political solution to the German Question was being laid.[43]

The Prussian finance minister had high hopes that this was only the beginning. In a memorandum for Frederick William, Motz enumerated the wide range of financial, military, political, as well as commercial advantages that he felt Prussia would gain by the new treaty. Most important, he said, were the political gains. If tariffs resulted from political separation, he reasoned, the unification of separate states in a customs or commercial union must lead to their constitution as a single political system. Through their economic union the German states would be united under Prussian aegis. Meanwhile, good relations with southern Germany would help guarantee the Prussian Rhineland in case of attack from France. Likewise, Prussia and the South German states would so surround Austria that she could be threatened simultaneously from Silesia and Bavaria, if necessary.[44]

This, the historian is forced to note, was the somewhat less than fraternal view of Austria that was held in 1829 by the finance minister of the power that Metternich considered Austria's most important ally—and most dangerous potential opponent—in German affairs. Austria's isolation in international affairs, because of the Eastern Question, threatened to lose her the cooperation and influence in Germany that she desired from both Prussia and the South German states. A new Prussian-South German political, as well as commercial, alignment was a fact.

But by late 1829 the course of European events was again changing, this time in ways that promised Austria advantages as well as dangers. As the Russo-Turkish War ended, faint rumblings of an approaching storm in France captured the attention of European statesmen. Metternich still insisted that his conservative principles were neither outmoded nor incorrect. He felt that only international efforts to preserve all legally existing institutions could ensure European peace and stability. Making these observations to Emperor Francis in October 1829, he predicted that Europe was about to enter a new era in which Austria's conservative principles would be indispensible. The old alliance system that had broken up over the Eastern Question would be brought together again by coming events. The Great Powers would be forced to return to their older conservative principles and to cooperation with an Austria that had always maintained them.[45] In fact, once again in Germany—as well as Europe—monarchs would soon look with favor on Metternich's solution to the still evolving and still unanswered German Question.

The period between 1824 and 1830 had hardly seen the continuation of Metternich's diplomacy at its zenith. Compared to the years between 1815 and 1824, which had witnessed the success of Metternich's policy in Germany and Europe, these were the nadir years. Federal duties so recently agreed upon at Carlsbad and Vienna were forgotten as revolutionary dangers proved specters of Metternich's imagination. German princes turned from thoughts of repression to thoughts of reform. Economic reform and the expansion of their own political influence through the creation of regional tariff unions were on the agenda. First it occurred in Prussia, then among the South German princes as well. Finally there were moves for the consolidation of a Prussian-South German economic union. It was obvious to all concerned that because Austrian economic interests did not lend themselves to joining in the solution to German trade problems, new leaders and new solutions were going to be offerd as alternatives. These alternatives, purely Prussian, purely South German, or a combination of the two as it turned out by 1829, were, although only answers to the economic portion of the German Question, answers with potentially high political significance.

Developments on the broader European scene replicated and reinforced developments in Germany. After the unity of the Concert of Europe at Troppau, Laibach, and Verona came years of discord. After the repression of the Italian and Spanish Revolutions of the early 1820s, European governments resumed their feelings of security and pursued their own interests. Danger of revolution in Western Europe had faded and with it the attractions of monarchic unity under the direction of the "Coachman of Europe." The only developments of interest lay to the east. There a Greek revolt against Turkish hegemony bled on since 1821. But in Greece the revolutionaries were seen as heroic. It was their Muslim masters against whom all but Metternich seemed to side. Tsar Alexander of Russia was gone. This one-time adversary of Metternich, but more recently reactionary friend, died in 1825. Tsar Nicholas was less subject to Austrian wiles and more interested in an autonomous Greece than in the Concert of Europe. He was joined by both the British and French governments, both with reformist constitutional systems and increasingly alienated by Metternich's predisposition toward the maintenance of the status quo. By 1828 even Prussia seemed to desert her German ally, not only by proceeding with the economic unification of Germany without Austria, but by siding with the other Great Powers regarding the Eastern Question. There were even rumors of a European war against Turkey and Austria, with the possibility of French gains on the Rhine and

Prussian gains in northern Germany. The balance of power in Europe seemed about to change. The Concert of Europe, at least the one conceived and led by Austria between 1815 and 1824, seemed at an end.

And in Germany, the former allies of Austria in the German Confederation were making the best of the changing situation. States' rights were being protected in new alliances and with little reference to the concerns of Austria. It would take a major international cataclysm to alter the new direction of European and German affairs. Such a cataclysm would be a revolution in France. Only then would the Great Powers allow Metternich to refocus their concerns toward the limitations of revolutionary change. Only then, in the broader spirit of European monarchic solidarity, would Metternich again be able to convince the German sovereigns that their survival depended upon the reaffirmation and performance of their German federal duties.

3

Search for Security, 1830

For Metternich the revolution that began in Paris on 27 July 1830, was not a French or German problem, but a European one. As such, of course, it was a factor of paramount importance in determining the course of Metternich's German policy. Experience had taught the Austrian foreign minister that a French revolution held a twofold danger for the European state system: it provided a model and catalyst for revolts elsewhere, and it unleashed the popular energies of the French people, energies that in the past had been directed into military adventures.[1] How the German rulers, particularly those with borders with France, would react to these dangers would determine to a great extent Metternich's ability to combat the dangers as they affected Austrian interests throughout Europe.

It was Austria's broader European, particularly Italian, interests that were disconcerting to important groups in Germany. Both in the South German states and in Prussia, influential forces within the ministries were not content that the states of the German Confederation might serve merely as pawns in Austria's European politics. Their own concerns were more "purely" German. Their answers to the German Question, as they had begun to emerge during the latter part of the 1820s, were significantly different from those of the Austrian foreign minister who saw Germany as a means—although a very important one—but not an end in his diplomatic considerations. Unlike Metternich, too, these elements within the South German and Prussian ministries hoped for compromise with the "spirit of the times." Through economic and constitutional reforms they hoped to retain the allegiance of Germans to the individual German princes. Unlike Metternich, their first thoughts were for cooperation between reforming states within the German Confederation rather than cooperative repression in the name of the Confederation. As a means to their end they became outspoken defenders of state sovereignty in the face of Austrian pleas on behalf of federal duty and the supremacy of German federal interests and German federal law. It was through invoking the supremacy of federal law that Metternich tried to restore both European security and recoup Austrian authority in Germany. The July Revolution presented Metternich with both a threat and an opportunity. It also provided Metternich's opponents in the South German states and Prussia with an opportunity to assess the viability of their own options for a solution to the German Question.

In the last years of the reign of Charles X, Metternich was not alone in recognizing the dangers inherent in the increasingly awkward handling of France by that sovereign. It was Metternich, however, who was most active in warning others of a potential French upheaval. He also was engaged in encouraging the French government to take measures against what he considered to be the major causes of political unrest: freedom of the press and a liberal suffrage law.[2] In Berlin and St. Petersburg the Austrian foreign minister's warnings were seen, at best, as the overzealous worries of a hopeless reactionary; at worst, they were regarded as part of an ill-conceived offensive to end the isolation that Austria had suffered during the Russo-Turkish War.[3] As long as Metternich could not regain the confidence of his European allies he could not hope to re-cement Austria's German bastion, of which Prussia and the South German states were becoming an alarmingly uncertain part.

When news of the success of the July Revolution reached Metternich on 4 August, he was in Bohemia patching up relations with Austria's Eastern allies through private talks with two important vacationers: King Frederick William III of Prussia and Foreign Minister Count Karl von Nesselrode of Russia.[4] Suffering from financial exhaustion and military unpreparedness, the Habsburg Monarchy was in no position to defend its own territorial interests, let alone to undertake a military offensive in the name of legitimacy against France. Metternich's first effort, therefore, was to try to reactivate a common front of the Continental Powers. Such a front might force the French government to contain revolutionary passions within its borders and give moral support to the Austrian government should it be forced to intervene against revolutionaries in neighboring Italy.[5]

When Metternich met Nesselrode at Carlsbad on 6 August, he proposed the creation of a three-power conference at Berlin to consider French developments before any official recognition was extended to the new government in Paris. His intention was

to impress Louis Philippe with the renewed unity of the conservative powers and to gain from him a promise that France
would not try to revolutionize neighboring states. The Russian
foreign minister, however, feared that Metternich might turn a
continental alliance to an offensive war against revolutionary
France. He agreed only to the principle that the Great Powers
would not interfere in the internal affairs of France as long as
France did not disturb the material interests or internal peace of
the rest of Europe.[6]

Metternich had no more success when he approached the
Prussians. They rejected three-power meetings as a compromis-
ing measure that could distort public understanding of Prussia's
non-offensive intentions toward the new French government.
Frederick William III had decided from the first news of the
French revolution that he would not provoke France—although
he feared that the situation for Prussia was like that in the years
after 1789, and sooner or later a French attack would come across
the Rhine.[7] Not waiting to see what part France would take in the
Belgian revolution that began on 25 August, Prussia became the
first of the continental powers to recognize Louis Philippe, doing
so on 9 September.[8]

As Metternich could not establish a common continental front
by which he might influence the foreign policies of the new
French government, he reluctantly advised his emperor to follow
what he considered to be the precipitous lead of Britain and
Prussia.[9] He concluded that, in any case, the real danger to
Europe from the July Monarchy would probably not be plans for
military conquest. Louis Philippe assured the conservative
powers that he had prevented the creation of a revolutionary
republic in France and that he intended to see that his countrymen caused no trouble abroad. What Metternich feared was
that Louis Philippe, although a fine fellow personally, would be
unable to control anarchy. The best way to combat anarchy,
Metternich believed, was to support Louis Philippe by agreeing
to recognize him. As it turned out, the Austrian letter of recognition was actually sent off a day earlier than that of Prussia, being
given to the French plenipotentiary, General Auguste-Daniel de
Belliard, on 8 September.[10] The tsar, separated by distance from
his allies, heard of the recognition post facto and grudgingly
followed suit on 30 September.[11]

While Metternich was striving for agreement with the Great
Powers—an agreement upon which he planned to base his policy

toward the smaller German powers—he avoided sending definite proposals to the German capitals other than Prussia. His pronouncements to South German diplomats, whose home territories seemed threatened most immediately by France, were hardly of the kind to reassure them that Austria's first concern was Germany. They were told that although Austria planned no interference in French internal affairs, she was developing plans by which the Great Powers might receive a quid pro quo for their recognition of the new French government. Meanwhile, the South Germans were asked only to stand together in firm and honest cooperation.[12] When pressed for a precise statement of Austria's intentions by the minister of Württemberg in Vienna, Baron August von Blomberg, Metternich would only assure him that Stuttgart would be informed of his ideas "shortly."[13]

The statement of policy that Metternich promised to the King of Württemberg was deliverd only in late August. On the request of Count François von Bray, the Bavarian minister at Vienna, the Austrian envoy to Württemberg also shared it with King Ludwig at Berchtesgaden, on 27 August, before delivering it to King William at Stuttgart on the 30th. The memorandum presented Austrian policy as based on the principle of reciprocal nonintervention between France and Europe. Most important, it called for the unity of all of the German powers in the face of uncertainty regarding the future course of French developments. Asserting a greater degree of agreement between Prussia and Austria than actually existed, it urged the South Germans to follow the lead set by these two great German powers.[14] In short, the memorandum was typically vague, as far as the lesser German states were concerned, except for the encouragement to follow the lead of Prussia and Austria.

Prince Alfred von Schönburg, who brought the Austrian memorandum to the two South German kings, reported that both men were worried by the ideological and military dangers eminating from revolutionary France. He found Ludwig of Bavaria concerned by the enthusiasm for the French revolution among Bavarian lawyers, men of commerce, and the educated. From the military standpoint, he admitted that he was quietly arming his forces against a surprise attack from France. The King of Württemberg, on the other hand, seemed to focus his attention on dangers in the neighboring German states, rather than in his own. He expressed particular concern about popular sympathy for the French revolution in Munich and for what he felt would be the

inability of the new Grand Duke of Baden, Leopold, to under-
stand and cope with the dangerous development in neighboring
France.[15]

Although Schönburg was not sent to Baden, his message to
King William of Württemberg included the request that the King
work on Duke Leopold in the sense of the Austrian memorandum.[16] The Austrian minister in Karlsruhe, Count Karl von Buol,
had already reported that the government of Baden hoped Great
Power unity would stabilize the European situation. Buol noted
that so far there were no signs of revolutionary disturbance in
Baden and, while the government expressed worry about the
revolutionary values of the French press, it refused to prohibit
the importation of French journals. This, according to Baden
officials, might only increase their readership while hindering
usual French-Baden trade.[17]

While the South German governments acknowledged some of
their political and ideological anxieties about the French revolution to Austrian agents, they expressed their most intimate concerns only in secret communications among themselves. Their
chief fear was being caught as helpless pawns in a military
struggle between a revolutionary France and the absolutistic
Continental Powers. Their primary concern was not an ideological one; it was the survival of their individual states. They were
interested in a South German, not European, solution to the
problems caused by the July Revolution.[18]

In fact, even before the Austrian position was stated in general
terms, an initiative was taken by the Bavarian foreign minister,
Count Joseph von Armansperg, to create a South German bloc, a
defense against both West and East. Armansperg, a Bavarian
patriot with French and Prussian sympathies and a deep-rooted
suspicion of Austrian conservatism, was certain that the South
German states were unprepared to hold out against a French
attack. Therefore, in early August, he proposed to the ministries
in Stuttgart and Karlsruhe that the South German states assume a
united, but unprovocative stand in regard to the government of
Louis Philippe. He advocated that they all avoid any commitment to the other German states in relation to the recent events in
France. Then they could act freely as South German interests
might command.[19]

The ministry in Karlsruhe seems to have expressed a qualified
interest in seeing the South German courts enter closer relations
along the lines Armansperg suggested.[20] The King of Württemberg's 13 August response to Armansperg's proposals indicated,

on the other hand, a complete willingness to cooperate with his Bavarian colleague to implement Armansperg's plan. King William was the leader of German trialism in the 1820s; the old urges were easy to evoke. He promised to use his influence on the Grand Duke of Baden to assure his cooperation too. His only regret, he said, was that Bavaria had already moved to increase her troops at the fortress at Landau—acting as did the Austrian and Prussian governments, who at the moment were reinforcing their contingents at the German federal fortresses at Luxemburg and Mainz. King William thought that the new French government was unlikely to take any offensive action for the moment, and he did not want to see her provoked. If war did come, however, he felt it important that popular opinion judge France the aggressor. Only then could the German governments expect to receive the full support of their people.[21]

The Federal Military Commission's decision, on 13 August, to propose the completion and reinforcement of the federal fortress at Mainz—thus preparing the Confederation to assume an armed, though defensive, attitude toward France—especially disturbed King William. He wrote to Armansperg to express his fear that federal defensive action might provoke France. At the same time, he told the Bavarian that he wanted to avoid the possible usurpation of South German troops by the Great Powers. He insisted that South German troops should not be called upon to reinforce Austrian and Prussian forces at the federal garrisons. If war did come, he wanted the South German armies grouped together so that they would be ready to implement the policies most advantageous to the South German governments.[22] To all of these ideas Armansperg could not agree more. Their implementation was to be his goal until he was forced from the Bavarian ministry by Austrian pressure in 1832.

One insuperable problem existed for Armansperg and his South German confederates: In the event of a French invasion of South Germany, the South German sovereigns really did not feel that they could do without Austrian aid. Their goal was to act independently of Austria—to avoid becoming the pawns in Austria's European power struggles—but to have Austria available to support them in case of their need. Therefore, neither the king of Württemberg nor of Bavaria could risk alienating Austria until they were certain that South Germany was safe and Austrian protection unneccessary. King William insisted that his minister in Munich avoid any irrevocable step and be very reserved with regard to South German communications so that nothing would provoke the displeasure of the Hofburg.[23] Each of the South German courts was standing close to the other, but each feared the indiscretion of its neighbor and the divulgence of its ideas to Austria or Prussia.[24] When, on 16 September, the Federal Military Commission proposed that the Confederation sanction the preparation of troops from Nassau, Electoral Hesse, and Grand Ducal Hesse for the reinforcement of Mainz and called for each of the German states to make contributions to the arming of the fortress, Württemberg delayed. The king tried to gain Bavarian agreement to resist the proposal, but then decided to support it. He wanted to avoid the appearance of provoking disagreement within the Confederation in a time of crisis.[25] He, like his confederates in the Bund, had developed a respect for their German federal security blanket.

It was Metternich's constant theme that the Confederation alone was the true protector of the German sovereigns against both foreign aggression and internal revolt. And internal revolts soon occurred. In the first half of September riots occurred in Hamburg and Leipzig, mobs forced the Duke of Braunschweig to flee his capital, and demonstrations intimidated the governments in Dresden and Kassel into promises of new and more representative constitutions.[26]

On 11 September, well before the Federal Diet considered the problems created by political unrest in the German states, Metternich wrote to his minister in Berlin asking him to consider with the Prussian ministry how the outbreaks could be met. The Prussian foreign minister delayed. Count Christian von Bernstorff did not want to commit his state until he saw what the Federal Diet said on the matter. Metternich, however, did not wait for an answer from Berlin. On 12 September he asked his presidential representative at Frankfurt, Count Joachim von Münch, to begin preliminary discussions on the need for federal measures.[27]

Acting under the impression of revolts in Braunschweig and Dresden, and considering it the right and duty of the Confederation—as stipulated in the Federal Act of 1815 and the Vienna Final Act of 1820—to uphold the safety and peace of Germany, Münch sought to ensure immediate federal military intervention to preserve endangered German governments. Before checking with Metternich, Münch called a special meeting of the federal delegates on 18 September to present such ideas. He proposed that the governments of the confederation mutually commit themselves to provide assistance upon the request of any endangered neighboring German government. They were thus to obligate themselves to intervene in the name of the Federal Diet, even before that body specifically delegated them to act on behalf of the Confederation. For this purpose each state was to keep its federal contingents in preparedness. Furthermore, Münch proposed that each government give its federal envoy extended powers so that the Diet could act quickly to develop any other measures necessary for Germany's internal or external defense. At the same time, on behalf of his government, he asked for the strict enforcement of existing federal censorship regulations within each state, particularly in regard to reports of recent revolutionary developments. Finally, the Austrian envoy suggested that the Federal Diet declare that any concession made by a government under duress should be considered null and void.[28]

Metternich was pleased with Münch's proposals and hoped that they would be quickly enacted by the Federal Diet. He expressed to the Prussian and South German governments alike the opinion that the proposed federal action was necessary both for its immediate defensive value for each of the German governments and for the moral support that it would give the individual princes. In short, it would prove to prince and subject alike the positive worth of the German Confederation.[29] This was to be Metternich's theme throughout the crisis years of the early 1830s as it had been in the twenties.

But there was a responding theme from the other German states that was also familiar: the fear of their subservience to the Confederation and their loss of sovereignty. Therefore, although the German diplomats at Frankfurt generally agreed with the Austrian presidential envoy about the need for federal action, they disagreed on its extent. More than a month passed before a vote could be held on the Austrian proposals.[30] The South Germans were especially worried that the proposed measures might lead to unwanted federal intervention in their internal affairs. They were not alone. They found a spokesman for their position in Austria's ally and rival, Prussia.[31]

In the last several years important elements within the Prussian government had become increasingly convinced that the road to Prussian leadership in Germany was not through participation in the conservative federalism of the Austrian-led Federal Diet, but through concessions to popular desires, economic and political. Finance Minister Motz told King Frederick William III, Prussian greatness could be realized through the expansion of free trade by means of the Prussian Zollverein.[32] Now there was talk also of the introduction of a limited form of representative government. Although the constitutional plans that circulated in the Prussian ministry in the early 1830s never got past the discussion stage, the existence of such plans did have some influence on policy and gave it an ambivalence that confused both friends and foes.[33]

A clear example of the progressive thinking going on in Berlin is seen in the 30 September memorandum that Foreign Minister Bernstorff sent to the Prussian diplomats at the other German courts. In it he set forth the major themes of his politics toward both France and the German states. He insisted that the first duty of government was to its people, and their good required the maintenance of peace as long as possible and compatible with honor and security. Although unstable, the new French government, monarchically constituted, should be tolerated in the face of worse evils. To maintain the Grand Alliance of 1815, the proper attitude of the other powers was the British one of watchful neutrality. Finally, illustrating his own current thinking—so appalling to Metternich—he concluded by noting that a state's military power depended upon the psychological outlook of its people. Their energies, he asserted, could only be fully mobilized to protect a state—or, in this case, the German nation—if a war was a defensive one.[34]

When Münch made his proposals on 18 September, the Prussian delegate at Frankfurt asked that the results of the proposed federal action be carefully considered before anything was done.[35] In the following weeks, he and the South German envoys enumerated the questions that they felt had to be contemplated.[36] Would German revolutionaries be provoked to extremes by a federal proclamation which stated that forced concessions would be considered null and void? Was it legal for the Federal Diet to issue a general delegation of its authority to suppress future, and as yet unspecified, revolts? Would this lead to undue interference of the Confederation in the internal affairs of the federal states?[37]

Despite Metternich's enthusiasm for Münch's original proposals, he was ready to have them modified to meet rising objections. In his instructions of 13 October to his federal representative, he outlined the information he had on the Prussian and South German positions and indicated his own feelings. He wanted to assure the Prussians and Bavarians that Austrian proposals were not intended to give the Confederation rights to intervene in state affairs beyond the legal limits set up in the Federal Constitution. If the German governments gave their delegates plenipotentiary powers, they would not be granting them the right to communicate directly with local administrative officials. The ministries would not be bypassed. The proposed plenipotentiary powers for the federal delegates were meant only to allow them to discuss more freely emergency measures, even the discussion of which would normally require prior ministerial approval. Finally, regarding the possible bad effect of a federal declaration against forced concessions, Metternich suggested that such a declaration could be eliminated: it would only reaffirm a principle that needed—as far as he was concerned—no reconfirmation.[38]

Fortunately for Metternich, the Prussian government acknowledged that however inefficient and bothersome the mechanisms of the Confederation, they alone provided the legal means necessary to check the collapse of governmental authority in Germany. Equally important the Prussians shared their feelings with the Bavarians.[39] Metternich counted on such Prussian convictions.[40] It was in no small measure thanks to Berlin's support that Münch's proposals were enacted, although with some modification. The stipulation about forced concessions was dropped and the provision for extended powers to the federal delegates was qualified out of existence. Nevertheless, Münch believed that Metternich would be pleased about the federal decrees that were enacted on 21 October.[41]

The Austrians had reason to be pleased. The new federal decrees extended existing federal legislation regarding federal intervention to support governments endangered by revolution. This was the key issue within the Confederation: Austria sought the extension of the federal right of intervention in state affairs in the interest of stability and other states tried to restrict those rights in the interest of state sovereignty. It was the perennial question of federal duties and states' rights. Now, according to the 21 October legislation, each confederate state was obligated to hold troops ready and to respond—in the name of the Confederation—to requests for help by neighboring federal states, even before being specifically delegated to do so by the Federal Diet. This help was to be given to the extent of the power of the supporting state and to be limited only insofar as its provision might endanger the territory or compromise the troops of that supporting state. Additional provisions obligated each government to inform the Federal Diet of revolutionary activity within its own borders so that appropriate federal action could be taken. Finally, Münch was particularly pleased to announce that—as Metternich wished—the press clauses of the Carlsbad Decrees were renewed and each state was called upon to censor the coverage of both foreign and internal political affairs.[42]

Metternich's joy was tempered by a growing awareness that there were competing claims to a solution for German problems. If the federal decrees of 21 October represented a victory for Austria's principle of conservative federalism, the discussion that led to their enactment indicated the extent of rapprochement that had developed between Prussia and the constitutional states during the 1820s. In the discussions before the vote of the Bundestag, Prussia and Bavaria joined in proclaiming that there would not have been any revolts in Germany had all of the princes fulfilled their federal obligations in regard to the institution of constitutional state governments.[43] Prussia, in fact, insisted that the final federal decrees should enjoin all the German governments to fulfill the just requests of their subjects, so that they would have no cause for unrest.[44] The Austrian envoy in Munich reported that King Ludwig and his foreign minister, Armansperg, were overjoyed by reports that Prussia intended to urge each state to fulfill its obligation under Article 13 of the Federal Act—the article that proposed that a constitution should be instituted in each German state. The Austrian envoy supposed that the Bavarians now hoped that Prussia would place itself at the head of an alliance of the constitutional German states.[45]

Bavaria was already engaged in what, since the succession of Ludwig I, had become a standard characteristic of Bavarian policy: a defense of states' rights against the "encroachments of German great power or European interests into the substance of the Bund."[46] Ludwig flatly refused to implement federal legislation that might limit the sovereignty of Bavaria. The Bavarian position was that sovereignty lay with the states. The Federal Diet was only an organ of the federation and could be afforded no recognition that might imply that it had authority independent of those states.[47] A case in point was the federal action of 30 September and 1 October that called for the formation and use of federal military contingents against revolutionaries—in this instance, mobs in the border areas of Electoral Hesse. The mobs, spurred on by the revolution in Kassel and by their own economic griefs, were burning customs houses and making disruptive incursions into border towns of Grand Ducal Hesse.[48] Bavaria was reluctant to permit federal action.

The federal action that Bavaria resisted was proposed by the Austrian president of the Federal Diet in an effort to assert the prerogatives of the Confederation. In view of the new French doctrine of nonintervention—a warning to foreign powers not to intervene against revolutionaries in states bordering France—Münch thought it wise to assert the right of the German Confederation to intervene against rebels within the territories of its member states.[49] On 30 September, he proposed, and the Diet approved, the mobilization of federal troops on the borders of Electoral Hesse. The Federal Military Committee was delegated to draw up plans for the employment of the troops should their presence in Hessian territory, or elsewhere, prove necessary.[50] On the basis of the committee's report of 1 October, the Diet voted to create mobile columns to a total strength of seven thousand men; a column each was to be formed by Nassau, Bavaria, Baden, and Grand Ducal Hesse. All of them were to be commanded by a general from Nassau. Three more corps, one each from Würtemberg, Bavaria, and Prussia, were to be held in reserve.[51]

Nassau, Baden, Württemberg, and Prussia admitted the general danger to Germany involved in the Hessian unrest and approved the federal measures of 1 October. Bavaria felt differently. Although the Bavarian representative voted for the new measures, his government emphatically rejected them.[52] King Ludwig was incensed that his envoy would bind Bavaria to federal action before consulting Munich. He and his ministry were insulted, too, that their troops would fall under the command of a general from the principality of Nassau. Ludwig's immediate reaction was to consider the dismissal of his ill-advised federal delegate. He refrained from this only because of the stir that it would have provoked in diplomatic circles.[53] However, on 6 October, Ludwig instructed his erring diplomat that Bavaria would not participate in the military measures approved by the Diet. The king noted that Bavaria had thirteen neighbors. She could hardly be expected to have her troops help all of them—except as might be arranged by individual agreement in each specific case. Moreover, in the Hessian affair, the Federal Diet acted before the threatened government requested aid.[54]

Although a preview of Bavaria's continuing preference for state sovereignty against federal duty, this first federal dispute proved something of a tempest in a teapot. On 7 October, the federal representative of Ducal Hesse reported that the incursions into his country by mobs from Electoral Hesse had stopped; the federal decrees of 1 October had lost their relevance.[55] A week later, on the recommendation of the Federal Military Committee, the Diet approved the reduction in strength of the mobile columns by 5,300 men and specifically noted that it would be unnecessary for Bavaria to mobilize her troops. At this point, in an apparent effort to save face for his government and to avoid the condescension of the Diet, the Bavarian delegate assured his colleagues that measures had been taken to reinforce the Bavarian troops along her borders. If they were needed for federal assistance—according to the stipulations of federal law—his government could rapidly bring into play a corps of five thousand men.[56] It was a belated gesture. On 21 October, the Diet decided that the mobile columns were no longer necessary and all of the contingents were ordered withdrawn from their staging areas.[57]

Metternich was concerned by the anti-federative sense of the Bavarian reaction to the federal measure of 1 October. It gave him one more reason for his decision to send the Bavarian minister in Vienna, Count François von Bray, to work personally on the Bavarian king to change his policies.[58] Metternich and Bray—much to the distress of the Bavarian foreign minister—shared a common concern that the Bavarian government misjudged the revolutionary spirit of its own people. They both felt that Bavaria needed, for its own good, to cooperate with federal efforts that alone could solve Germany's current problems and discourage the intervention of revolutionary France. Already, on 21 September, Metternich had informed Emperor Francis that reports from Bavaria showed a dangerous spirit abroad among King Ludwig's subjects. At that time, he explained that the reports had motivated him to encourage Bray's own fears and feeling that he should personally warn his king.[59] Moreover, by early October, Metternich was worried by more than the spirit of the Bavarian citizenry. He was concerned as to how the Bavarian government would react if Austria violated the French doctrine of nonintervention in Italy. Bray informed Ludwig that the Austrians had heard rumors that, if Austria should provoke a war with France by its determination to help Italian princes against their native revolutionaries, the South German states might declare their neutrality.[60]

Thus Metternich's motive for sending Bray to see King Ludwig was twofold: to prevent Bavaria from falling prey to revolution and to discourage her government from any idea of South German neutrality. Either development would weaken the German Confederation and prevent it from serving as Austria's northwestern bastion. Ludwig was to be reminded of the Austrian emperor's personal concern that Bavaria set a good example of cooperation for the maintenance of the security of the German Confederation. Bray was chosen to convey this concern because Metternich wanted to bypass the Bavarian ministry. After its performance in the past, he correctly assumed that it would not be very sympathetic to Austrian views on the Bavarian and German situation. He concluded that a message would have the greatest impact on King Ludwig if Bray acted as the go-between in a direct emperor to king—brother-in-law to brother-in-law—communication.[61] This was personal diplomacy at its best—or worst.

The Austrian message that Bray carried to King Ludwig summed up the Hofburg's attitude toward the German Confederation and its place in European politics in the fall of 1830. It was elaborated in a conversation that the Austrian emperor had with Bray and in a memorandum prepared for the Bavarian by Metternich. The essence of both was an appeal to Ludwig's German federal consciousness. He was to be reminded that under the present circumstances it was necessary to make good use of the German Confederation to settle Germany's internal problems and to secure the general peace of Europe as well.[62]

In the memorandum that Metternich presented to Bray, he recalled the revolutionary dangers facing all the European states after the July Revolution. He concentrated, however, on the German dangers—made worse by the combination of liberal and nationalistic agitation. Still, he asserted, Germany—unlike Italy, for instance—was blessed with a confederation that offered a means of securing safety. To make the confederation effective, however, all jealousies had to be put aside. Germany had to act as a common unit against the dangers of both French revolutionary doctrines and the subversive Paris-centered revolutionary organization that spread them. Similarly, although Metternich claimed that war was not a great danger at the present—unless France fell into civil war and Louis Philippe was unable to control the revolutionary and expansionist tendencies of the mob—he insisted that Germany had to be united and prepared for such an eventuality. In defense against both internal and external danger, the German states had to act as a strong federal unit; a unit that, being a great European power itself, should act in concert with the other great European powers.[63]

Bray's unexpected arrival in Bavaria in mid-October surprised and irritated King Ludwig. His minister had not even requested permission to leave his Viennese post. The proud king was greatly provoked that his own servant acted as an emissary for another power.[64] Foreign Minister Armansperg believed it was necessary to intervene with the king, because of Bray's age and long service, to spare the erring diplomat a severe royal reprimand.[65]

After being directed to confer with Armansperg near Landshut, Bray was allowed to present the Austrian emperor's personal note to Ludwig at Straubing on 19 October. Although the king did not conceal his displeasure at Bray's mission, he assured him that Austria would be informed that things were under control in Bavaria, that he was making needed military preparations, and that he hoped the three monarchs of the Continental Powers would not doubt his good intentions.[66] On 24 October, Bray was sent Ludwig's personal note for the Habsburg monarch. It perfunctorily thanked Emperor Francis for the expression of his views and assured him that the Bavarian king's sentiments were those of a patriotic member of the German Confederation.[67]

In fact, Ludwig and Armansperg were greatly disturbed by Bray's visit. They could not believe that the Austrian foreign minister had sent such an extraordinary mission merely to repeat clichés. They surmised that Metternich was trying to make other states believe that Bavaria's relations with Austria were particularly close.[68] For this reason, Ludwig decided to act at once to inform the governments at both Stuttgart and Berlin regarding the Bray mission. He also had copies of the Austrian emperor's note and Metternich's memorandum sent so that they could see for themselves the innocence of the Austro-Bavarian exchange.[69]

Ludwig did not want to assume an anti-federative role in German affairs, but neither did he wish to be subservient to Austria or Austrian-directed federal legislation. Foreign Minister Armansperg continued to cherish high hopes for the development of a South German neutrality alliance in case of a Franco-Austrian war over Italy. Such an alliance, whether there was a war or not, would be the basis for the creation of a new balance of power within the Confederation and a new direction in federal policy. But such a course required the backing of Prussia.

Since August, Armansperg worried that Austria would provoke a European war by acting to repress revolts in Italy in defiance of the French doctrine of nonintervention. In a Franco-Austrian war the members of the German Confederation would be caught as helpless pawns unless they were prepared with a plan for neutrality and self-defense against both France and Austria.[70] Of course, since the Belgian revolt of 25 August, the possibility existed that the states of the German Confederation might also be drawn into a European war by some federal action to preserve Luxemburg—part of the German Confederation— from Belgian rebels. Yet Austria was too involved watching Italy to force action in Luxemburg; and Prussia, although she had a more logical interest in conditions in neighboring Luxemburg, seemed disinclined to risk a war with France.[71] Since 15 October, the king of the Netherlands, the sovereign of Luxemburg, had been petitioning the Federal Diet for armed aid. But he had received no encouragement from Berlin.[72]

Armansperg put his faith in Prussia to keep the German Confederation out of a war with France. Such a war, he felt, would bring disruption to Germany and the overthrow of all the German thrones. Although a relative Francophile, the Bavarian foreign minister saw the French government as too unstable to be trusted to guarantee South German neutrality in an international struggle. He counted, therefore, on Prussia to maintain her own neutrality and that of the German Confederation. Should Berlin not act as he hoped, however, Armansperg wanted the South German ministries to be prepared to act on their own.[73]

Prussian plans were to play an increasingly important part in the development of the policies of the South German governments and thus in the problems that Metternich confronted in his efforts to bend those policies to his purposes. Ludwig's attitude toward a neutrality alliance was problematic because of his erratic personality and impetuous German patriotism, but he was enamored with the idea of some alliance with Prussia.[74] He was particularly interested in concerting with Berlin on military matters, and he intended to send Field Marshal Prince Karl von Wrede to the Prussian capital for consultations in October. As things turned out, the Prussian government was involved at the time in military talks with a Russian plenipotentiary and could not accept a visitor from Bavaria. It assured Ludwig of its interest, however, and promised to send a representative to Bavaria and to the other South German courts to initiate military discussions in the near future. Meanwhile, the Bavarian king was told that Prussia would fight a war with France only if it were a national one. Only if France actually threatened German territorial integrity would war be necessary. Then it would be a war for self-preservation.[75]

The Prussian reply indicated the similarity of Prussian and South German views regarding the role to be played by Germany in a potential European war: it would be limited to a defense of

German territory, not extended to a defense of non-German interests. Neither Prussia nor the South Germans had any interest in fighting a war for the protection of Austrian influence in Italy. Thus, the Prussian foreign minister, Bernstorff, was unshaken when he was informed of the enthusiasm in southern Germany for a system of neutrality among the German constitutional states. He was certain that if the South German governments felt their interests ensured by closer alliances, their ultimate position would be in the best interests of Prussia and Germany.[76]

Unlike Bernstorff, Metternich had to be concerned about rumors of a neutrality alliance. For him the unity of the Confederation behind Austria in the face of any revolutionary war was a keystone of his European policy, second only to his pursuit of the unity of the three great continental powers. His response to the rumors was to continue to encourage the South German monarchs to help Austria build up the defensive strength of the moral and material powers of the German Confederation. That was the purpose of the Bray mission. It was also the purpose of his communications with the King of Württemberg. Responding to a report that King William personally—if not officially—favored the idea of a monarchic crusade against the French source of the present revolutionary contagion, Metternich wrote to discourage the idea of an offensive war. Instead, he encouraged the king to cooperate with his efforts to strengthen the Confederation. To indicate his ideas on the subject, he enclosed a copy of the memorandum that Bray had taken to the King of Bavaria. He also assured King William that the government of his Russian relatives in St. Petersburg supported this conservative and federative program, even if the Bavarian government might not.[77]

In apparent confirmation of Metternich's assertions of Russian support for the Austrian position, Russian diplomats in Munich and Stuttgart posed the rhetorical and cathartic question as to the truth of the rumors of South German neutrality.[78] Naturally the response of Bavaria and Württemberg was that of innocent surprise. They both asserted their firm intention to participate wholeheartedly in any federal defense of Germany. Such an answer, they did not explain, was not a promise to support just any Austrian interpretation of a "federal defense of Germany." Nevertheless, such assurances impressed the French minister in Munich. He reported that the neutrality ideas that Armansperg had shared with him had to be considered invalid. The neutral intentions of Bavaria, Baden, and Württemberg now had to be considered unworthy of confidence.[79]

Although the French diplomat might be given credit for foresight, it was a precognition that was not accepted by important men in both South Germany and Prussia. Armansperg, for one, did not give up his ideas of an independent South German policy based upon a neutrality system. After the Bray mission, he felt that it was absolutely necessary to give immediate substance to his plans.[80] The initiative, however, was taken by King William of Württemberg. It was he who proposed a South German military alliance and a potential neutrality pact. This was the purpose of a secret memorandum of 22 November he sent to the King of Bavaria. Officially Armansperg knew nothing of this initiative.[81] But whether or not he was directly responsible for motivating the communication, he was definitely in on the plan. The proposal to King Ludwig was made directly by the King of Württemberg, because it was feared that the stubborn Bavarian ruler would resist ideas introduced by his own ministers.[82] It seems it was not Metternich alone who recognized the value of informal personal diplomacy outside regular channels.

William's memorandum concentrated principally on a plea for a South German military alliance. The alliance that it proposed was designed to give these states the security and influence in Europe that each one of them could not achieve alone. Second, the memorandum expressed the possibility that the proposed military alliance might develop into a neutrality pact to protect South German territorial and political integrity in case of a European war concerning non-German interests. South Germany, placed between Austria and France, had always become the battlefield of these factious powers. The South German princes were pawns in struggles in which they had little interest and nothing to gain. In the past their troops had died on the far-flung fields of Spain and Russia without gain to their own countries or sovereigns. Divided, the South German princes were weak. Yet their peoples had qualities of religion and enlightenment in common; they also enjoyed constitutional governments and close trade relations. In light of all this, the King of Württemberg asked, why should the South German states not act together as a third force within the German Confederation? As a bloc they would be able to determine what European alliances they would or would not join.[83]

King William's memorandum also hinted at the possibility of

securing Prussian support for the proposed South German alliance. It called attention to the similarity of ideals and interests
held by the South Germans and Prussians, as compared to the
great difference between the progressive interests of the South
Germans and the archaic, multinational, and economically exclusive interests of the Austrians. In any case, the memorandum
concluded, while abiding by the rules and obligations of the
Confederation, the South Germans should be prepared to defend
themselves against non-confederates and confederates alike. The
governments of Württemberg, Bavaria, Baden, and Grand Ducal
Hesse should agree to arm their troops and have them operate as
a single unified force under its own South German commander.
Thus prepared, the participating states would face the inse-
curities of the future in safety and be prepared, if need be, to
await the development of events behind the shield of armed
neutrality.

Ludwig, without even informing his foreign minister, Armansperg, responded favorably to King Williams's proposals on 2
December. The Bavarian king agreed to the value and necessity of
a South German military alliance and indicated his desire to see
one developed. He hesitated, however, on one (to him very important) point: for a South German alliance to be successful, it
would have to include Bavaria's territorial rival, Baden. But Ludwig felt that to achieve a Bavarian-Baden alliance it was imperative first to obtain a settlement of their long-time territorial
differences.[84] Therein lay the major obstacle to the Armansperg-
King William plan: the same particularism that led Bavaria to
resist Austrian direction of the Confederation was the obstacle to
the formation of a sub-alliance system within the Confederation
that might prevent Austrian dominance.

The obstacle of particularism was also evident in the reaction
of Baden to the South German alliance plan. Grand Duke
Leopold of Baden was kept abreast of the top secret communications between Stuttgart and Munich by his minister at the Bavarian court, Baron Friedrich von Fahnenberg.[85] Leopold could
see the value of a South German military alliance arranged in
cooperation with Prussia. He wanted, however, to maintain the
German Confederation basically as it was. He was worried by
Fahnenberg's report of the belief in Munich that the Prussian
ministry wished the dissolution of the existing federal structure.[86] Fahnenberg was instructed to inform Armansperg, therefore, that Baden would cooperate in a South German alliance and
would work closely with Prussia, but only so long as this could

be done within the context of the existing German Confederation.[87]

Armansperg's response was that the goal of a South German-Prussian alliance was not the destruction of the German Confederation, but its neutrality in a Franco-Austrian war. This neutrality could be guaranteed, he said, by organizing a bloc of federal states that would vote against committing the Confederation to a war. As the federal constitution required a two-thirds majority in the plenum of the Federal Diet to declare a federal war, a bloc of states with twenty-four votes could assure German neutrality. Armansperg counted, at the very least, on the four votes each of Prussia, Bavaria, Württemberg, Saxony, and Hanover; the three votes each of Baden and Grand Ducal Hesse; and the two votes of Hohenzollern-Hechingen and Sigmaringen.[88]

Once these ideas had been aired, Armansperg could not resist urging King William to bring the proposed alliance into fruition. As 1830 drew to a close the Bavarian foreign minister was especially anxious. He felt that King Ludwig was more inclined than ever to agree to the plans. The minister of Württemberg in Munich, Baron Philipp von Schmitz-Grollenburg, reported Armansperg's feelings and his own personal fears that the Austrian federal delegate would return to Frankfurt in the new year with proposals for a general arming of the Confederation. With this in view, Armansperg called for King William to follow-up his earlier memorandum to the Bavarian king and try to secure a final agreement.[89]

But by mid-December, William was reluctant to push further his proposals.[90] The cautious and conservative attitude of the Prussian king apparently convinced the King of Württemberg that it was useless to attempt to gain Frederick William's support for an alliance that was designed for the protection of purely German interests. William felt sure that since the Polish rising against Russian rule on 27 November, the three partitioning powers of old—Austria, Prussia, and Russia—had entered a general anti-revolutionary coalition.[91] Metternich's German policy was aided once again by the apparent unity of the Continental Powers. As 1831 began, however, neither Metternich nor the King of Württemberg could be certain of what the future policy of the Prussia government might be. That policy would be decisive in determining a solution to the German Question.

4
South German, Prussian, and Austrian Options, 1831

The success of Metternich's approach to the German Question, no less than that of Armansperg and his royal ally in Stuttgart, depended on the attitude of Prussia. Armansperg desired a Prussian-supported South German neutrality alliance so that Bavaria would not be drawn into a war with France in support of Austria's non-German interests. Metternich, on the other hand, needed Prussian support so that the other German states would be compelled to defend his interventionist policy in Italy despite French threats and possible military intervention. Metternich and Emperor Francis decided that Austria would not undertake a war of aggression, but if attacked, "would defend [Austria] to the last man, united with Russia, Prussia, Germany, and Spain."[1] Metternich thought of the German Confederation, along with the Great Powers, as the pillars of the European—and thus the Austrian—security system.

Metternich's pursuit of Great Power and German cooperation, based upon anti-revolutionary principles and organized to force the July Monarchy to contain the spirit of revolution within its own borders, was thwarted initially by Prussia's decision for an early unconditional recognition of the government of Louis Philippe. Metternich had hoped that by his willingness to support Prussian interests in Luxemburg—first at the London Conference and then by working for federal occupation and defense of the Duchy—he could involve Prussia in a policy of mutual support should either government feel the necessity to act against revolution on its own borders.[2] He found Berlin as reluctant to risk provoking France by a federal occupation of Luxemburg as she was to support his efforts to make the German Confederation a bulwark for the defense of Austria's Italian interests.[3]

The South German advocates of a South German-Prussian alliance, aimed at preventing Austria from turning the Confederation into a mere pawn in Austria's non-German policy, could only be encouraged by the lack of agreement between the two great German powers. More and more in 1831, Metternich's German diplomacy had to be turned to preventing the development of a Prussian-South German solution to the German Question.

All parties were interested in protecting Germany from a French attack. The likelihood that any French revolutionary expansion would involve an attack on the Rhineland and the necessity of Austrian assistance to repell such an attack was always an advantage that Metternich had in his dealings with the other German states. It was such a potential French invasion—which the South Germans hoped to prevent by a neutrality alliance with Prussia—that led Berlin to seek Vienna's views on the proper defense of Germany. In October 1830, the Prussian foreign minister, Count Christian von Bernstorff, encouraged by Bavarian military overtures, suggested to Frederick William III that Prussia initiate military talks with the more important German governments. He urged that Prussia take the lead because she would probably have to bear the greatest burden should there be a war between France and Germany. The king insisted, however, that any Prussian planning be conditioned upon the approval of his mightiest German ally, Austria. So it was that in the first days of January 1831, General Friedrich von Röder was sent to Vienna to seek such agreements.[4]

Röder's instructions were written by Johann Albert Friedrich Eichhorn.[5] Thus they bore the mark of the progressive ultra-Prussian party that so alienated Metternich in the 1820s by its advocacy of reforms such as the Prussian-South German commercial union. Eichhorn, along with Finance Minister Motz and Foreign Minister Bernstorff, would soon come to be identified by Metternich as the "Eichhorn-Bernstorff party," whose Prussian-German reform ideas were aimed at a Prussian-dominated Germany. Metternich felt that in the process they were thoughtlessly and unconsciously undermining the Confederation and preparing Germany for a revolutionary catastrophe. Whether we agree with Metternich's evaluation or not, some of the tendencies that the Austrian foreign minister identified can be seen in the Röder overtures in Vienna. They would be more obvious in talks that another Prussian general, Rühle, had with the South German courts later in the year.

Prussia, Röder was instructed to tell the Austrians, intended to fight only a defensive war. In the event of such a war, however, she would provide nearly 200,000 men as opposed to the 80,000 required by federal agreement. Meanwhile, the Prussian government volunteered to act as the intermediary between Austria and the South German states during the formulation of any defensive program. This, according to Eichhorn, was because of the "many points of collision" between South Germany and Austria, and because of the South Germans' particular trust in Prussia. Adding insult to injury, Röder's instructions proposed a specific defensive system for Germany in which Prussian troops would predominate and a Prussian general would be the obvious choice for overall commander-in-chief. The proposal was for a tripartite division of the German federal armies: Prussian troops on the right flank with the North German Ninth and Tenth Federal Corps, a Prussian-supported middle German army of the South German Seventh and Eight Federal Corps, and Austrian forces on the left.[6]

Metternich, retreating as he perennially did in such cases to a position of political strength through Great Power consensus, insisted that an agreement between the three Continental Powers was necessary before specific German military plans could be formulated. His position was that such an agreement and a joint declaration of principles was needed to increase the strength and decisiveness of the allied states. This, Metternich declared—hinting at the rumors of neutrality from South Germany—was absolutely necessary before the independent bent of the South Germans could be catered to by a tripartite division of German federal forces.[7]

The Austrian foreign minister had good cause to insist that a political agreement precede a military one. He was all too aware of the sentiment in South Germany for a system of independent neutrality. Under these circumstances, Metternich had to wonder what the course of Prussian politics would be if a Prussian general became the commander of all the German forces. With obvious reference to the ambiguity of Prussia's attitude toward potential Austrian intervention in Italy, Metternich questioned Röder closely as to what the King of Prussia felt the German Confederation should do if a war broke out over the Belgian question. What should the Confederation do if there was no *casus foederis* for a federal war? The threat of a quid pro quo may have been thinly veiled when Metternich reminded Röder that Austria's interest in the Belgian affair was similar to that of Prussia's interest in Italian affairs. Was the implication that if

Prussia wanted Austria to use her influence to help Prussia in Belgium, Prussia had better not abandon Austrian interests in Italy? It seemed so.[8]

In the midst of his discussions with Röder, Metternich received word on 11 and 12 February of the revolutions in Modena, Bologna, Ferrara, and Parma—states bordering on Austria's Lombardy-Venetia. The Austrian foreign minister and Emperor Francis had already decided that, for its own defense, the Habsburg Monarchy had to save the Italian princes, no matter what the French reaction. Metternich had long known, from the reports of his ambassador in Paris, that despite his good intentions, Louis Philippe might not be able to control the warlike passions of his own people. Nevertheless, in January 1831, Metternich had informed the French government that, although Austria wanted peace, she would intevene in Italy to defend her own perimeters.[9] He hoped that the French authorities would not try to oppose this policy, and he based this hope on the fact that France could not attack Austria without declaring war on her buffers, Piedmont-Sardinia and the German Confederation. An attack on either buffer would bring about a general European war. That was something that Metternich was sure Louis Philippe wanted to avoid; it would give free rein to his opponents, the bonapartists and anarchists in France. Therefore, after hearing of the Italian revolutions, Metternich reminded the French government that anarchy was their common foe. Furthermore, if the Habsburg Monarchy were mortally threatened by anarchy as a result of the moral support the French government gave to Italian revolutionaries, the Habsburgs had Napoleon's son with whom to threaten Louis Philippe.[10]

Although it is uncertain what part Metternich's warnings played in convincing the French government not to try to thwart Austrian intervention in Italy, the Austrian foreign minister was correct in assuming that Louis Philippe would try to see peace preserved. By 2 March, Metternich had already learned that the government in Paris would agree to a limited Austrian intervention in Italy.[11] By then, however, Metternich seems to have fired himself to meet any French opposition with war. The new bellicose language in Vienna seemed to be part of an Austrian plan to prepare her German allies to support her should defiance of the popular French doctrine of nonintervention bring a declaration of war from Paris. That, at least, was the view of the foreign minister of Württemberg, and he warned his envoy in Vienna not to commit the government at Stuttgart to any such support.[12]

The time was at hand for which Metternich had so long tried to prepare a Great Power and German defensive system. Now he could not accept the Prussian military proposals brought by General Röder. Reports from South Germany and the warnings of his military advisors made it impossible for Metternich to agree to plans that would give Austria so little control of the German federal armies. From Stuttgart and Munich came rumors of neutrality plans. The idea was openly advocated in the press.[13] Field Marshal Friedrich von Langenau warned Metternich that in case of a Franco-Austrian war there would be a need for at least 130,000 to 150,000 Austrian troops to protect the South German states and to see that they did not turn from allies into opponents.[14] A similarly pessimistic view was held by Archduke Carl, the man who Emperor Francis wanted to be the German federal commander. Carl discounted completely the reliability of the German federal contingents. The German princes, he felt, would most likely disarm or join the first army that touched their soil.[15]

Increasing the danger of a South German neutrality alliance was the apparent Prussian willingness to encourage such a project. The Austrian minister in Berlin, Count Joseph von Trauttmansdorff, reported that on 13 March the government-sponsored newspaper carried an article that made it seem that the proclamation of a representative constitution in Prussia was imminent. The same article proclaimed that the Prussian government intended to resist the bellicose promptings of Austria and Russia and to avoid a war with France for non-German interests. At the same time, Trauttmansdorff reported that the Prussian chief of staff, Baron August Rühle von Lilienstern, was on a mission to South Germany. Its purpose the Prussian foreign office seemed unwilling to disclose.[16]

Metternich expressed to Röder his extreme regret that Rühle was sent to the South German courts without previous consultation with the Hofburg. He complained that such a lack of Austro-Prussian coordination was especially bad at the moment, because there were consultations going on in Munich that could lead to a project for South German neutrality.[17] Metternich insisted that the Prussian plan for a tripartite division of the German armies was not advisable now. An independent middle German army composed chiefly of South German troops might prove dangerous. Depending on the course of events, the South Germans might neutralize themselves and take up an independent position. Metternich expressed the opinion that no one should be surprised if there existed plans for such a contingency in Bavaria and Baden. As to the King of Württemberg, he had always had an inclination to want to play a special role.[18]

Röder concluded that the sudden hardheadedness of the Austrian foreign minister and his insistence on a bipartite—Austrian and Prussian led—division of the federal armies was the result of Metternich's fear that Austria could not control an independent South German army. The Prussian general reported that, if Prussia ever wanted to gain Austrian acceptance of her proposals, special care had to be taken not to nourish the suspicion in Vienna that Prussia was trying to gain a predominant influence over all of the German federal troops. He attributed Metternich's desire to have Archduke Carl chosen head of these armies to the decisive influence over them that his command might ensure to Austria.[19]

Before the Prussian general left Vienna on 2 April, he persuaded Metternich not to press for immediate selection of a federal field marshal. For his part, Röder tentatively accepted the idea that division of the federal armies should be in only two parts: the northern half under Prussian command, the southern half under Austrian command. Nothing, however, was accomplished beyond an exchange of ideas and a tentative agreement on these generalities. But this was the basis, Metternich told Röder, upon which he was going to open talks with the South German states, if he could get them to send military representatives to Vienna.[20] This information was all that General Röder left Vienna with, except for a familiar sounding Metternichian memorandum for the Prussian king.[21]

The main thesis of the memorandum was that all of the evils that occurred since the July Revolution were the result of a moral malady that had been extending itself over Europe during the previous twenty years. According to Metternich, the only way to survive this sickness was through the strength to be gained by a frank accord between the rulers of the three Continental Powers—the only princes who were still in total possession of their sovereignty. They alone could provide the nucleus around which could assemble all the rulers who still preserved the ability to act in the interest of their own salvation. Then, through uniformity of action, the Great Powers—especially the two great German powers—could assure their own safety and that of their German confederates.[22]

No doubt Metternich's memorandum to the Prussian king would have been more vigorous had he known the course that

General Johann Rühle von Lilienstern's visit to South Germany was taking at that moment. That the Austrian foreign minister did not know is evident from his angry reaction when he finally learned of the German military and political options that came out of the Rühle discussions.[23] Of course, it was a long time before even the South German ministries involved understood what to make of the Rühle mission and its meaning for Prussian policy.

Some of the South Germans were quite concerned about the nature of that policy. Undeterred by their failures in the fall of 1830, Armansperg and his intimates—Count Philipp von Schmitz-Grollenburg, the envoy of Württemberg in Munich; and Johann Friedrich Cotta, the publisher and friend of the two South German kings—had continued to encourage the King of Württemberg to ask the Prussian ruler to support their ideas for South German neutrality.[24] They saw here the basis for a South German-Prussian alliance that would replace the current power structure in the German Confederation. But King Frederick William had to be contacted if the South German kings were to agree to put such ideas into effect. The problem was that King William had been reluctant to approach the Prussian king, because he felt that Prussia had already agreed to a continental anti-revolutionary alliance.[25] The real attitude of the Prussian king had remained unlearned.

Then, in late February 1831, Armansperg received word from Berlin that General Rühle was coming on a confidential mission to the South German courts. His reported objective was to learn their attitudes toward France.[26] King William of Württemberg was informed of the Rühle mission, at about the same time as was the Bavarian government, by the resident Prussian minister in Stuttgart. According to his information, Rühle was coming for military discussions that were to prepare the way for the creation of a new German military policy by the Federal Diet.[27] The opportunity for a South German-Prussian political and military understanding seemed to be at hand.

When Rühle arrived in Munich on 4 March, he found Armansperg and King Ludwig eager for a close military understanding with Prussia. In a joint interview, along with the Prussian minister resident in Munich, Johann von Küster, Rühle was told to banish all fears that Bavaria would join France or proclaim a one-sided neutrality. Ludwig declared that he was willing to follow Prussia's lead, because he did not trust the machinations of Metternich. He was in full agreement with the Prussian proposal for a tripartite division of the federal armies. He also liked the proposal that no federal field marshal be named and that strategy should be worked out by joint planning sessions at a common headquarters in the field. The assurances were one-sided, however. The Prussians had to admit that, because of their lack of instructions, they could not answer the Bavarians' question as to what Prussia would do if France invaded only Italy or Switzerland.[28]

Armansperg kept saying he was certain that Prussia intended to preserve the peace of Germany: that she would join to herself a compact South German alliance and make sure that Austria could not assemble the votes necessary to move the Federal Diet to a declaration of war.[29] The course of Rühle's language in the next few days, however, made it appear that Armansperg's hopes were to be disappointed. More and more it seemed that the Prussian general was trying to keep the second rank powers dependent on Prussia and Austria and that he was merely trying to speed the arming of their federal contingents. His language indicated that Prussia intended to include Austria in any agreement that she reached with the South German states.[30]

Rühle was at best noncommittal. So too was the nature of his memorandum of 13 March, designed to represent to the Bavarian ministry his impressions and proposals after talks with the Bavarian foreign minister. Although Rühle noted that both Prussia and Bavaria earnestly wanted peace and were convinced of the necessity of a purely defensive stand against France, he left it up to Bavaria to propose a specific common policy toward France, Austria, and the German Confederation. He only committed himself to carrying such proposals to the other South German courts. It was up to them to develop a set of common proposals for him to take back to Berlin. Meanwhile, he warned of the need for moderation in public statements so that Austrian mistrust would not be aroused. Bavaria, he asserted, still needed the security and protection that Austrian good will could provide. He also advised the Bavarian government to aid Prussian efforts to prepare South Germany for a defensive war and to cooperate with Prussia and Austria should it become imperative to initiate some immediate federal military action.[31]

If Rühle was noncomittal about Prussian policy, he seemed open to Armansperg's perceptions and proposals. He was surprised at first by the antipathy and distrust toward Austria that he found in the Bavarian king and his foreign minister.[32] Gradually, however, in his conversations with Armansperg and the envoy from Württemberg, Schmitz, he began to speak as they did. He also became convinced of the need for Prussian-South German cooperation to prevent the mobilization of the federal armies and the election of a federal commander. He too became certain that Austria had to be prevented from diminishing Prussia's influence in Germany and, with it, the chances for German peace. Rühle expressed shock in the face of rumors that Austria planned to defy the French doctrine of nonintervention by further military action against revolutionaries in Italy and Poland. When he heard that the Hofburg was preparing to send an emissary to South Germany to win these courts to such plans, he decided to prolong his stay in Munich to personally counter that effort.[33]

Because the time of arrival of the Austrian emissary was in doubt, however, Armansperg convinced General Rühle to leave at once for Stuttgart and Karlsruhe with Bavaria's proposals for a Prussian-South German alliance. These were given to the Prussian as an unsigned memorandum on 28 March.[34] Tentatively approved by King Ludwig, Armansperg's memorandum presented the outline of an alliance system that was designed to protect Germany against French aggression and keep the Confederation from becoming merely an instrument of Austrian policy. Armansperg also hoped that out of the proposed alliance system would grow a common tariff system that would make its founders—Prussia and Bavaria—the first and second states of Germany.[35]

The immediate purpose of the proposals, Armansperg explained to King Ludwig, was to "strike the intrigues of the Federal Diet at their roots" and to place the question of war and peace in the hands of Prussia and Bavaria, in union with any other cooperative German courts. The combined votes of these states could prevent a federal declaration of war, a declaration that the Confederation was endangered, or the election of a federal field marshal. Armansperg feared that any of these federal actions could be perverted by Austrian intrigue so as to involve the Confederation in the implementation of purely Austrian policies. Nevertheless, he recognized the real value of Austrian cooperation should the defense of Germany actually become necessary. After a firm alliance was secretly concluded between the members of the new political alignment, Austria was to be informed and permitted to join too. The condition for her membership would be a guarantee that the Habsburgs would not threaten France or otherwise endanger Germany through international problems arising out of their own Italian concerns.[36]

Armansperg's memorandum was a remarkable document that showed both antipathy toward Austria as a power with non-German interests, and the recognition that that same Austria was still an integral part of Germany. Here, then, was a new option for the solution of the German Question: a reorganized Confederation led by Prussia and Bavaria, with Austria as the new pawn in German affairs. Turnabout was fair play: Metternich wanted the German states to be the pawns in his European policies.

With Armansperg's memorandum in hand, Rühle arrived in Stuttgart on 30 March. In the capital of Württemberg, as later at Karlsruhe, he found the government friendly and interested in his mission, but more circumspect with its own views than was the government in Munich.[37] King William was still unsure of the real purpose of Rühle's mission. The Prussian minister in Stuttgart and his own envoy in Vienna informed him that the Hofburg approved the Rühle mission and had asked the Austrian ministers in South Germany to support the Prussian's proposals.[38] However, when the king specifically asked his envoy in Vienna what the Austrians thought of the Rühle mission—hinting at its possible anti-Austrian character—Baron Ludwig von Blomberg reported that the Austrian government knew nothing about the details of the mission. They merely assumed that Rühle's mission was like that undertaken by Röder.[39]

The memorandum that Rühle presented to the foreign minister of Württemberg on 4 April showed the impact of the Prussian's talks in Munich. While asking for proposals to take to Berlin, Rühle now admitted that the Prussian government wanted to learn South German views regarding a possible Franco-Austrian crisis over Italy. It also wanted to cooperate with the South German courts on an appropriate response by the Federal Diet. Although Rühle continued to urge military preparations for the defense of Germany, he indicated that it would be wise for Württemberg to vote negatively on any federal measure to declare Germany in a state of danger. This, he insisted, would needlessly provoke France.[40]

The response that the government of Württemberg made to Rühle on 6 April took the form of an unsigned memorandum, following the form used by Bavaria.[41] Its contents were circumspect and stressed the desire of the Stuttgart government to remain in conformity with Confederation laws. This, however, did not prevent the ministry from expressing a great interest in avoiding a provocation of France. Armed neutrality had great appeal. It provided a means by which South Germany could avoid a war but be prepared for any eventuality. Nevertheless, Württemberg wanted to be better informed of Prussian views concerning such matters before entering further into their discussion.[42]

When Rühle arrived in Karlsruhe on 10 April, he received a reception similar to that in Stuttgart: favorable but discreet.[43] The government of Baden was well informed regarding the course of Rühle's talks in Munich and Stuttgart.[44] Armansperg had confidently communicated to Karlsruhe the Bavarian proposals and had received the assurance that Baden agreed with them.[45] Nevertheless, the memorandum given to Rühle in Karlsruhe was still just as cautious as the one he received in Stuttgart.[46] While Prussia was to be assured of Baden's German patriotism and her readiness to defend the fatherland, she was to remember that Baden was forced by her geographical position to maintain a certain degree of friendship with France. Baden was willing, however, to cooperate with Prussia to prepare measures for Germany's defense. Not only that, but she encouraged Prussia to take the lead generally in developing the common institutions of the German Confederation. Thus German nationalism was to be given a legal basis and brought to the support of the German princes in their struggle against foreign influence.[47] Cautious or not, such encouragement to Prussia sounded essentially like a mandate for Berlin to seek new answers to the German Question. Thus when Rühle, while in Darmstadt, learned of Austrian opposition to the Prussian ministry's South German initiatives, he urged Foreign Minister Bernstorff to make clear to the South Germans the approval of those initiatives by King Frederick William.[48] It was such approval that all sought.

Rühle and his reforming friends had good reason to be pleased with his mission to South Germany. When he returned to Berlin, after a final visit to Munich in May, he was convinced that the South Germans felt that their future lay in close relations with Prussia. They were pleased by Prussia's Zollverein efforts and now put their trust in her to help preserve the safety and independence of Germany. As for Austria, Rühle concluded that the South Germans viewed her as too involved in the affairs of Italy, Poland, and Turkey to give impartial consideration to Germany's problems. She could take part selflessly in neither Germany's internal prosperity nor in her external defense. As Rühle saw it, the South German governments felt that when old Emperor Francis died Austria would suffer terrible internal governmental and financial problems. Then, instead of being able to fulfill her role as the protector of European peace, order, and legitimacy, Austria would sooner or later need the help of the German Confederation to preserve her own existence.[49] And although we now know that Rühle and the South Germans were somewhat premature in anticipating events (the general nature of which would not occur for eighty-three years), the road certainly seemed open in 1831 for a Prussian-South German answer to the German Question.[50]

The views of the South German governments notwithstanding, the Prussian government had good reason not to rush into any project that would alienate Austria—her European as well as German ally. With a goodly number of troops on her eastern border guarding against the spread of revolution in Poland, Prussia was vulnerable to a French attack. Because of Austrian preoccupation with Italy, the Prussian government felt the necessity of sending Rühle to South Germany to ensure the participation of those states in a general German defense.[51] Of course, in March 1831, the French government under the new minister president, Casimir Perier, banished the popular notion that a broad application would be given to the French doctrine of nonintervention. The danger that Germany would be drawn into a war with France because of Austrian intervention in Italy was greatly diminished.[52] But the Belgian crisis remained. The Belgians loudly claimed Luxemburg. At the same time, the King of Holland rejected even the Eighteen Articles, by which an international conference in London was trying to ensure the peaceful establishment of the new Belgian state. If war did develop out of this situation, military support of the Habsburg Monarchy would be more valuable to Prussia than that of the weaker South German states. Close cooperation with Austria offered Prussia more advantages than disadvantages.[53] Naturally Metternich stressed the advantages as he pursued the continental alliance he deemed necessary for the successful implementation of his European and German policy.[54]

Metternich was still seeking a continental alliance system that would preserve the current European status quo—not make war against France, as his critics charged. He was sure that even the French government sought nothing more than he did: international peace and the end of revolutionary subversion at home. He advised Emperor Francis that defensive armament had to be continued, however, because well-meaning Louis Philippe might lose control of his countrymen. With him or without him, the French nation might still launch a program of revolutionary expansion. Nevertheless, the financial strain on Austria caused by the increasing armaments led Metternich to propose to Emperor Francis that Austria work for a general European agreement for the limitation of armaments. At the same time, he underlined the necessity for an international agreement according to which each state would seek to preserve the peace of Europe by repressing revolutionary propaganda within its own borders.[55]

Metternich felt that a close understanding between the two great German powers would assure the acceptance of his ideas in South Germany as well as in the rest of Europe. He was concerned, therefore, that the Rühle mission was a sign of disunity between Austria and Prussia. As such, it was most inopportune at a time when the South German press extolled the virtues of an independent South German–Prussian neutrality alliance. The fact that the official Prussian newspaper carried articles that encouraged belief in Prussia's progressive constitutional intentions and neutral inclinations could only further encourage an independent South German attitude.[56]

Metternich decided to attack the divisive Prussian influence at its source. In a dispatch for Trauttmansdorff on 2 April, he ordered his envoy to talk to the acting Prussian foreign minister, Johann Peter Friedrich Ancillon, about the provocative articles in the South German press.[57] Specifically, Trauttmansdorff was to advise the Prussian minister of the necessity of cooperating with the Austrian government to persuade the South German governments to censor articles that portrayed Prussia as interested in constitutionalism and neutrality.[58]

The approach was direct, but the response not altogether satisfactory. Ancillon said that the Prussian ministry would consider what could be done, but the constitutional guarantees of freedom of the press in the South German states limited the possibilities. He assured the Austrian minister, however, that the government in Berlin had no thought of a neutrality system in cooperation with the lesser German states. It recognized too well the dangers to Prussia's own Rhine provinces from a French attack. Neither was there, according to Ancillon, any real thought of introducing a new constitution in Prussia. There was, he admitted, a party that hoped otherwise, but it was a minority and the king would never agree with its ideas.[59] Ancillon was to be proven right, but not before more was heard from "the party."

"The party" in Prussia and its supporters in South Germany were a major concern for Metternich. In his estimation, they diverted attention from the true danger of the day: revolutionary decay within the European states, increasingly even in Germany. He saw the possibility of the Confederation's dissolution through the weakening of monarchic authority in each German state. He was angered that the governments did not stand together to prevent such developments. Instead they acted individually and made concessions to revolution. In March 1831, the Saxon government granted its subjects a constitution, declaring it a voluntary act instead of resisting popular pressure with the backing of Austria and Prussia. Metternich still had hopes that at least the Elector of Hesse might repent of his constitutional concessions and, admitting that they were the result of coercion, provide an excuse for federal intervention. But what particularly became a source of concern for Metternich—a stimulus for his desire for some action to secure a stricter application of the monarchic principles of the Confederation—was the revolutionary spirit that he viewed as dominant in the diet of Baden.[60] Because of the decision of the government of that state to allow the debates of its diet to be carried in the German press, the whole nation was being aroused by attacks against censorship, the Carlsbad Decrees, and the German Confederation in general.[61]

By April 1831 Metternich was concerned, not just by the possibility of a South German-Prussian alliance in military and political affairs, but by the whole system of South German permissiveness to anti-monarchic expression. Both concerns motivated the memoranda that the Austrian foreign minister had Prince Alfred von Schönburg take to Munich and Stuttgart in the last days of that month. They were part of a political offensive by which Metternich hoped to regain the direction of policy in the South German courts. He had long seen the need to reach some understanding with the kings of Bavaria and Württemberg, but he had felt the need to await the appropriate moment. It had been necessary to see what would happen in Italy and to be sure of the intentions of the French government before he concentrated fully on Germany. Because things had evolved most satisfactorily in these areas by mid-April, Metternich decided that the time had come to deal with Germany, particularly the South Germans.[62]

On 21 April, Schönburg received orders to carry a political and military memorandum to the Austrian minister in Munich, Count Kaspar von Spiegel, and then on to King William of Württemberg. Although he was not to take a copy of the memoranda to Baden, King William was to be asked to use his influence on the Grand Duke in the sense of the communications that he received. Instructions that accompanied the memoranda explained to Schönburg and Spiegel how they were to convey the documents and the purpose for which they were sent. The political document, for instance, was written so that it could be seen by both kings. The military memorandum was only to be read to King Ludwig of Bavaria; it was not to be let out of Spiegel's hands. Such caution, the instructions noted, resulted from Austria's past experiences with the Bavarian foreign minister, Armansperg. What he learned, said Metternich, was soon known in Paris. The memorandum could be shown to King William of Württemberg. He was to be trusted as a true supporter of the common good.[63]

Metternich's diplomatic offensive was on: he was appealing to the German patriotism of the South German sovereigns and trying to separate them from members of "the party" among their advisors.[64] The goal that Schönburg and Speigel were to work for in their talks with the South German monarchs was fourfold: unity among the German governments and a strong trusting relationship with the two great German powers; strict adherence of the German rulers to the principles of the Confederation and its laws; mobilization of military forces and cooperation with Austria and Prussia in case of a federal war; and avoidance of any offensive action against France, but preparation for resistance against any French attack.[65] In short, Metternich was restating the Austrian solution to the German Question: the preservation of the monarchic status quo through the defensive unity of the German monarchs within a confederation led by Austro-Prussian dualism.

The political memorandum for each of the South German kings was essentially the same call for German federal unity under the direction of the Continental Powers that Schönburg had delivered in August 1830. But it was more: it was a resounding clarion of praise for the benefits of the German Confederation, described as the true source of German greatness and security. The document reminded the South German sovereigns that since the July Revolution, the "crass principle of popular sovereignty stood against that of historic right." The French were held responsible for this grave threat to all institutions of society, and their influence, as seen in the revolutions in Belgium, Poland, Italy, and even in Saxony, Electoral Hesse, and Braunsch-weig, denounced. Now, the document continued, the revolutionary parties everywhere had thrown off their liberal masks and shown their real radicalism. The salvation of Europe depended on all the governments uniting to preserve the status quo. The only method of salvation for Germany was the unan-imous cooperation of the German princes within the Con-federation. "Only thus," said Metternich, "can we preserve the individual states and the independence of Germany as a power of the first rank." Therefore now, the memorandum concluded, the Emperor of Austria asked his allies for unity in the implementa-tion of German federal laws, complete trust in the views and intentions of himself and his allies among the Great Powers, and the armament of Germany to withstand any French attack.[66]

The accompanying military memorandum was part of Metter-nich's effort to convince the South Germans of Austria's military preparedness and her close understanding with Prussia. While urging the preparation of plans and armaments for the defense of Germany, it outlined the federal context in which South German plans should be developed. This, according to the memorandum, was the bipartite division of the federal armies—with the Ninth and Tenth Federal Corps to operate with the Prussians and the South Germans, along with Austria's forces, to defend the left flank, as had been agreed to by Röder during his visit to Vienna. Now, to finalize these plans, it was suggested that the South Germans find some pretense to send representatives to Vienna for complete military discussions. Without arousing undue atten-tion in France, these meetings were to determine the manner in which advancing Austrian troops could reinforce South German units as they retreated before an initial French attack.[67]

If the two memoranda were intended to gain for Austria the hearts and minds of the South Germans, the end result was just the reverse. South German sensibilities were injured by the sec-ondary place they were assigned in federal affairs. Suspicions were also aroused by the enunciation of military plans very different from those discussed with General Rühle. For Metter-nich there was only one immediate benefit from the Austrian initiative: the distrust that Metternich showed of Foreign Minis-ter Armansperg led King Ludwig to suggest that in the future Metternich might wish to correspond through their mutual confi-dant, the conservative monarchist, Field Marshall Prince Karl von Wrede.[68] This circumvention of Metternich's opponents within the Bavarian ministry was a major coup, the first of several that Metternich would secure against "the party" within the inner councils of the various German courts. But Foreign Minister Armansperg's suspicions of Austria had already taken their toll. King Ludwig and King William continued to seek the benefits of a closer alignment with a Prussia that proffered a reformist answer to the German Question. Austrian answers seemed both outdated and threatening.

King Ludwig was convinced that Austria was trying to place the South German corps under her exclusive control; he told General Wrede that he would never agree to that.[69] Nor had he any intention of sending to Vienna the military representative that Metternich requested. Ludwig felt that it would be better to have Prussia represent South German interests at any military talks. King William, on the other hand, suggested that Bavaria send someone in the name of all of the South German governments so as to avoid Austria's suspicions. This was not done.[70] Instead, the South German monarchs continued their own mutual military planning and proceeded to choose Field Marshal Wrede as their supreme commander.[71] They still hoped for implementation of the proposals they had made to General Rühle. They still hoped, although Wrede's requests for an official Prussian response to those proposals remained long unanswered.[72]

But if the Prussian government delayed in satisfying the pleas of their aspiring South German allies, neither did they give assurances to a troubled Metternich. On 29 April, the Austrian foreign minister sent his South German memoranda off to Berlin with the request that Prussia back Austrian efforts by having her diplomats speak in a similar sense. Ancillon's reply was that they had long had such instructions. He did not hurry to guarantee any further support for Metternich's conservative federalist ideas. He merely expressed interest in Metternich's views of the need for action to stem the liberal outbursts of the Bavarian diet, to withhold federal sanction from the recent constitution in Electoral Hesse, and to control disorders in Saxony. He also pointed out the opposition that Metternich's good intentions would face from other German states, even those that were already the prey to the spirit of revolution.[73]

By May 1831, Metternich was convinced of the necessity for an immediate understanding between the German monarchs if the monarchic principle were to be upheld in Germany. He felt it was time for a renewal of the efforts begun at Carlsbad and Vienna in 1819 and 1820. Those undertakings had not withstood the liberalizing pressures of the decade that had followed. Reports from

Germany more than proved that. According to Austrian sources, the diet of Baden was acting like a German national convention.[74] There and in Bavaria the ministries were under pressure to reject their obligations to the German Confederation and to proclaim complete freedom of the press.[75] In Saxony mobs freed jailed agitators.[76] In Electoral Hesse a new representative constitution was proclaimed and, worse, its approval by the Federal Diet was even backed by Prussia.[77] At the Federal Diet, nearly a majority of the German states—including Prussia— wanted to recognize a ruling prince in Braunschweig whose brother had been forced by a mob to abdicate.[78]

Metternich considered calling together an assembly of the German princes to discuss what should be done. In fact, he called home his federal envoy, Münch, to consult with him on the matter. To his advisors and to South German diplomats alike, he pictured Germany threatened by great dangers that required equally great preventive measures. If not a congress of the princes, at least a ministerial congress might have to be assembled to lay the basis for a new federal offensive to save monarchy in Germany.[79]

Despite the attention that all this aroused in diplomatic circles, no immediate action resulted from the Metternich-Münch discussions in May 1831. The minister of Württemberg in Vienna guessed that Metternich was going to be careful to prepare the ground better before coming out into the open with plans for reactionary reforms.[80] He was right. Metternich decided that he had to counter the influence of "the party," both in Berlin and South Germany, before he could be sure that they would not thwart his plans. To do this he first had to bring the Prussian and South German monarchs to share his own distrust of "the party" as it existed within the Prussian ministry itself.

For this Metternich used Münch's return trip to Frankfurt in late June. The means was another memorandum on the contemporary German situation that the Austrian presidential envoy read to King Ludwig when they met in Munich on 26 June. It started, not surprisingly, with a declaration of the need for close cooperation between the members of the German Confederation in order to halt the attempts of state diets to transfer to themselves the powers of their princes. Then, however, the focus shifted. It warned of the revolutionary aspects of the expanding Prussian Zollverein which, it asserted, a revolutionary faction sought to use to make Prussia the center of a German federation governed by the representative system. Münch went on to name

Johann Albrecht Eichhorn, the new head of the German division of the Prussian foreign ministry, as the most prominent of a group of Prussian ministers who were working toward such a goal.[81] Münch assured Ludwig that the Austrian government recognized the need for better trade relations between the German states; the Hofburg knew, however, to differentiate between such a worthy goal and its use as a means to another end.[82]

Metternich also saw to it that the King of Prussia learned of the revolutionary aspects of his ministry's commercial policies. Through the Prussian minister in Vienna, Maltzahn, he informed the king of the hope of German revolutionaries that those commercial policies would lead to the unification of the constitutional states under Prussian aegis.[83] In a letter of 5 August to the king's most conservative and influential advisor, Prince Wilhelm zu Wittgenstein, Metternich continued and sharpened the attack. He warned that Eichhorn was "blinded by liberal and doctrinaire views and errors" and had become mistakenly convinced that the plans of the "German faction" offered Prussia a means to greatness.[84]

All of these attacks were part of a plan that Metternich prepared to implement more fully during Frederick William's visit to Teplitz in August 1831. As Metternich saw it, unless some action was soon taken monarchic Germany would be no more. "So much remains certain," he wrote to Baron Münch, "something must happen or Germany will go to ruin."[85] To achieve the necessary reforms to prevent this, Metternich sought the close cooperation of Prussia. Without it, he could not count on the help of the influential South German governments—though in his eyes, they were most endangered by the current trends. While Metternich relied on the "enlightened personal disposition" of the Prussian king, he wanted to assure the implementation of any Prussian commitment by forcing the Prussian ministry to agree to the king's "true views." If he could do this, an Austro-Prussian understanding would lead to joint proposals to a select number of German rulers. When their agreement was assured, action could be taken at the Federal Diet. Even if the Prussian ministry resisted his efforts, Metternich hoped that something would be gained: the king would then "get to know the spirit of his own staff."[86]

According to plan, Baron Josef von Werner, the counselor of the Austrian legation in Berlin, arrived in Teplitz in late July to present Metternich's views to the Prussian king. A memorandum for Frederick William proposed a close entente between Austria,

Prussia, and Russia for the formulation of their European policies and an equally close entente between the two German states to stabilize German affairs. Without help, Metternich's memorandum asserted, the middle-sized states would become the booty of revolution; there would be a general dissolution of some of the oldest princely houses in Germany. According to Metternich, for years there had been a tendency in Germany toward a fusion of the separate German states into a single whole. Now only in the older states and among the lower classes was there to be found loyalty to the princes. The middle classes were alienated. In the post-Napoleonic acquisitions like the Frankish and Swabian provinces of Bavaria and the Rhineland Palatinate of Baden, there could be no loyalty to tradition in any case. Everywhere revolutionaries were given aid in their quest for a united Germany by writers, university students and professors, and the opposition in the state diets. Measures had to be taken to halt these developments.[87]

Metternich made it clear that the first and basic necessity was unbreakable unity between Austria and Prussia in all federal affairs. Otherwise the larger secondary states would be tempted to play one of them off against the other. In a like manner, revolutionaries might try to bring Prussia to support their programs by presenting her with the possibility of great gains. The two great German states had to remain united in their policies and efforts. It was up to them, Metternich wrote, to save Germany by convincing all the German princes to hold true to their federal principles. They had to remember that the German Confederation was an organization of princes, not of their subjects. They had to be made to see that the laws of the Confederation, as the will of all its members, had to stand above the laws of the individual states. If Frederick William agreed, Metternich requested that he empower the Prussian minister in Vienna, Baron Maltzahn, to discuss with the Austrian government the means to halt the evils of the day in Germany. Once the two great German powers reached an understanding, then the other German princes could be appealed to.[88]

Metternich's Teplitz strategy seemed to bring the desired results. Frederick William was convinced that his best interest lay with the conservative policies of his Great Power ally. On 12 August, Werner reported that Wittgenstein had just shown him an order for Maltzahn in Vienna. The Prussian envoy was empowered to begin talks with Metternich and a Russian representative concerning the creation of a common continental entente and with Metternich alone concerning the means to stabilize German affairs. Moreover, Maltzahn was instructed to clear with Metternich all of his reports regarding the meetings before sending them, so as to assure their accuracy. They were then not to be sent to the Prussian foreign ministry, but directly to the king.[89] As in Bavaria, royal officials who might have dissenting views were to be bypassed by what amounted to direct correspondence between Metternich and the king. Metternich could now be more assured of the successful outcome of his efforts. He might save the German monarchs and, among them, the Habsburgs.

5

Undermining the Opposition, 1831–1832

Metternich was preparing to develop the strategy that he had initiated at Teplitz when he was jolted into the recognition that "the party" in the Prussian and South German ministries was far from defeated. The jolt came in the form of two Prussian circulars dated 15 August 1831. Addressed to the South German courts, they were the answer of the Bernstorff ministry to the South German proposals made to General Rühle. For Metternich they represented renewed Prussian concessions to South German liberalism, particularism, and antifederalism. They were proof that Austria did not yet possess the cooperation in Berlin necessary for the reconsolidation of the German bulwark against war and revolution. Metternich's efforts in the second half of 1831 were turned to destroying the influence of the Prussian and South German ministers responsible for the ideas contained in the August circulars. Only after that was done could he hope to achieve the Austro-Prussian unity necessary for the acceptance of the Austrian answer to the German Question.

The August circulars were sent to the South German courts at a time when officials in Berlin feared a war over Belgium.[1] On 4 August the Dutch, in an extreme provocation of the July Monarchy, invaded revolutionary Belgium. Louis Philippe's government decided to intervene to protect the Belgians. Despite French promises to leave Belgium as soon as the Dutch did, the Prussians did not know that those promises would be kept. In the face of such danger adjacent to Prussia's Rhineland territory, the government in Berlin wanted to ensure the sympathies of their South German confederates.

The content of the Prussian circulars manifested a combination of trust in the peaceful intentions of Austria, faith in the benefits of German nationalism and liberalism, and a continued willingness to cater to South German particularist sensibilities. They presented the argument that had there been a Franco-Austrian war in Italy, because of Austrian's defiance of the French principle of nonintervention, German armed neutrality might have been appropriate. Now things had changed. All of the European powers had shown their desire to avoid a war of principles. Now a French attack—anywhere in Europe—had to be considered the work of a faction that sought French territorial aggrandizement. Neutrality would be impossible. Germany would have to fight a truly defensive war. If that were the case, the best protection for the German princes would be the common German patriotism of their subjects. All of the German governments should cooperate, therefore, for the creation of German institutions that would encourage that kind of patriotism.[2]

Because a defensive war against France would require military planning, a military circular was paired with the political one. It suggested that the South German states have their military units form an independent central division of the combined federal German armies. If they objected to the selection of a federal field marshal, Prussia could agree to a joint command system such as had been used during the wars against Napoleon in 1813 and 1814. To develop the details of these arrangements, Prussia proposed a German military conference. The South German governments were invited to send representatives to participate in the planning of an overall German defensive system.[3] The South German courts responded favorably, although cautiously, to these Prussian overtures. Armansperg feared that Prussia and Austria were now in basic agreement and the South German states would be forced to follow their lead.[4] Metternich had no such view of Prussian policy. When Bernstorff sent him a copy of the circulars on 21 August, he was irate. In a dispatch to Werner, the counselor of the Austrian legation in Berlin, Metternich attacked the circulars as proof of an attempt by the "Bernstorff-Eichhorn party" to exclude Austria from active participation in the affairs of the German Confederation. The circulars implied, he said, Prussian acquiescence to the French principle of nonintervention. More than that, they indicated that Prussia intended to make concessions to revolutionary ideas by implementing reforms designed to give German subjects a strong feeling for a common fatherland.[5]

Metternich concluded that without ending the influence of the Prussian party responsible for the August circulars, he could not hope to achieve the Austro-Prussian cooperation he needed to fulfill any of his plans. All progress toward calling a ministerial conference for the discussion of political reforms or even a purely military conference had to be postponed until Metternich had recaptured his influence over Prussian policy. Therefore, when asked by the South Germans if Austria was ready to participate in the Prussian-called German military conference, Metternich replied that there were some details that first had to be considered by Austria and Prussia alone.[6] He also had his envoy in Berlin, Count Trauttmansdorff, inform the Prussian ministry that he was sending General Karl von Clam-Martinitz to discuss the August circulars with them. He suggested that in order not to arouse attention, it could be said that the Austrian general was in Berlin to discuss a cordon against the current cholera epidemic.[7] In fact, Metternich instructed Clam to discover the reason for the divergence between what Röder agreed to in Vienna and what Rühle apparently told the South German states.[8] This was to be Austria's first step toward ending the divergence between the two great German courts.

Metternich was intent on keeping "the party" in the Prussian ministry from obstructing his plans for the rejuvenation of the German Confederation along the lines that he desired. On 5 September, he sent to Berlin renewed proposals for the creation of a center of entente for German affairs that the Prussian king had agreed to at Teplitz.[9] Bernstorff's response, through a dispatch of 26 September to his minister in Vienna, Maltzahn, seemed relatively positive and at least opened the way for further Austro-Prussian discussions. But Bernstorff focused on the need for governmental, not princely negotiations, and he called for new cooperation between the German states, not new laws. He stressed the necessity of trust and cooperation among the German governments and admitted that problems had emerged, not because of the dearth of federal laws, but because of the lack of will to use them. He blamed that partly on the inactivity of the German Confederation in the past, but noted the German princes' false sense of honor and their reluctance to call upon the Bund. What was needed now, Bernstorff insisted, was not new laws, but a new will. At the same time, the Prussian foreign minister expressed his fear that any attempt to change the federal constitution would both arouse mistrust among the German princes and encourage foreign political intervention. The appearance of a union of princes against their subjects had to be avoided for that would only aid revolutionary propoganda.[10] Bernstorff's caution and his repeated references to "governments" rather than to "princes" was unsettling to Metternich. In his response of 9

October, he stressed the differences that existed between the German cabinets and their sovereigns. That, in Metternich's view, was the cause of compromises with the forces of revolution. Thus, again he stressed the need for close collaboration between the German princes themselves.[11]

Actually, Metternich had not waited for Bernstorff's opinion before he approached the South Germans. He already had begun to prepare the ground for the general monarchic conference that he hoped would follow an Austro-Prussian agreement. As he wished to bypass the opponents of his ideas in the South German ministries, just as he wished to bypass them in Berlin, he communicated as directly as possible with the monarchs themselves. Ludwig's most influential conservative adviser, Field Marshal von Wrede, was the approved intermediary in Munich, and the Austrian envoy, Prince Schönburg, spoke directly to King William in Stuttgart. Through similar messages to both South German kings on 8 September, Metternich sought to involve them in the development of his plans. His tactic was to propose that the monarchs themselves suggest to him the kind of measures they felt were needed if the monarchic principle were to be preserved in Germany. It was the old Metternich tactic of agreement through participation.

In his dispatch to Schönburg, Metternich declared that the King of Württemberg had to be convinced, as Emperor Francis was, of the pressing need to secure internal order within the German Confederation. Without such order the federal relationship was unthinkable and the individual German states would face dissolution from within. If the king doubted this he had only to look at Electoral Hesse, Braunschweig, Baden, and Bavaria. The government of Electoral Hesse was forced to proclaim a liberal constitution. Braunschweig had lost its legitimate prince. The Baden and Bavarian governments were subject to the verbal attacks of their own diets. What, the Austrian foreign minister asked, did King William feel was necessary to end this trend of affairs? Schönburg was to obtain from the king his confidential views on this question.[12]

So that William would have some point of reference from which to respond, Schönburg was to share the Austrian view of the Confederation and its problems with him. Basically, he was to say, Austria recognized the Confederation as an independent power whose members were sovereign princes and free cities. They alone were empowered to preserve or change the federal constitution. Its bonds, however, were indivisible. Its principle purpose was the preservation of Germany's internal peace and security. Its goal was to uphold the sovereignty of the German princes. For this reason, Metternich argued, federal laws had to have precedence over those of the individual states. Current revolutionary ideas stood opposed to the foregoing principles. To defend them Austria now sought an agreement among the major German princes that would pave the way for appropriate defensive action by the Federal Diet.[13]

Metternich's letter to Wrede of 8 September had the same purpose as the dispatch to Schönburg. It did not, however, go into details concerning Austrian policies. Such details were promised in forthcoming communications. What Metternich wished to learn was Wrede's views—ultimately those of the King of Bavaria—concerning Germany's current problems and the means of their solution. Metternich explained that he felt the end of the Polish revolution was near. When it ended both revolutionaries and good citizens alike would expect the major German powers—secure on their eastern frontiers—to turn their attention to problems in Germany. Metternich did not want to disappoint them.[14]

The responses to Metternich's overtures were typical of the men from whom they came. King William, anxious to prove his soldierly qualities, seemed to want to restore German security through war. Wrede, more cautious and defensive regarding the Bavarian constitution, wanted things to be talked over carefully before committing Bavaria to anything.

William expressed the view that war was necessary against France, the ultimate source of all revolutionary propaganda. From it stemmed the evils of the day: the license of the German press, the metamorphosis of German diets into revolutionary conclaves, the lack of German commercial unity, and the failure of the Federal Diet to end all of these evils. The King of Württemberg felt that there was little hope of bridling the press, changing state constitutions, or expanding the influence of the Federal Diet in internal states affairs through legal means. The Bavarian constitution, for instance, did not acknowledge the supremacy of federal over state laws. Ministers in constitutional German states would be attacked by their diets if they instructed their delgates at Frankfurt to work for reactionary reforms. A war alone would justify extraordinary measures to reform federal and state institutions. Whatever was decided, however, William expressed the hope that Austria and Prussia would cooperate to lead Germany to its salvation.[15]

Wrede, too, proposed that Austria and Prussia take the initiative. But he did not speak of war. He suggested that the two great German powers call a German ministerial conference to organize measures to protect the German governments. He reminded Metternich, however, that although Bavaria would be willing to participate in such a conference and do her duty as a member of the German Confederation to preserve the internal peace of Germany, it had to be remembered that she was a constitutional state. Her government would abide by its constitution and insist that the Confederation observe the limits of competence assigned to it by the Federal and Final Acts of 1815 and 1820.[16]

Metternich indicated to Baron August von Blomburg, the minister of Württemberg in Vienna, his satisfaction with King William's views.[17] Well he might; if they went far beyond Metternich's intended tactics to achieve reforms, they at least admitted the need for federal reforms to preserve monarchism in Germany. Metternich felt it necessary, on the other hand, to prod Wrede to a more agreeable response: one not so typically Bavarian in its assertion of state sovereignty over federal duties. He assured the field marshal that Austria had no intention of overturning the German constitutions. Instead, she wanted to preserve them as they had been created originally. The question, Metternich insisted, was how to defend the monarchic principle against the principle of popular sovereignty. Wrede was to consider this and suggest how, in this light, the federal and state constitutions could best be preserved. As to his idea of a German ministerial conference, Metternich told him that such a conference could only follow a thorough exchange of opinions on a more confidential level.[18]

Metternich learned from this initial correspondence with King William and Field Marshal Wrede what he already knew. Any broad program of reform for Germany would be left up to the joint initiative of Austria and Prussia. He had hoped that a basis for such an initiative had been laid at Teplitz. He was so upset by the Prussian circulars of 15 August because they showed how far apart the views of the ministries of the two courts still were. General Clam's mission to Berlin was one attempt Metternich was already making to end the differences.

By the time Clam arrived in the Prussian capital on 16 September, Metternich's violent reaction to the Prussian circulars had already had an effect. Metternich's letter of 29 August denouncing the "Bernstorff-Eichhorn party" was the vehicle. Werner had planned to modify Metternich's harsh criticisms of the Prussian foreign ministry before passing them along to Prince Wilhelm zu Wittgenstein, but he did not get the chance. Wittgenstein had grabbed the note and hurried off with it to the king. The result was all that Metternich could have asked. Frederick William instructed his foreign minister, Count Bernstorff, that he had no wish to pursue a German policy independent of Austrian cooperation—still less act against his ally. Henceforth, no memorandum of any importance was to leave the ministry without the king's personal approval. Frederick William rejected Bernstorff's explanation that, by raising no objections to their content when Bernstorff showed them to him at Teplitz, the king himself had tacitly approved the August circulars.[19]

Much to the chagrin of South German diplomats in Berlin—some of whom thought the Austrian general was encouraging Prussia to an offensive alliance against France—Clam settled in for a prolonged stay in the Prussian capital.[20] New orders instructed him to try to end independent Prussian-South German military planning and to get Prussia to enter a preliminary political understanding with the other Continental Powers. His job was to convince the Prussian government that her European responsibilities were more important than consideration for the smaller German states. If necessary, Clam might accept the Prussian-South German military agreements in thesis, but he was to question their feasibility. How, for instance, Clam was to ask, could Prussia guarantee the reliability and faithfulness of an independent South German army? Forced to face such unanswerable questions, the Prussian ministry was to be influenced to reject what Metternich felt to be its mistaken views.[21]

Metternich was ready for stiff Prussian resistance. He knew that Bernstorff believed that if Prussia rescinded her proposals to the South Germans that would alienate those proud and independent princes and make them less reliable. Metternich assured Clam, therefore, that he should tell his conservative Prussian contacts that Bernstorff was in error in thinking that it was the South Germans who were really pushing for the Rühle plans. Certainly the South Germans were pleased by the military proposals contained in the August circulars. They had two great attractions: they flattered South German self-esteem and they excluded Austrian influence from an important German affair. Metternich felt sure, however, that the original ideas behind the proposed military system were developed by the "Prussian-German party" and the "pure Prussian party" within the Prussian government. The first cherished visions of a Germany under Prussian aegis. The second group, Metternich said, could think of nothing but the campaign of 1806 and the Saale Valley.[22]

While having Clam turn the conservative elements around the Prussia king against their more progressive colleagues, Metternich laterally pursued his plans for a German ministerial conference. In Vienna on 9 October, Metternich and Baron von Maltzahn, the Prussian minister to the Habsburg court, signed a memorandum that tentatively established the form for the proposed German affairs talks in Vienna. According to this preliminary agreement, they were to take the form of secret meetings between the most intimate advisors of a select group of German princes. Metternich proposed that these include the kings of Bavaria and Württemberg, the Grand Duke of Hesse-Darmstadt, the Duke of Nassau, and the Grand Duke of Mecklenburg-Strelitz. The exact selection was left up to the King of Prussia. By the secrecy, selectivity, and intimacy of the talks, Metternich hoped to negate the influence of the liberal parties within these courts and more easily influence their sovereigns.[23]

While waiting for approval of the Metternich-Maltzahn memorandum to arrive from Berlin, Metternich decided to independently approach the South German monarchs so that talks could begin as soon as possible. Through dispatches to his envoy in Stuttgart and to Wrede, the wily Austrian laid before the South German kings the principles and proposals that were still under consideration in Berlin. Both messages also contained attacks on the liberal parties in the Prussian and South German ministries. Metternich felt that they were obstructing efforts necessary for the preservation of the German Confederation. They weakened its defensive strength, and it was defense against revolution in Germany that was Metternich's aim. He confided to Schönburg that Austria intended no war against France such as the bellicose King of Württemberg wished. A war would only help to spread the revolutionary virus. His goal, he said, was to consolidate the Confederation. By its moral and material impregnability it would confine revolutionary activity to France and have it smother itself there.[24]

Metternich's message for the King of Württemberg consisted of a dispatch and a memorandum for Schönburg to share with the king. The dispatch, which introduced the memorandum, declared Germany's most pressing need to be the preservation of the monarchic principle. This was made difficult, Metternich asserted, by the growing strength of the principle of popular sovereignty within the individual German states. Governments like that of Baden—an object of William's own constant complaints—were no longer in a position to save themselves without federal help. Revolutionaries knew this too; more and more they were aiming their denunciations directly at the Confederation.[25]

Metternich explained to William that he, like the king, believed that a close understanding between Austria and Prussia had to be the basis for action by the German princes to halt such developments. For that reason, he had already approached the ministry in Berlin. There, as in most of the German ministries, Metternich explained, there existed a liberal and a monarchic party. He placed his trust in the monarchic party around the king, however, and had already reached an agreement with that party on some general principles. These he wished to present to King William in the accompanying memorandum. Furthermore, as the two great German powers were about to open new discussions in Vienna, Metternich invited the king to empower his envoy to participate. He requested only that the meetings be kept strictly secret until their results were acted upon by the Federal Diet. To ensure this secrecy, he requested that the minister of Württemberg in Vienna be permitted to report directly to the king. He warned that the liberal parties in all the governments were so closely linked that secrets could not be kept in any other way.[26]

The memorandum itself was presented as the view of the current German situation held in common by the governments of Austria and Prussia. This view was that the state of popular unrest in Germany could be attributed originally to the mistakes of the German princes whose first error was the introduction of representative constitutions into their states. They had then further facilitated revolutionary intrigues by their laxity in enforcing the press provisions of the Carlsbad Decrees. Since the July Revolution, a large number of German states were in a condition of revolutionary dissolution as a result of these past mistakes. In Electoral Hesse, revolution was already given legal form through the enactment of a new representative constitution. In Baden, Bavaria, Grand Ducal Hesse, and Saxony representative forms were being implemented in the face of existing federal laws. Except for Austria and Prussia, only Württemberg, Hanover, and Nassau had rulers who were still in a position to assert their sovereign authority.[27]

According to Metternich, it was the view of the two great German powers that the German Confederation had been created to preserve peace and order in Germany as well as in Europe. Its organization was designed to protect the sovereignty of the princes of each of the federal states. Since 1815, however, the German princes had made the mistake of neglecting to observe federal laws. By asserting their own sovereignty they had only helped that faction that aimed at the unification of the German people into a single state. Now the diets of Baden and Bavaria daily denounced the Confederation. The *Constitutionelle Deutschland* in Baden and the *Deutsche Tribune* in Bavaria openly advocated German unification. Implementation of existing federal laws could put an end to all of that. Austria and Prussia had to take the lead in preparing the means for the reassertion of federal power, but the other German states had to cooperate. They had to realize that the Confederation was the only support for individual German princes threatened by revolution.[28] As the reader can see, from Metternich's point of view, that said it all. There is hardly a more perfect statement of Metternich's evaluation of the nature of and solution to the German Question.

Metternich's letter to Wrede, and thus to King Ludwig, expressed the same views and proposals that were sent to King William. The wording of Metternich's communication to Wrede, however, was designed as a rejoinder to the Bavarian's response to the earlier Austrian request for reform proposals. Wrede had said that he and Metternich seemed to agree on what was wrong in Germany, but not on the means to correct it. Metternich now tried to show Wrede how similar their thoughts were on the means as well. He agreed with Wrede that the means for the defense of the monarchic principle had to be found in the principles and institutions defined by the Federal and Final Acts of the German Confederation. Like Wrede, he felt that on the basis of these principles and institutions the Confederation had to gain new functionality and life or be discarded as useless. Unlike the Bavarian, however, Metternich expressed confidence that new life could be given to the federal body if each government conscientiously applied the existing federal laws. In his opinion, there were no federal legislative gaps that needed filling.[29]

Metternich repeated his earlier rejection of Wrede's suggestion that Austria and Prussia immediately call a ministerial conference to deal with Germany's problems. Before any such conference could be held, he insisted, there had to be secret, free, and formless talks between the most influential German courts. According to Metternich, many of the German governments could not even control their own officials, let alone their diets. If there were a public conference the participating governments would be faced with two enemies: their own ministers and "so-called public opinion." Therefore, Metternich noted, he had already proposed to Prussia that the major German powers hold secret talks in Vienna. He said he expected an affirmative answer from Berlin shortly. Meanwhile, he requested that the Bavarian minister in Vienna be authorized to take part in the talks when they did begin. Finally, to ensure secrecy, Metternich asked that the Bavarian ministry know nothing about the talks. To guarantee this, he further requested that King Ludwig's envoy be instructed to report only to Wrede or to the King himself.

In an accompanying secret communication for Wrede alone, Metternich attacked the liberal members of the South German governments. He blamed the rulers, however, for being so weak as to allow their liberal ministers and the middle-class members of their diets to run their affairs. Metternich was disturbed that these people were able to use the modern representative system as their instrument. It was a system of government, he said, that was a poor caricature of the English system without the necessary historic prerequisites.[30]

Metternich let Wrede know that he was describing the situation in Bavaria, too. He suggested that there were provisions in the Bavarian constitution, however, that still gave Ludwig some possibility of reasserting himself. Metternich warned that if the king sought popularity through a policy of concessions, there would be no hope for him. Even now, in the discussion of press regulations before the Bavarian diet, the king's ministers, Count Joseph von Armansperg and Baron Georg von Zentner, asserted that Bavarian state laws took precedence over federal laws. If such things continued, Metternich said, there would finally be open revolt.[31]

While Metternich exhorted the monarchs of Bavaria and Württemberg to more monarchic and federalistic policies, he waited in vain for the Prussian agreement he needed to open secret discussions in Vienna. In a dispatch of 24 October, Trauttmansdorff reported that Bernstorff would not agree to talks in which the German rulers, but not their ministers, were participants.[32] This convinced Metternich that the liberal party in the Prussian ministry wanted to include the liberal South German ministries so that together they could counter Austrian aims and influence. He was so infuriated that he told intimates that, if his efforts were thwarted, he might propose that Austria leave the left bank of the Rhine to France and create a new Germany with

French help.[33] Although this was probably empty talk, as his advisors supposed, it indicated Metternich's anger at the liberal Prussian and South German ministers. It also indicated, no doubt, his interest in using the German Confederation to maintain the governmental status quo in Europe rather than the territorial status quo in Germany.

It was not the perfidity of the liberals in the Prussian and South German ministries, but their stupidity, that attracted Metternich's attention. He confided that view to Prince Schönberg in a private letter of 2 November 1831:

> The Prussian and South German clubs—for these ministries deserve this name too—believed they could surely maneuver Austria out of the Confederation. As nothing is so thoughtless and awkward as a German doctrinaire and *Freitummler*, these good people have forgotten a few things. For example, Austria is a ponderous mass that one can not easily shove to one side. If Austria set itself to one side, a tremendous breach would develop that could not be easily filled with theories. Finally, the day of the victory of their plan would also be that of the downfall of the German princes.[34]

Metternich's view of the liberal party in the Prussian ministry did not become any more sympathetic after he received the dispatches from Berlin of 6 and 8 November. They aroused him to quite a storm.[35] The 6 November dispatch from Bernstorff to Maltzahn illustrated the extent to which Bernstorff and Metternich had completely different views on solving the German Question. Trauttmansdorff's report of 8 November merely elaborated on those differences and drew harshly negative conclusions from them.

Bernstorff's note to Maltzahn, accompanying the 6 November memorandum for Metternich, insisted that Prussia and Austria had to have full agreement between themselves on any measures for Germany before there was any discussion with other German princes.[36] Little did he know that things were already beyond that stage. But the contents of his memorandum help to explain both his search for a preliminary agreement with Metternich and Metternich's attempts to work around such a reformist Prussian minister.

Bernstorff's memorandum illustrates both the similarities and stark differences between the Prussian and Austrian solutions to the German Question. Although Bernstorff agreed with Metternich's ideas for having Prussia and Austria invite a select group of German princes to send representatives to Vienna for talks, he warned of the need for secrecy to avoid the mistrust of those excluded, false publicity, the clammer of state diets, and possible protests from France or England.[37]

Regarding the problems of the Confederation, Bernstorff blamed a party spirit that encouraged the particularism of the German states and led them to neglect the authority of the Bund. It was this same spirit, Bernstorff said, that criticized the Federal Diet and sought the dream of a united German people in a single German state. That, Bernstorff agreed, had to be stopped by the German princes themselves through the establishment of proper maxims regarding the worth and productivity of their relationship as members of the Confederation.[38]

Up to this point in the memorandum, there was much with which Metternich could certainly agree. But then Bernstorff's "reform conservatism" became obvious. Bernstorff felt that serious efforts had to be made to improve the public image of the Federal Diet. This, he felt, could be done by speedier work by that body and by common efforts of the German princes in the interest of all Germany. He argued also for the publication of the protocols of the Federal Diet—so long suppressed.[39] He advocated the educational value of prompt publication of a yearly edition of the protocols, perhaps going back to the year 1824. Thus although he concluded his memorandum with his positive assessment of the German Confederation as the true protector of monarchic power and urged the need for police cooperation between the German states to stop the spread of French revolutionary propoganda, Bernstorff fatally aroused Metternich's fears by invoking the benefits of public opinion.[40]

Trauttmansdorff's dispatch of 8 November elaborated further on Bernstorff's position and reported that the Prussian minister's disagreement with Metternich's plan for direct communications between the German rulers might be backed by the king. In fact, Trauttmansdorff presented the Prussian reaction to all of Metternich's current proposals as both disappointing and provocative. The disappointment came with Prussian reluctance for federal action. Metternich had proposed that the two great powers consider how to deal immediately with two of Germany's most pressing problems: the weakness of the government of Baden in the face of the liberalizing pressures of its diet and the dangers of the revolutionary propaganda of a Strasbourg-based German language newspaper, the *Constitutionelle Deutschland*. The Prussian ministry felt that nothing could be done about the situation in Baden before the end of the current session of the Baden diet.

It was also unwilling for any federal action to be taken to limit the circulation of one newspaper until general rules had been set up by the Federal Diet to deal with all of them[41]

Trauttmansdorff's explanation of the Prussian ministry's position was guaranteed to make it provocative. The envoy's analysis was that the Prussian liberals, with the help of their counterparts in the South German ministries, were working for the creation of a confederation within the Confederation. They were tired of having Prussia play the role of helpmate to Austria and wanted her to be the center of a new political alignment. To achieve this goal, they had tried to develop a separate commercial and military system within the Confederation. To escape entirely from Austrian influence, however, they also had to play up to liberal opinion in Germany. Bernstorff permitted these efforts by Eichhorn's liberal party because he feared being pushed too far into reactionary policies by the Austrians. He underestimated the importance and dangers of the efforts of the Prussian liberal party. Trauttmansdorff warned that Eichhorn would continue to work for closer relations between Prussia and the constitutional states until finally the Prussian king also granted his subjects a representative constitution. Prussia could then put herself at the head of a unified constitutional Germany that was the dream of Prussian and German liberals alike.[42]

Metternich was determined neither to give in to the plans of the liberals in the Prussian ministry, nor to allow them to delay his efforts for an agreement with the South German monarchs. He decided, therefore, to trick the Prussian liberal faction into committing itself to a reactionary program by seeming to accept its proposals. While agreeing to pursue preliminary negotiations with the Prussian ministry alone, he laid the basis for an agreement with the South German monarchs—without the involvement of their ministries. Thus on 15 November, Metternich secretly sent to the kings of Bavaria and Württemberg the memorandum that he had planned to present at the first secret meeting of the envoys in Vienna.[43] It would have already taken place if it had not been for the reluctance of the Prussian ministry: the envoys from Bavaria and Württemberg had been already empowered to participate on the terms that Metternich had suggested.[44]

Metternich's memorandum of 15 November was introduced to the South German monarchs as the basis for continuing discussions until Prussia could be brought to agree to the secret talks in Vienna that Austria had proposed. Metternich explained that the

Prussian ministry could not agree to the form for the talks. It felt that Prussia and Austria should come to some agreement among themselves and only then contact all of the German princes and their ministries. Metternich said that he did not want this disagreement to hold up continuing communications between Austria and the South Germans. To facilitate the desired exchange of ideas, he was sending the monarchs an outline of Austrian principles. He asked that they comment on this outline point by point. He also requested that they keep his communication to them secret from Prussia. Metternich explained that, while the Prussian ministry said that its objections to the form of the discussions were based on a desire to maintain secrecy and to avoid the jealousy of the uninvited governments, the Prussian liberals had other grounds for their objections. The form of talks that they wanted, he explained accusingly, was intended to allow them—in cooperation with the liberals of the South German ministries—to thwart Austrian influence.[45]

The memorandum itself was almost a restatement of his communication of 14 October. In it the Austrian foreign minister portrayed the goal of the German revolutionaries to be the creation of a union of "free states" patterned after their ideal, the United States of America. The realization of their goal necessitated ending the sovereignty of the individual German princes. According to Metternich, the revolutionaries sought to bring this about by the development of the democratic principle in the German states through the debates of the state diets and the propaganda of the periodical press. Through these media they would denounce the individual German governments and the laws and constitution of the German Confederation as well.[46]

Metternich was quick to point out that the principles and institutions of the German Confederation offered it the means to both its own salvation and that of its members. A monarchic organization, its first duty was the preservation of the monarchic principle. Its laws, flowing from the unity of the German princes, stood above the laws of the individual states. No state law could keep a German prince from fulfilling his duty to the German Confederation—especially the duty of applying federal laws designed to preserve the monarchic principle. These laws included the Federal Act, the Carlsbad Decrees, and the Final Act of Vienna. This view of the Confederation—its attributes, its laws, and the responsibilities of its members—Austria offered as the basis and point of departure for the secret talks to be opened in Vienna.[47]

Metternich's offensive against the liberals in the Prussian and South German courts continued on two fronts: the political and the military. While he worked to split monarchs from liberal advisors on the question of federal reforms, he also proceeded along the same route with regard to military questions. He had his envoys in South Germany tell King William and Field Marshal Wrede that the military plans that had been revealed in the Rühle mission were the work of Prussian and South German liberals who aimed at developing a constitutional Germany under Prussian aegis. Although neither of these South Germans were convinced by Metternich's picture of liberal intrigue and both denied any such intention in the Rühle talks,[48] Metternich had more success in Berlin. General Clam was able to enlist prominent conservative advisors to the Prussian king—Prince Wilhelm zu Wittgenstein, Friedrich Ancillon, Duke Carl of Mecklenburg, and General Karl von Knesebeck—to convince Frederick William III of the false principles of his ministers.[49] Their influence seemed to be effective. In his dispatch of 14 November, Clam reported that he felt sure that the Prussian monarch now rejected the Rühle plans and would cooperate only with Austria.[50]

In a reserved dispatch on 2 November, Metternich expressed his pleasure at the success of General Clam's efforts in Berlin. Now that the designs of the liberals in the Prussian and South German ministries were uncovered, he felt that appropriate defensive plans could be worked out. He intended that they be plans that were based on the Austrian view that defense against France was a European question. It was one that had to be worked out by the Continental Powers before the South German states had their wishes consulted.[51]

Metternich asked Clam to see to it that the Prussian king and his conservative intimates informed neither the king's own ministers nor the South German courts of the course of Clam's mission. They were to know only what Metternich had told the King of Bavaria: the Austrian general had gone to Berlin to obtain an explanation of the August memorandum, not for negotiations. "The plan of the *Deutschtummler* has been shattered," Metternich exulted. They were not to know how. In his estimation their plans had been bad ones. To begin discussions concerning a European war with plans for the unification of two unreliable South German corps was an absurdity. Their goal, however, was not a military one, according to Metternich. He felt that they had been seeking a means to unite Prussia with the constitutional states. In fact, they caused dissension between the German governments from which only their common enemy would benefit— "the all devouring revolution."[52]

By early December 1831, Metternich had won one round in the struggle to restore Austro-Prussian cooperation—the basis for his solution to the German Question. Austro-Prussian cooperation was apparent on the question of a German defensive system. Before General Clam left Berlin on 5 December, he received new Prussian proposals to take to Vienna. They still called for a tripartite division of the German armies, but one in which the center was to be made up of equal numbers of Prussian, Austrian, and South German troops.[53] There was no longer to be an almost completely independent South German army.

Despite Bernstorff's resistance, Frederick William had come around to Metternich's thinking in regard to the wisdom of the cooperation of the two great German powers. The Prussian foreign minister argued that the continued danger of war with France made a military agreement between Prussia and the South Germans more important than a political understanding with Austria.[54] However, on 14 October, a Great Power conference in London agreed on a peaceful settlement of the Belgian question. By mid-November, all of the major powers except Russia had agreed in principle to a plan for mutual disarmament.[55] At about the same time, the tsar empowered his ambassador in Vienna to begin discussions with Metternich and the Prussian envoy for the creation of a common continental policy for the handling of future European problems.[56] Things had changed. Frederick William decided to change his policies to fit the times.[57]

The change in policies in Berlin gained momentum with Prussia's agreement to accept Metternich's proposals for the secret political talks in Vienna. The South German monarchs had already agreed. The Austrian minister in Munich, Kaspar von Spiegel, reported that King Ludwig had been worried by Austrian insistence that the Confederation was indivisible and that federal laws always had preeminence over state laws. But Spiegel had assured the king that these propositions were grounded in the Federal Act and the Final Act of Vienna.[58] On 24 November, Wrede sent Metternich Ludwig's cautious, but positive response to Metternich's 15 November memorandum.[59] The official response from Württemberg apparently came in the first days of December. Before that, Schönburg reported the King of Württemberg's favorable reception of Metternich's memorandum. William agreed with Metternich that no German government with a representative constitution could continue to exist by its own power.[60]

By 1 December, Metternich learned that he had prevailed in Berlin as well as in Munich and Stuttgart. The Prussian minister in Vienna informed him that his government had given up its scruples regarding direct negotiations between the German princes. It was ready to cooperate in joint overtures to the two South German monarchs if Austria would agree to its most recent proposals. Metternich told Wrede that he was not sure of the reason for the happy change at Berlin.[61] There is little doubt, however, that the Prussian conservatives who helped General Clam influence Frederick William on the military question exerted some influence in this political one as well. In part, too, Bernstorff was being tricked by Metternich. Although agreeing to Bernstorff's proposals of 25 November, Metternich, in fact, edited out provisions that he did not care for. These included references to publication of the full proceedings of the Federal Diet.[62] Bernstorff was right to have reservations about the talks in Vienna, and he did. He feared that his government might have little influence on their outcome. Trauttmansdorff had tried to reassure him. He promised that the Prussian minister in Vienna would participate in the development of all the proposals that were to be presented to the South German monarchs. Moreover, the Prussian diplomat would have to give his consent before the proposals were actually delivered.[63] That proved to be no obstacle for Metternich: he convinced Maltzahn to accept the Austrian edited version of Bernstorff's 25 November memorandum for their joint overture to the South Germans.[64]

After six months of secret diplomacy, Metternich had overcome the influence of the Prussian and South German liberals enough so that he could look with some confidence to the acceptance of his military and political policies for Germany. He had undermined his liberal opponents by accusing them of being nearsighted opportunists, whose efforts to exclude Austrian influence from Germany would only pave the way for the creation of a single German republic. In an atmosphere charged by the anti-monarchic declarations of the German diets and the political press, the monarchs of Prussia, Württemberg, and Bavaria were ready to listen to Metternich's proposals for ensuring their safety. Whether or not the South Germans would feel compelled to follow Austria, however, still depended on decisions in Prussia. Was there still a viable Prussian option to the Austrian answer to the German Question? It was hard to tell. By the end of 1831, it looked increasingly as though King Frederick William III, despite the influence of Bernstorff, saw his interests best served by cooperation with the monarchic and federalistic policies of his Great Power ally, Austria.

6
Fear, Finesse, and Federal Duties, 1832

In the last months of 1831, Metternich had sufficiently vilified the liberals of the South German and Prussian courts so as to greatly weaken their influence on their conservative masters. Once this hindrance to his military and reform programs had been substantially reduced, Metternich could concentrate on their implementation.

Military planning, however, was now less pressing than it had been earlier in the year. The desire for peace among all the Great Powers was evident. Austrian military intervention in Italy in March had taken place without provoking France. Moreover, that affair had culminated in an international conference in Rome and the withdrawal of Habsburg troops from Bologna in July. The French military action to counter the Dutch invasion of Belgium in August had been sanctioned by the international conference at London, and French troops left Belgium at the end of September. By October, the Great Powers were discussing mutual disarmament and were making tentative agreements for the resolution of Dutch-Belgian differences. Even the French occupation of Ancona in February 1832, in response to renewed Austrian intervention in the Papal States, would be considered by Metternich a mere bagatelle.[1] Thus by 1832, the Austrian foreign minister's interest in securing the adoption of his military program was nothing more than part of his general policy of ensuring that Austria would be protected in the future by a German federal military system that met Habsburg needs—or at least did not endanger Habsburg policies.

More important than Metternich's military program, at the moment, were his reform plans. In his eyes, Austrian security required that he save the German states from internal revolution. Revolution there was inevitable, Metternich felt, if the antimonarchic tendencies of the German press and state diets were not controlled. The press seemed more republican and nationalistic daily. The diets were becoming democratic conventions, abrogating to themselves the powers of their sovereigns. Both of these phenomena had been most conspicuous in Baden and Bavaria in the fall of 1831. Metternich planned to stop these developments there and throughout Germany during 1832 using fear, finesse, and federal duties.

The year 1832 opened auspiciously for Metternich. On 26 December 1831, he had gotten the Prussian agreement that he needed to commence the long-planned secret talks in Vienna. Shortly thereafter, he received news that boded well for their success. A complete change of ministry in Munich at the end of the year brought the dismissal of Metternich's most persistent South German ministerial opponent, Count Joseph von Armansperg. Since the spring of 1831, Metternich had warned King Ludwig of Armansperg's liberal and Francophilic tendencies. The Austrian minister's efforts to bypass the Bavarian foreign minister in all of his correspondence with Ludwig made it clear that he considered Armansperg an obstacle to good Austro-Bavarian relations. Because of Armansperg's skill at handling the Bavarian Diet, Ludwig had decided to keep him until the end of its current session, but the king's Francophobia made Armansperg's fall inevitable. Adopting Metternich's view that his foreign minister had pursued his own policies at variance with those of the official ministry—thereby creating, in effect, a second or "shadow" ministry—Ludwig let it be known that he would no longer tolerate the existence of a "double ministry."[2]

The trend toward acceptance of Metternich's views and policies by the major German governments—heralded by Armansperg's fall and Prussian agreement to the form for the talks in Vienna—was, for the moment, more apparent than real. Of the German sovereigns represented at the Vienna meetings, the King of Württemberg alone was immediately receptive to Metternich's ideas concerning the need to control the state diets and to suppress the radical press.[3] The new Bavarian foreign minister, Baron August von Gise, was no less intent than Armansperg on defending Bavaria's own constitutional principles. Metternich had to reassure Ludwig that an increase of federal powers to control the state diets would protect his sovereignty, not endanger it. He assured the king that, contrary to suspicions in Munich, neither Austria nor Prussia intended to try to change the Bavarian constitution.[4]

The problem was not that of Bavarian suspicions alone. As long as Bernstorff was foreign minister in Berlin, Prussian policy remained much too liberal for the Austrian foreign minister. Still hoping to accommodate to the liberalizing trends of the day, Bernstorff allowed Eichhorn to work up plans for a new Prussian press law that might also serve as a model for a federal censorship law that could replace the harsh Carlsbad Decrees. The Prussian foreign minister had already confided to Metternich back in November how he hoped to make the Federal Diet more popular and to give it new positive connotations by increasing public awareness of its discussions. Although he did not want the press to be able to comment on the daily affairs of the Federal Diet, he did feel that all but a few protocols might be published in a single volume at the end of each yearly session.[5] On these and other points, however, Bernstorff had kept Vienna in the dark since December. On 27 February, Metternich complained that nearly two months had passed since the opening of the Vienna talks without an official communication from Berlin.[6]

Such a delay could not but worry Metternich. While he waited for Prussian cooperation at the Vienna meetings, Germany's defenses against revolution seemed to crumble. True, the close of the sessions of the Baden and Bavarian diets put a temporary end to the excesses of the spirit of popular sovereignty in these two bodies. The press question, however, afforded no such respite. On 28 December, after two and a half months of debate in the Baden diet, a press law was proclaimed that ended the requirement of prepublication censorship. The government in Karlsruhe, intent on bending rather than breaking before its diet's demand for press freedom, and unable to persuade the other South German courts to cooperate in some broader German press reform, agreed that this law was to become effective on 1 March 1832.[7] It ran directly counter to the federal press law provisions in the Carlsbad Decrees.

In the fall of 1831, Metternich had wanted Berlin to support him in some action to prevent the enactment of the new press law in Baden, but Bernstorff insisted that any action had to wait until the Federal Diet was prepared to enact new censorship guidelines for the whole Confederation. Only after the new press law was officially published in Baden on 12 January did Bernstorff reluctantly agree to Metternich's proposal that the Federal Diet question the compatability of the law with existing federal legislation. On 9 February the Prussian delegate at Frankfurt, Karl von Nagler, secured the consent of the Federal Diet to have its commission for press affairs decide to what extent the Baden press law could be permitted to exist unchanged.[8]

The federal press commission's report of 20 February advised the Federal Diet that Baden's press law was entirely incompatible with existing federal legislation.[9] This pronouncement, however, merely focused attention on a more basic problem—the failure of the individual states to enforce federal press legislation. In this, Bavaria, not Baden, was the worst offender. The Bavarian government allowed the *Bote aus Westen* and the *Deutsche Tribune* to become Germany's most daring proponents of nationalism and democracy.[10] As Austrian diplomats noted, the basis of the entire German press problem was that influential Bavaria did not suppress her own radical press. She claimed this could not be done in accordance with her constitution, thereby asserting the uniquely Bavarian principle that state legislation was superior to that of the Confederation.[11] Until Bavaria acted, neither Baden nor any other state would incur the anger of its subjects by enforcing federal press regulations.[12]

It was on Bavaria, therefore, that Metternich decided to exert his greatest diplomatic efforts. On 25 February, he approved the suggestion of the Austrian minister to Württemberg that that diplomat find some excuse to visit Munich and work personally on his old friend and classmate, King Ludwig. Metternich equipped Schönburg for his mission with a list of subjects on which Ludwig's agreement was to be sought. Most important, the king was to be brought to accept the principle—generally accepted, but not specifically stated in the Federal Act of 1815— that federal legislation took precedence over state legislation.[13] Specifically, Ludwig had to be persuaded to apply the federal press laws to the periodicals of his own Rhineland province. Finally, he had to be convinced of the correctness of the federal press commission's views regarding the press law in Baden.[14]

Before Schönburg could arrive in Munich, the antifederative attitude of the Bavarian government became poignantly obvious. On 2 March, on the initiative of the federal press commission, the Federal Diet decreed the suppression of the *Deutsche Tribune,* the *Bote aus Westen,* and the *Neue Zeitschwingen.* These papers—the first two published in Bavaria and the third in Electoral Hesse—were condemned for containing articles threatening the honor and safety of the Confederation and its member states.[15] On 8 March, when the Bavarian delegate presented a declaration of his government's compliance with the decrees of the 2nd, this compliance was tenuous indeed. The declaration asserted that, by an ordinance of 1 March, the Bavarian government itself had suppressed both the *Deutsche Tribune* and the

Bote aus Westen—for as long as they did not comply with the censorship clauses of the Bavarian constitution.[16] In effect, the Bavarian government said that it was going to observe its own rules, not enforce those of the German Confederation.[17]

Schönburg reported from Munich that the Bavarians seemed to think that, because their own press law did not provide for the total suppression of newspapers, they need not enforce federal decisions to that effect. Although King Ludwig felt a need for the German Confederation and the support that it could provide the German princes, he undercut it, because he loved to preserve the appearance of independence from outside direction. In an attempt to change the king's attitude, Schönburg employed a mixture of moral persuasion and implicit threats. He told Foreign Minister Gise that Bavarian laxity in enforcing federal press legislation was responsible for the dangerous new press law in Baden. He also reminded Field Marshal Wrede of Bavaria's political position and geographical location and warned that federal protection had to be paid for by obedience to federal laws.[18]

The Austrian envoy was convinced of the basically conservative nature of the Bavarian king and his ministers. They felt the need of the Confederation to limit the powers of their diet. However, they were ready to prove their independence of the German Confederation whenever the diet seemed unlikely to present them with problems. As Schönburg saw it, Bavarian ambivalence was a result of a mania to have that state recognized as a major European power: that status would be impossible if Bavaria submitted to the supremacy of the German Confederation. The Bavarian government wished to regain the degree of independence it had enjoyed under the aegis of Napoleonic France. But in 1832, as Schönburg noted, France, the homeland of revolution, was no longer a suitable protector.[19]

In a note to Wrede on 26 March, Metternich took up Schönburg's theme. He reminded the Bavarian field marshal that since the July Revolution, Bavaria could no longer maintain an independent policy by seesawing between the influence of the major European powers. And now, Wrede had only to read the German press to find that the German radicals saw in Bavarian resistance to federal law the salvation of the Baden press law. Metternich insisted that there could be no doubt that the future of this law would determine the fate of Germany. If it were allowed to stand, there could be no hope for the preservation of order.[20]

For now Metternich focused all his diplomatic efforts on Bavaria. He asked Schönburg to persuade King William of Württemberg to add his influence to the Austrian attempt to bring King Ludwig to strict adherence to the federal press law.[21] As it was, Munich already bore the brunt of Prussian and Austrian protests against its intransigence. Alienated by what it considered the insulting tone of Austria's protest notes, the Bavarian ministry refused even to answer them. Still, to avoid diplomatic isolation, the Bavarian government decided to try again to satisfy Bavaria's federal obligation using a carefully worded publication of the 2 March decrees.[22] On 12 April, the Federal Diet was informed that on 31 March the official newspaper in Bavaria proclaimed the efficacy of the 2 March decrees. The article noted again, however, that Bavarian ordinances of 1 March had already suppressed the two Bavarian papers. It added that the Bavarian government would, of course, now prohibit distribution of the Hessian *Neue Zeitschwingen* in its territories as well.[23]

Metternich did not always force members of the Confederation to such slippery conformance with Austrian wishes. In his continuing effort to gain the revision of the Baden press law, he was capable of compromise to achieve his final goal. Faced with Prussian sympathy for Baden's insistence that its press law remain in effect until new federal press legislation replaced the Carlsbad Decrees, Metternich compromised. He agreed to Bernstorff's proposal that federal action against Baden wait until such federal legislation was developed at the secret Vienna talks. That would help to disguise for the government of Baden the loss of face involved in federal action against itself alone.[24] Also, on 26 April, Metternich had the substituting federal president, the Prussian delegate Karl von Nagler, propose to the Federal Diet the creation of a commission to consider new federal guidelines for the press. Gratified by this initiative for a general revision of the federal press laws, the Prussian, Württemberg, and even Bavarian delegates cast their votes with Austria to express the hope that Baden would adhere to the current federal press laws until they were replaced.[25]

Meanwhile the secret discussions in Vienna had come to an end.[26] There had been many delays. Partly responsible were the suspicious advisors of King Ludwig, who demanded caution and clarity in each communication.[27] Then, of course, there was the long initial delay between communications from Berlin while the liberal Prussian ministers fought their losing battle against the influence of conservatives like Wittgenstein.[28] Finally, however, conservative federalistic principles triumphed. On 4 April, Metternich was able to achieve agreement with his fellow con-

ferees on a program of federal measures that were expressed in
six articles. Except for the Bavarian government's insistence on a
limitation of six years to the article providing for a federal commission to monitor state diets, there remained no apparent disagreement. Even this qualification was omitted, however, in the
text of the Six Articles that Metternich sent to the German courts
in a secret memorandum of 12 April.[29]

The memorandum was designed to explain the principles behind the Six Articles, their intent, and their text. First, however,
it explained how Austria and Prussia, then Bavaria and Württemberg, and now all of the German courts were called to participate
in secret discussions to consider the way to combat contemporary German evils. The major premise explicit in all of the discussions was the principle that the German Confederation had
been created to ensure the internal as well as the external, security of Germany. Thanks to the Vienna Final Act of 1820 the
Confederation possessed all the organic legislation necessary to
fulfill this task. No new laws were needed. New federal laws, the
memorandum explained, might only encourage a "dangerous
spirit of innovation" that would destroy the German federal body.
Furthermore, the avoidance of new laws would prevent mistrust
from arising among the German governments or their European
neighbors. It would silence the rumors of the malevolent that
there was an attempt being made to separate the interests of the
princes and their peoples and to create among the sovereigns an
alliance to oppress their subjects.[30]

According to the memorandum, what was to be chiefly com-
batted at the moment were the "demands of the democratic spirit
that masked itself in the constitutional garb of the parliamentary
opposition." It was an opposition that was demanding concessions incompatible with the public order, was openly attack-
ing the German Confederation and its diet, and was giving force
to its demands by threats of rejecting governmental budgets. The
German princes were called to unite and to end such attacks on
their own authority and that of the German Confederation. Six
articles were offered: their implementation was to restore to the
Federal Diet the power it needed to uphold the rights of the
Confederation and its members against the pretensions of the
state diets. The resulting restoration of public confidence in the
authority of the German Confederation was to nullify the efforts
of the "destructive party spirit." Then there would be no more
credence given to assertions that the Confederation would not
last and that it had to be replaced by a single German state.

The Six Articles were presented as corollaries of the Vienna Final Act of 1820. According to its provisions, sovereign power in the confederate states was to reside in the chief of state. Therefore, the first article of the Six Articles obligated the German princes to reject parliamentary petitions that ran counter to their authority. In a similar vein, the second article proclaimed that state diets could not be permitted to use the threat of budgetary opposition to limit princely sovereignty. According to the third article, no state was permitted to make laws that conflicted with those of the German Confederation or prevented a government from fulfilling its federal obligations. The fourth stipulated that the Federal Diet would name a special commission to safeguard the dignity and rights of the German Confederation and its diet and to facilitate in the various states constitutional rapport between the governments and their diets. The principle duty of the commission would be to keep the Federal Diet informed of propositions and resolutions of the state diets that might be directed against the German Confederation or the governments that it guaranteed. The fifth article obligated each government to take measures to prevent attacks by its diet against the Confederation—insofar as the provisions of its constitution permitted such measures. Finally, the sixth article asserted that the German Confederation alone—through the Federal Diet—possessed the right to interpret the Federal and Final Acts upon which it was grounded.

These Six Articles found a good reception in Stuttgart and Karlsruhe. Of course, they were hardly a surprise to the rulers of these courts. King William had been involved in the formulation of the articles throughout, and Grand Duke Leopold had secured information on the Vienna discussions from both Metternich and Field Marshal Wrede.[31] In fact, Count Karl von Buol, the Austrian envoy to Baden, who brought the proposed Six Articles to both courts in April, was returning from a trip to Vienna, the purpose of which had been to give the Grand Duke a chance to express his views to the delegates assembled there.[32] According to Schönburg's report from Stuttgart, King William expressed his complete agreement with the articles almost as soon as Buol arrived with them on 17 April.[33] By 27 April, Buol could report from Karlsruhe that Leopold was in agreement too.[34]

King Ludwig was in a less cooperative mood. Spiegel reported on 3 May that Foreign Minister Gise presented him with a note indicting his government's disapproval and disavowal of its envoy's agreement to the Six Articles as they stood. Bray was not to have agreed to make permanent the federal commission for monitoring the state diets. When the Six Articles were presented to the Federal Diet, the Bavarian government intended to insist that the commission's initial duration be limited to six years. It also proposed to introduce a reservation that would prohibit any extended application of the Six Articles by generalization or analogy.[35]

Metternich did not just wait for favorable replies to his 12 April memorandum. His goals for 1832 included the enactment of the Six Articles by the Federal Diet and the repeal of the Baden press law. He applied his own diplomatic charm and finesse to ensure the realization of both objectives. The particular recipients of his personal efforts were confidants of the King of Bavaria and the Grand Duke of Baden whom he invited to visit him in Vienna at the end of April and in early May.

Metternich's first visitor was his Bavarian correspondent, Field Marshal Prince Karl von Wrede. In a letter of 25 March, Metternich invited Wrede to make use of his spring vacation in Austria to find an excuse to come to Vienna. With King Ludwig's permission, Wrede accepted on 1 April[36] and appeared in the Austrian capital on 21 April. Wrede's own interest in the visit lay in his desire to learn what Austria's position would be at the long-delayed German military convention. It was, therefore, to military discussions that the visit was largely devoted.[37] Metternich, however, used the occasion to reinforce the Bavarian's conservative inclinations and to encourage him to work for Ludwig's acceptance of the Six Articles and a better enforcement of the federal press decrees of 2 March. Wrede's language during the talks indicated to Metternich that he could count on the field marshal to work for these ends.[38] This, in fact, he would do. By 16 May, Metternich was able to note a more cooperative attitude in Munich, and he praised Wrede for thus fulfilling the task to which he had set himself.[39]

Meanwhile, Wrede had hardly left Vienna when Metternich's next distinguished South German visitor arrived. He was Baron Franz Anton von Falkenstein, a member of the upper house of the Baden diet in 1831, but otherwise unconnected with the Baden administration. The origins of his mission lay back in February, when Austria first took a strong stand against the new press law in Baden. At that time the government in Karlsruhe considered sending a trusted, and ostensibly objective, emissary to explain to the Austrian emperor the difficulty of its position and to request his patience and understanding. When the Austrian minister in Karlsruhe was called to Vienna in March, the Baden government requested that he propose the subject to Metternich and inform Karlsruhe if he felt it would be appropriate to send a special advocate.[40] By the time the Austrian envoy, Buol, returned to Karlsruhe in April, however, Baden's interest in such a mission had waned. Buol reported that the government apparently wanted to avoid the attention that such an ostensible effort for better Baden-Austrian relations might arouse. Buol was able, however, to convince the ministry that it was too late for a change of heart. He implied that his superiors in Vienna would think little of a government that refused to send a mission for which it had so fervently sought approval.[41]

Falkenstein arrived in Vienna on the evening of 5 May. He was well received. In fact, he had nothing but praise for the sympathetic hearing that he was given. But Metternich had Falkenstein come to Vienna to listen rather than to talk. When his guest from Baden noted that the constitution of his state and the state's proximity to France made it difficult for the government in Karlsruhe to act vigorously against subversives, Metternich insisted that it was for these very reasons that he expected that government to enforce federal measures designed to ensure its own peace and security. Then, assured by Falkenstein that Baden would prove its readiness to fulfill its federal duties by its complete adherence to the Six Articles, Metternich concentrated on the question of the Baden press law. He told his visitor that Austria, unlike Prussia, did not insist on the complete revocation of that law. Austria would be satisfied with its suspension until the Federal Diet decided on new press laws for the entire Confederation. The hope of the imperial court, Metternich said, was only that in the future Baden would cooperate with the other members of the Confederation in the pursuit of their common goal—the preservation of peace and legality within all of the federal states.[42]

Throughout the end of April and May, while Metternich was meeting with Wrede and Falkenstein, he received reports from the various German capitals assuring him that the respective German governments would vote for the Six Articles at Frankfurt.[43] There is little doubt that this positive response to Metternich's 12 April memorandum was the reaction of the German princes to the increasing state of popular unrest in this period. Buol reported from Karlsruhe on 22 May, that, as the time grew closer to when Metternich hoped to erect a dam against revolutionary movements in Germany, the revolutionaries seemed to become more active. Newspapers were increasingly passionate in their appeals to the German citizenry to resist the German Confederation and to free themselves from those sovereigns who submitted to its decrees. There were popular assemblies in Pforzheim, then Mannheim and Heidelberg. Still, the excitement in Baden, although it had increased in recent weeks, gained real importance, Buol felt, because of the reigning spirit in neighboring areas—especially the Rhineland province of Bavaria. The Austrian diplomat noted the special concern among Baden officials about an assembly set for 27 May at the old Hambach castle in the Bavarian Rhineland. The fact that the Bavarian authorities had first prohibited the gathering, then revoked that prohibition, only strengthened apprehensions in Karlsruhe.[44]

The famous Hambach Festival of 27 and 28 May came too late to have more than an indirect influence on the passage of the Six Articles. Contemporary popular opinion was incorrect in seeing one as the impetus to the other.[45] Metternich even feared that the occurrence at Hambach might confuse his efforts to bring federal action on the Six Articles.[46] The Hambach Festival, however, vindicated Metternich's warnings to the German rulers.

The Hambach Festival set off its own wave of reaction. It was only one of many such gatherings in the spring of 1832 at which speakers denounced the German Confederation and called for the unification of Germany under a representative constitution. The festival at Hambach Castle at Neustadt an der Haardt, however, was well publicized in advance and compared with similar and contemporaneous meetings in Gaibach, Frankfurt, and Zweibrücken, drew the largest crowd—perhaps 25,000.[47] It worried the neighboring government of Baden enough for it to call troops from Freiburg to Karlsruhe. In the capital they were to be safe from revolutionary contagion and ready to defend the government should the spirit of Hambach take a practical turn. Baden took the lead in enacting ordinances against popular assemblies and the display of the German tricolor insignia. Her government also contacted Württemberg, Grand Ducal Hesse, and Bavaria to propose the consideration of further measures to be taken in common by all of the South German governments.[48]

As early as 30 May, the Federal Diet acted on warnings of the military government at Mainz to vote to have the German governments prohibit revolutionary insignia such as were seen at Hambach. On the same day, the Diet also voted to ask the governments to take measures to prevent and suppress future public assemblies.[49] It was only on 7 June, however, after receiving further news of the Hambach Festival, that the disturbed Diet opened discussion on the means to secure German order. Karl von Nagler, the Prussian delegate and substituting president of the Diet, was even then uncertain what either his own court or that at Vienna wanted done. He limited himself, therefore, to securing the creation of a commission to discuss appropriate measures. Even this had to be done over the objections of the Bavarian delegate, who incurred the ire of his colleagues by urging delay rather than overaction.[50]

Metternich wanted to ensure that the Hambach Festival provided an excuse for federal action that would prevent such manifestations in the future.[51] He insisted, however, that the federal reaction to the festival not be confused with the business of the Six Articles. For him the Hambach affair was a new and separate business, and he urged Wrede to have the Bavarian government see it as such, too. For the moment, he was satisfied to prod the government in Munich to take swift police action against the leaders of the festival and to move troops to the Rhineland to ensure order.[52] Nevertheless, he maintained that as the Hambach Festival endangered all of the German monarchs it required the attention of the federal government as well as that of the government of the state in which it occurred.[53] At the same time, he urged the Prussian government to join Austrian efforts to give this attention the proper impetus.[54]

The first order of business, however, was the conversion of the Six Articles into federal decrees. On 21 June—even before he sent the details of the Hambach Festival to the Emperor—Metternich sent to Berlin a copy of the presidential proposition that was to introduce the Six Articles.[55] He wanted to ensure the cooperation of the two great courts. But it was from Bavaria that Metternich most expected resistance. Therefore, when Münch left Vienna for Frankfurt in mid-June, he carried a special memorandum that he was to share with Wrede in Munich. His mission was one more effort by Metternich to convince King Ludwig of the necessity of supporting the Six Articles and all the other Austrian efforts to bring Germany back from what Metternich called the brink of revolution.[56]

The memorandum that Münch presented to Wrede portrayed Metternich's "truth of the present German situation." That truth consisted of several basic facts. First, the German constitutional systems in themselves fostered revolution. They were too easily perverted by demagogues to their purposes. Secondly, revolutionary principles had crossed the Rhine from France and had been at work in Germany for at least fifteen years. Finally, according to Metternich, inspiration for the recent events at Hambach, as for an uprising that occurred in Paris on 5 June, came from a revolutionary directorate based in the French capital. In existence since the July Revolution, that directorate planned the revolts in both France and Germany. France, however, like a house that had already burned, might have little to lose in a new conflagration. Germany still had everything to lose. In Metternich's view, if a general revolutionary blaze did not start in Hambach it was only because the fuel was not yet sufficient. If something were not done, the conflagration would be general next time.[57]

Unfortunately for Münch's mission, his arrival in Munich was poorly timed. His presentation of the memorandum and plea for cooperation on the Six Articles came just after Ludwig received disturbing news from Berlin. The military conferences there between Austria, Prussia, and the South German courts were not developing as Metternich had said they would. Austria's lack of concern for South German interests was only too evident. Ludwig was so angered that he preemptorily cancelled a family visit with Emperor Francis at Innsbruck. In regard to the Six Articles, he was in no mood to modify his insistence that a six-year limit be placed on the existence of a federal commission to monitor the German diets.[58]

Because of Bavarian dissatisfaction, Münch had to move carefully if the Six Articles were to be enacted with the unanimity necessary to make them effective. After arriving in Frankfurt on 24 June, he worked behind the scenes to prepare a smooth passage for the long-prepared measures. First, there were discussions with the Prussian delegate, Nagler, and some slight editorial changes in the presidential proposition to please Berlin. Then Münch contacted Baron Maximilian von Lerchenfeld, the Bavarian delegate, and convinced him to revise the declaration he was preparing to give in regard to the articles. Münch saw to it that the declaration would have an agreeable tone so that Bavarian suspicions and ill will would be less evident.[59]

On 28 June, the Six Articles were formally presented to the Federal Diet as the joint proposals of the Austrian and Prussian courts. In accordance with Bavarian wishes, Münch allowed a six-year limitation to be appended to the article creating the new federal commission. Otherwise the articles were passed unchanged. The Bavarian delegate was satisfied and, although he told Münch he needed to contact his court first, he felt he could sign the protocol of the session when it was done on 5 July. Münch confidently assured Metternich that the danger of schism in Germany—a possible result of Bavarian resistance to the Six Articles—was now almost passed. On 8 July he sent to his chief a printed copy of the finalized protocol of the 28 June session, proof of the Federal Diet's ratification of the Six Articles as federal law.[60]

The day that the federal protocol containing the Six Articles was signed was also the day that the Diet enacted the Ten Acts. They were the Federal Diet's real reaction to the Hambach Festival and represented the work of the commission of five delegates—from Austria, Prussia, Saxony, Grand Ducal Hesse, and Holstein—who had been chosen on 7 June to consider federal action for the restoration and preservation of German order. They sprang from the commission's study of recent state ordinances and like them were aimed at taking away from demagogues the means by which they disturbed the legal order. The distribution of German language political papers and books under twenty *Bogen*[61] was prohibited except under conditions of prior censorship and approval by the government of the state in which they were to be circulated. All political clubs and assemblies were declared illegal and the display of all unauthorized insignia and flags was forbidden. The portion of the Carlsbad Decrees concerning the measures for the control of the universities was renewed, and the states were made responsible for exchanging information concerning the secret activities of students and nonstudents alike. Foreigners were to be kept under careful surveillance and provision was made for the extradition of political suspects. Finally, the members of the German Confederation reaffirmed their guarantee of mutual military assistance and promised to inform the Federal Diet of their efforts to apply all of these measures.[62]

Like the Six Articles, the Ten Acts were approved by all of the delegates at Frankfurt. But this did not happen before the specter of South German independence had shown itself again. Münch confirmed what Metternich had already heard from other sources about a Bavarian attempt to organize South German measures outside of federal channels. Münch reported that the Bavarian delegate had held conferences with the representatives of Württemberg, Baden, and Grand Ducal Hesse and tried to persuade them to accept his government's own anti-revolutionary propositions. The caution of the other South German diplomats, however, kept them from acting independently of their other federal colleagues.[63]

The desire to protect state sovereignty in the face of federal duty remained characteristic of the thinking of the South German governments. It was a major recurring obstacle to Metternich's efforts to strengthen the German Confederation as the bulwark of German monarchy. But there were other problems even after federal action on the Ten Articles preempted Bavarian attempts for an independent South German initiative to make federal measures unnecessary. Metternich still had to deal with Baden's resistance to his plans for press reform. Karlsruhe continued to try to forestall federal action against its press law. It pleaded that the press in Baden was no worse than that in neighboring states: that prepublication censorship was unnecessary. This tactic, however, was no more successful than Baden's fruitless attempt to secure support on this issue from the self-possessed government of Bavaria. Yet, even when, on 5 July, the Federal Diet voted for the suppression of the long discussed Baden press law, Baden's delegate at Frankfurt continued to request that the Confederation stipulate that only individual clauses of the law be repealed. Finally, he insisted that at least suppression of the law be delayed until the federal press commission proposed new general legislation.[64]

The Austrians had had enough of South German opposition. Münch guided the Federal Diet to a rejection of all of Baden's pleas. Finally, in a private meeting with Baron Friedrich von Blittersdorff, the Baden delegate, the Austrian representative threatened Baden with force. Implying Austrian readiness to enforce the will of the Federal Diet by military means, Münch showed Blittersdorff a letter from Metternich indicating that the Austrian general in Vorarlberg awaited his instructions. Isolated and threatened, the government in Karlsruhe was forced to comply with the will of the Austrian-led German Confederation. On 31 July, Blittersdorff informed the Federal Diet that his government had fulfilled the wishes of the Confederation and modified its press law out of existence.[65]

With the end of the Baden press law, it would seem that Metternich had accomplished his goals for 1832. Continued efforts were required, however, to ensure that the South Germans would act with the vigor needed to make the new federal legislation effective. The Six Articles were under popular attack, and the South German governments were given cause to consider the wisdom of their enforcement. Although none of the new federal provisions was a departure from established federal laws and principles, they were portrayed as such by aroused liberals in the political press. It was asserted that the two great German powers were destroying the power of the South German diets so that the South German princes could be mediatized—deprived of their sovereignty.[66] Such ideas made the rounds in diplomatic circles also. The ministers of Baden and Electoral Hesse in Munich told members of the Bavarian ministry that the Six Articles had no other purpose than to gain Austrian hegemony in Germany.[67] Worse still, the idea caught on in London and Paris. British and French diplomats warned the smaller German states of their loss of independence and complained to Austria and Prussia about this development. The French foreign minister, Horace Sebastiani, even chided a Bavarian diplomat that now that Austria and Prussia controlled German affairs he supposed he should correspond only with them.[68]

Metternich rejected any foreign intervention in German affairs. He informed the French that it was difficult to see how anyone could speak of the German princes voting to mediatize themselves. He was confident that the French government would find it in its best interest to see the suppression of revolutionary tendencies in a neighboring nation. He warned Paris, however, that he would see to the defense of the German sovereigns no matter what the French attitude.[69] At the same time, the Austrian representative at Frankfurt moved to limit popular attacks on the recent federal decrees and to keep the state governments firm in their intention to apply them. On 19 July, Münch had the Diet vote for the suppression of two Baden papers, the *Freisinnige* and the *Wächter am Rhein*, because they attacked the Six Articles. On 9 August, he persuaded the Diet to order the German governments to prohibit the circulation of petitions and addresses against the federal decrees. Finally, on 23 August, he saw to it that the state governments were asked to report to the Federal Diet their progress in the implementation of the recent decrees.[70]

Despite all these efforts, Metternich still had to worry about the lack of conservative conviction in the Prussian and South German ministries. In Württemberg, for instance, the ministry published the Six Articles with an accompanying assurance that the new federal decrees neither could nor would affect the constitution of Württemberg.[71] Worse still was the effort of the Bavarian and Prussian delegates at Frankfurt to persuade the Federal Diet to give the German people a similar guarantee with regard to all state constitutions. Both Münch and Metternich felt that a federal proclamation along such lines would put the Confederation on the defensive. It would only seem to confirm accusations that the Six Articles were aimed at something other than what was said. Metternich ascribed the Bavarian-Prussian proposal to wrongheadedness rather than to treachery. "I think that it can be assumed that the reason for the agreement [between Bavaria and Prussia on this issue] is to be sought rather in common perversity than in calculated treachery to the common cause," Metternich confided to Münch.[72] Metternich wanted no dilution of the federal decrees in any case. He saw to it, therefore, that the Federal Diet declared, on November 8, that no qualification appended to the Six Articles in their publication was meant to, or could, restrict their application.[73]

Metternich continued to be concerned that the weakness of the South German rulers and the irresolution of their ministers might endanger his German policies. He had cause, however, to be more reassured in the fall of 1832. When the Austrian envoy to Württemberg, Prince Schönburg, visited Munich in October, he found King Ludwig and his foreign minister, Gise, firm in their conservatism. On 17 October, the Bavarians finally published the Six Articles, and Schönburg could not have been more pleased. He felt that the official proclamation referred to federal duty in wording that the Bavarian government had never used before. Never before had it ever officially suggested to its people the idea of federal duty and the subordination of the Bavarian constitution to the purposes of the German Confederation.[74]

Schönburg was pleased with the apparent new subordination of Bavarian officials to their king and the revived general trust and adherence to Ludwig among the Bavarian people. He was equally pleased with the situation in Württemberg. He reported to Metternich that, although "inner dissolution" had never gone as far as in Bavaria, there was a noticeable quieting of spirit and a lessening of press offenses in Württemberg. Schönburg attributed the cautious manner of publication of the Six Articles in Stuttgart to the personal revolutionary fears of the king's chief advisor, Baron Paul von Maucler. Maucler was responsible for the government's public assertion that the Federal Decrees would not affect the constitution of Württemberg. Since then, the king realized that he had been ill-advised to make such an announcement and consulted Maucler much less than formerly. In any case, in Schönburg's estimation, the good intentions of King William were beyond doubt.[75]

Encouraging reports came also from Karlsruhe. In May, the Grand Duke of Baden had called Baron Sigismund von Reitzenstein to become his minister president. Reitzenstein was Baden's elder statesman, the chief minister of the Karlsruhe government during the final battles against Napoleon and the creation of the Baden constitution. He was, moreover, the man responsible for renewing the prestige of the University of Heidelberg. He enjoyed respect and confidence both at home and abroad as a progressive, but judicious, statesman. Since his appointment, except for the delay in retracting its press law, the record of the government of Baden was perfect in its response to federal measures. At the end of September, Reitzenstein assured the Austrian minister in Baden that he planned to reform the basis of the Baden government so as to please Austria, Prussia, and the Federal Diet. He agreed that Baden had been confused for too long. He intended to calm things down in his country and expressed the hope that Metternich would appreciate the purity of his intentions.[76]

Even when his federal policies were vindicated and apparently accepted in South Germany, Metternich could not rest. His efforts had to be directed to making certain that the South German rulers resisted the attacks on the Six Articles that were to be expected when their diets opened in 1833. The violent denunciation of the Six Articles in the Darmstadt Diet in December seemed an omen of things to come in Württemberg and Baden. Metternich wanted the princes to resist intimidation. His efforts in late 1832 and the beginning of 1833 were directed, therefore, to organizing a princely defense of the German Confederation against the slings of the South German parliamentarians. Through Prince Schönburg he communicated to King William his desire to see the ruler of Württemberg organize a common front among the German princes concerned. He explained to the king that street radicalism had declined since the Hambach Festival, but in its place would develop a more insidiously dangerous liberalism.[77]

7

Politics by Other Means: The Berlin Conference, 1832

Metternich's German policy in 1832 called for the consolidation of the Rhineland and South Germany against the dangers of revolutionary France. Simultaneous, therefore, with his attempt to convince the Prussian and South German sovereigns to join a common ideological front of the Continental Powers was his effort to guide them into a military system of Austrian design. He felt he could not allow the South Germans an independence that might force them into alliance with France or into a neutrality pact with Prussia. He had to overcome the influence of important factions, not only in the South German ministries, but in the Prussian one as well. To implement his military as well as ideological policies in Germany, Metternich had especially to overcome the influence of the "Bernstorff-Eichhorn party" in Prussia. Then only could he have some hope of convincing the Prussian and South German kings that their real interests were best served by military plans that had the approval of the Austrian government.

Since General Rühle's visit to the South German capitals in the spring of 1831, Metternich felt that the Prussian ministry was encouraging the development of a South German neutrality league. Convinced of the reality of this danger by the Prussian circular of 15 August 1831, the Austrian foreign minister moved to correct the situation in Berlin. He was certain Frederick William III recognized the necessity of a firm Austro-Prussian alliance no matter what the feelings of his foreign ministry. Counting on this, Metternich sent General Clam to the Prussian capital to confront the Prussian king with Austria's disturbing view of the Prussian ministers responsible for the Rühle mission. Metternich characterized them as members of a faction that sought to push Austria out of the Confederation and to reform it along liberal and nationalistic lines. With his encouragement,

Prussian conservatives were urged to warn the king against alienating Austria for the sake of dangerous policies that would bring little assurance of South German reliability in any case. When Clam returned from Berlin in December 1831 with new Prussian military proposals, it seemed that Metternich's efforts had brought a conservative turn in Prussian policies. At least it appeared that the Prussian government would no longer encourage the South German demands for an independent South German army.[1]

But the German military question was not to be settled so easily for Metternich. When Clam returned to Berlin in January 1832, he found that Foreign Minister Bernstorff was using all of his influence to nullify the proposals made to Austria in December. Bernstorff insisted that Prussia had to stand by its earlier concessions to South German pride and independence. The result was that the Austro-Prussian military talks were at an impasse.[2]

Metternich tried to end the impasse by writing directly to Frederick William. The memorandum that he sent was designed to impress the King with Austria's continuing desire for close cooperation with Prussia in the development of a general defensive system for Germany. Such a system, however, the memorandum explained, had to be based on the needs of the whole German Confederation, not on the narrow desires of the South German governments. Certainly they had to be given some options that were in their interest. In the formulation of a grand strategy, however, the importance of South Germany's 60,000 men could not be equated with that of the 200,000 troops of the two great German powers. The wishes of Austria and Prussia had to have precedence. Thus, if the Prussian government still agreed to its proposals of December—with the Austrian reservation that the contingency line of retreat be toward the Danube rather than toward the Main—Metternich suggested that they invite a representative of each of the South German federal corps to Berlin. There, in discussions based on this Austro-Prussian understanding, they could help plan the defense of Germany from Tyrol to the Main.[3] Metternich proposed Berlin for the meetings so as to discredit claims by the "party" that behind his proposals lay an Austrian scheme for German hegemony.[4]

Metternich's memorandum had the desired effect. King Frederick William agreed completely to the Austrian proposals.[5] Bernstorff was so angered by Metternich's successful separation of the king from the advice of his own foreign minister that, on

4 March, he requested that he no longer be required to take part in the military discussions. His request was granted on 12 March.[6] Metternich's first step toward removing Bernstorff from German affairs was achieved. Nevertheless, when General Clam reported the Prussian king's agreement to Metternich's proposals, he was right to warn the Austrian foreign minister that Bernstorff and the Eichhorn party could still put many obstacles in Austria's way. His warning was that at the coming military conference they might try to win back the position of strength that they had had when the conference was originally proposed. Clam felt that for that purpose they would probably try to have the South Germans insist that the Rühle negotiations form the basis for the discussions in Berlin. They would make it seem that it was the South Germans who wanted their troops to fall back toward the Main River—to be supported by Prussian, rather than Austrian, forces. Clam left it up to Metternich to find a means to block such efforts.[7]

The means Metternich chose to counter the efforts of the Prussian "party" was to try to convince the South German rulers that the methods and goals of the "party" were incompatible with their own. He felt certain that the South German monarchs were antagonistic toward France and would rather fight alongside Austria than see the expansion of French power.[8] The appeal of the defensive system that was conceived during the Rühle talks was that it would make the South Germans independent of Austrian influence. Such an idea flattered South German vanity. However, as Metternich saw it, it was not the rulers but their liberal ministers who, encouraged by the Prussian "party," contrived the idea of concentrating South German and Prussian forces. Metternich felt that the principle result of such a plan would be political rather than military; namely, the creation of the basis for an independent German political alignment under Prussian aegis. As Metternich saw it, if the French really attacked Germany—as would be necessary if they were to get to Austria— the Rühle system would leave South German territory open to immediate French occupation. He knew that the South Germans could never accept that.[9] To regain the upper hand in German military planning, Metternich decided that he had only to point out the danger inherent in the Rühle plan and to introduce a better one.

On 25 March 1832, the day before the Austrians and Prussians sent out their joint invitation for the representatives of the South German corps to come to Berlin, Metternich wrote to Field Marshal Wrede to invite him to come to Vienna for private discussions. The effect of these talks on Bavaria's agreement to accept the Six Articles and to enforce federal press laws has already been mentioned.[10] Military affairs, however, had an equally important part in the talks. Metternich had assured Wrede that he would send him a copy of the instructions that were to guide the Austrian representative at the military conference in Berlin. As a result, Wrede delayed the departure of the Bavarian representative of the Seventh Federal Corps until he could see these instructions. When they arrived on 10 April, however, they were so vague that Wrede continued to hold up General Franz von Hertling's departure for the conference. Wrede also advised Württemberg to delay the mission of the representative of the Eighth Federal Corps too, until he could learn firsthand in Vienna more about the Austrian position.[11]

Wrede's visit to Vienna at the end of April offered Metternich a chance to counter in advance any attempt by the Eichhorn party to confront Austria with a firm Prussian-South German alignment in Berlin. His efforts toward that end were twofold. He sought to discredit the Prussian ministers responsible for earlier Prussian-South German military planning, and he warned that the strategy they proposed involved a dangerous retreat from South German territory.

To discredit the Prussian ministers, Metternich showed Wrede a secret Prussian memorandum of January 1831 that he had recently sent to Berlin to undermine the Eichhorn party. The memorandum, written by Eichhorn and presented to Frederick William by Bernstorff, was an answer to the king's question as to how order could be preserved in Germany in case of a European war. The answer given by Eichhorn and Bernstorff was that a policy of concessions to liberalism and nationalism would be necessary if popular contentment and internal security were to be assured. Most damaging to the Prussian liberal party was the fact that they had circulated the memorandum in South Germany without the king's permission. Having obtained a copy of the memorandum from an informant in Nassau, Metternich sent it to Berlin to expose the infidelity of the Bernstorff-Eichhorn party to Frederick William. Metternich showed it to the strict monarchist, Wrede, to discredit Bernstorff and Eichhorn in his eyes as well. Later, in May, Metternich boasted to the field marshal that they both knew the reason for Bernstorff's resignation from the Prussian ministry—implying that the discovery of the memorandum was the cause.[12]

Metternich was not content, however, to discredit the men responsible for the Rühle plan. He wanted to convince Wrede that the strategy that it entailed would leave South Germany open to French occupation. He told Wrede that Austria, unlike Prussia, would not support a system of defense that called for a retreat from a portion of German territory. In fact, he was so persuasive that, on 22 April, Wrede wrote to his friend in Berlin, General Karl von Knesebeck, to check if Prussia really was in favor of an initial evacuation of the German border areas.[13] At the same time, Wrede was reassured enough by the supposed Austrian policy that he told the minister of Württemberg in Vienna, Baron August von Blomberg, that he was now going to have the Bavarian delegate leave for the convention in Berlin. He asked that Stuttgart send their man as well.[14]

Metternich's assurances to Wrede involved not a little dissimulation. The truth was that Metternich, not unlike his Prussian rivals, felt that the best defense of Germany lay in gathering federal forces back from the frontier. Only then could a counterattack against a French invasion be made with sufficient force. The Prussians thought the Main River to be the best point from which to begin the counterattack; the Austrians chose the Danube. For each country the protection of its own territories determined its evaluation of the best location for the weight of the assembled federal forces. It was not long before this was obvious to the South Germans.

The fears that led Wrede to write to Berlin regarding a preliminary retreat were soon given tangible grounds. Knesebeck's reply of May 12—one upon which he consulted the Austrian delegate to the convention, General Clam—was not at all reassuring. It explained that, because there was to be no thought of an offensive war against France, the French would have the advantage of the attack. An immediate German counterattack would, by necessity, be of unequal strength. Because of this, it was considered advisable for German forces to avoid an engagement before they could be gathered in sufficient mass.[15] To Wrede, who feared that the retreat of South German forces in the face of the French would cause demoralization and even revolution in South Germany, this was not acceptable. He complained to both Knesebeck and Metternich. At the same time, he asked the Austrian foreign minister to instruct General Clam to see to it that South German interests were given more consideration.[16]

Metternich assured Wrede that he found his views worthy of study and that he had instructed Clam to bring them to the attention of the convention in Berlin.[17] The first reports of the South German delegates, after the convention opened on 26 May, did not indicate that this was the case. Neither the Austrian nor the Prussian delegate seemed willing to give attention to South German interests and concerns. In the first session, General Knesebeck declared that the earlier Prussian propositions were void: new accords had to be reached.[18] General Clam then proposed that the South German Seventh and Eighth Federal Corps be separated and that at least the Seventh be placed on the Danube in contact with Austrian forces. Despite the insistence of the South German delegates that the two corps not be divided, Knesebeck seemed content to allow Clam to reject the idea in the name of both of the great German powers.[19] Württemberg's General Joseph Konrad von Bangold concluded that neither Austria nor Prussia was inclined to exert herself to defend the Rhine Valley.[20]

Metternich seems never to have intended to support a plan any different than that which Clam was enunciating in Berlin. His soothing words to Wrede appear to have been only a tactic to ensure that the South Germans did not agree to earlier Prussian ideas for a South German retreat toward the Main River. Such an arrangement would have placed most of the Confederation's forces under Prussian control and created a danger that a new Prussian-South German alliance would pursue a policy independent of Austrian influence—and potentially dangerous to Austrian security. If, on the other hand, the Prussian "party" were unable to persuade the South Germans to insist on a retreat to the Main, the Prussian military might be persuaded to adhere to its most recent understanding with Austria. Metternich counted on this Austrian and Prussian military understanding to produce a German defense system that would better protect Austrian interests.

In his correspondence with General Clam, Metternich expressed his impatience with South German resistance to a defensive retreat and his belief in the necessity of Austro-Prussian cooperation for the implementation of an adequate German defensive system. Three things, he felt, influenced South German thinking at the military conferences. First was the hope they had to preserve their independence through the unification of their Seventh and Eighth Federal Corps. Second was the desire of Field Marshal Wrede to attain through that unification an important command. Finally, there was the fear that the South German governments had of the result of an evacuation of their territory in the face of a French advance. This evacuation and the resulting entrance of revolutionary influence, was, Metternich granted, an important consideration. Yet, as he saw it, there were two evils that had to be dealt with—revolution and war. In case of a French attack, war, not revolution, would be the most pressing problem and the one to be dealt with first.[21]

Metternich concluded that Austria and Prussia had to determine what was the best means to defend Germany. In a war, he reminded Clam, power—not pretensions—was what counted. The Rühle mission to South Germany was a great misfortune because it reversed the priorities. Metternich suggested that one way to reestablish them was to invite the representataives of the northern German Ninth and Tenth Corps to the Berlin conference. As long as they were not present, the South Germans would continue to have a certain parity with the great powers. Therefore, if the Prussians wanted to include the northern Germans, Austria would be ready to agree. Because of their geographic position—surrounded by Austria and Prussia—they could be counted on to stand by the great power.[22] When their representatives arrived at the conference in August, this proved to be the case.

Meanwhile, tensions mounted between the South German and Great Power negotiators because of the issue of an initial strategic withdrawal from South Germany. It was because of the apparent deadlock on this issue, however, that General Clam was able to turn the convention to Austria's benefit. While Wrede rained protests on Metternich for abandoning the South Germans,[23] Clam proposed an unexpected concession to those very states. As the South German delegates insisted that the two great German powers support the South German Seventh and Eighth Corps in a forward position, Clam suggested that perhaps Austrian troops could perform that function. He volunteered that, should the South Germans be attacked, Austria would immediately bring up an advance echelon of sixty to seventy thousand men to support them.[24] The idea behind this proposal, Clam told Metternich, was to ensure that, at least at the outset of a Franco-German war, the formation of the federal forces in the South German theater would be such that Austria would have predominance—thus a decisive influence over their use.[25]

Thanks to Clam's proposal, the conference was about to enter a more active stage. Metternich, however, could not yet be sure that that would be the case. He intended to damage the liberal Prussian-South German alignment beyond repair. He continued to tell the South Germans that it was not Austria, but Prussia, that had always been for a strategic retreat. The mention of such a plan in the current talks, Metternich told Württemberg's minister, Baron Blomberg, was merely the last trace of the "Rühle intrigue" and a plan for the establishment of German neutrality under Prussian aegis. According to Metternich, Clam had allowed these old views to be discussed but had never been instructed to support the idea of a retreat—even a retreat to the Danube. The Austrian foreign minister wanted the South Germans to believe that he approved completely of Württemberg and Bavarian resistance to a system that required the division of the Seventh and Eighth Corps and the abandonment of any part of South Germany.[26] He, of course, had not believed it himself. Now things could change.

If Clam's proposal for Austrian reinforcement of the Seventh and Eighth Corps could be agreed upon, there would be less need to continue irritating the South Germans by demanding the division of their troops and their retreat to the interior. Austria would have enough direct control over the South German armies so that their reliability in the defense of the South German approaches to Austria could be ensured without requiring that other conditions be agreed upon. Meanwhile, by his harsh portrayal of the Prussian position and a dissimulation of his own, Metternich hoped to convince both the South Germans and the Prussians of something that he had felt to be the case from the start: Prussian-South German defense schemes were based more upon political than military considerations; they were just trying to band together to escape Austrian influence. Metternich wanted both sides to see that Austria alone had plans appropriate for a general German defense. His wayward confederates were to be brought to the realization that they had been mutually deceiving each other. They were to see for themselves that plans aimed at German neutrality under Prussian protection would not be applicable if there were a defensive war against France.[27]

By the time the representatives of the Ninth and Tenth Corps joined the military conference at Berlin on 19 August 1832, Metternich was confident that he had achieved his goal. He wrote to Wrede that the "Rühle neutrality garbage" was set aside and the field opened for proper negotiations.[28] Now some movement developed at the talks. The South German military men had less cause for opposition after they received some assurance that the two great German powers would support their efforts to stave off a French attack as close to the Rhine as possible. Austria's position seemed to become more pliable too. Since May, and the replacement of Bernstorff as head of the Prussian foreign ministry by the more conservative Johann von Ancillon, Metternich could be more confident that Prussia would not pursue political aims opposed to those of her Austrian ally.

Now Metternich decided that he could agree to a final German defense plan that was much like the one that developed out of the Rühle talks. There could be a tripartite division of the federal armies with Prussian and north German forces on the right, the Prussian-supported South Germans in the center, and Austrian forces on the left. Prussian forces would be predominant and Prussian overall influence inevitable—just as it was according to the Rühle plan. Because of Clam's proposal, however, a large number of Austrian troops would come to the aid of South German forces at the outset of a war, thus giving Austria initial predominance in the South German theater.[29] There would be little possibility for a South German-Prussian neutrality system to develop. Although Metternich did not explain all of these implications to Wrede, he did explain that Austria was making no concession to Prussian supremacy by the adoption of her final mobilization plan. Austria was not accepting the plans of the liberal party in Prussia. According to Metternich, he and the "pure party" in the Prussian ministry now agreed to a defensive system that was in the best interest of all of Germany. There was no concession involved now that the Prussians wanted the same thing as the Austrians.[30]

Despite Metternich's effort to impress Wrede with the happy turn of events in regard to Germany's defense, the Bavarian continued to protest to Metternich the Austrian attitude toward German military affairs. He was indignant at Metternich's exultation over setting aside the "Rühle neutrality garbage." Wrede denied that there was ever any word of neutrality during the Rühle talks. He insisted that they had only concerned the development of a system of defense that would guarantee the security of South Germany in case of a French attack. That system, which Wrede felt would defend South Germany at the Rhine, was largely disregarded by Austria and Prussia at the Berlin talks. Wrede had to admit that the conference had recently taken a turn toward greater consideration of South German wishes. He felt, however, that in calling the representatives of the Ninth and Tenth Corps to Berlin, Austria and Prussia changed the focus of the talks and skipped over another basic question in regard to South German defense. He insisted that, as long as the German powers did not agree to a fortification of the middle and upper Rhine, South Germany could never be assured of its defense. Without fortresses there, the fulfillment of any promise of immediate support on the Rhine depended too much on the contingencies of each situation.[31]

Metternich was concerned by the protests of the man who had been selected by the South German sovereigns to lead their troops into battle. He was convinced, however, that much was being accomplished at Berlin, despite the remaining disagreements of the South Germans. After all, a system of mobilization had been outlined that could provide for rapid defensive action by the German Confederation. Metternich was especially pleased that complete agreement had been reached on this by Austria, Prussia, and the states whose troops made up the Ninth and Tenth Federal Corps. He was convinced that the firm union of these powers had created a German defense system from which, should Germany ever be attacked, the South Germans would be unlikely to separate themselves.[32]

Nevertheless, this conviction did not satisfy Metternich. He sought immediate South German adhesion to the Berlin agreements. He told Wrede that Bavaria alone was now preventing the conclusion of the conference at Berlin. Her insistence on a settlement of the fortress issue had to be ended. Metternich asserted that the adamant Bavarian stand on the issue was caused by the unfounded suspicion that ulterior political motives lay behind the plans of the great German powers: that they were ready to sacrifice military considerations so that they could force the South Germans to support this or that political plan. Metternich denied that there existed any such motives. There were, he assured Wrede, no isolated Austrian or Prussian political plans any longer. Both powers were cooperating in the common interest to formulate plans for the protection of all of Germany. In any case, the question of permanent fortifications at Germersheim, for instance, was something to be decided later by the Federal Diet. The Berlin conference was concerned only with wartime field operations. Regarding Wrede's related and continuing insistence on the absolute necessity of South German forces defending the Rhine, Metternich appealed to Wrede's experience as a soldier. He urged Wrede to remember the dangers involved in the isolation of small advanced units. The loss of small battles could result in the loss of great wars.[33]

While Metternich was seeking to end South German obstruction by writing to Wrede, Schönburg worked directly on King

William of Württemberg. The Austrian minister saw that the king was tired of supporting Bavarian intransigence. William was beginning to suspect that it was the result of Wrede's desire for a substantial command or a Bavarian scheme to secure federal funds for constructing a fortress for Bavaria's own defense. Schönberg made use of these suspicions to make any future Württemberg advocacy of the unification of the Seventh and Eighth Corps under an independent Bavarian command seem ridiculous and subservient. His hope for success lay in the fact that William's consent to Wrede's command of the South German armies was motivated solely by a desire to ensure Bavarian cooperation with the other South German states. Back in June 1831, William feared that a war with France was imminent, and he wanted to stabilize the politics of the Bavarian government when it was guided by a liberal ministry and a wavering king.[34] Now Schönburg tried to manipulate William's second thoughts to Austrian purposes. It was an effort in which Metternich was very interested, for he attributed the recent tractability of Bavaria to the attitude of the King of Württemberg.[35]

In fact, by early November, the Bavarian government had decided that it would agree, at least conditionally, to the work of the Berlin conference. Although still insisting that the Seventh and Eighth Corps be allowed to act together to thwart an attack on the Rhine, the government in Munich felt that it could agree to a general plan of preparedness. It was satisfied to let the question of federal fortresses be handled by the Federal Diet, since, on 25 October, the Austrian president of the Diet introduced the problem for discussion at Frankfurt.[36] In view of Bavaria's increasing isolation at the Berlin talks, Ludwig decided that it was wise to have his delegate sign the military protocol. It could be ratified, with reservations, later. Meanwhile, Bavaria could escape criticism and solemnize the first steps toward a federal defense of Germany.

The secret military protocol that was signed in Berlin on 3 December 1832 was described by the representative of the Eight Corps, General Franz von Hertling, and by the Bavarian envoy in Berlin, Court Friedrich von Luxburg, as conceived in the spirit of the talks with General Rühle.[37] The final federal mobilization plan called for a tripartite division of the federal armies. As was agreed during the Rühle discussions of the year before, Prussia and Austria were to hold positions on the right and left flank of a center South German army. The change was that contingents from Prussia and northern Germany were to be added to this South German army. Also, since it was agreed that the formation of the final tripartite federal formation would take time, an emergency provisional army was to be mobilized in case of immediate danger. Consisting of the Seventh, Eighth, and Ninth Corps, along with 30,000 Prussians and 70,000 Austrians, it was to protect the Rhine from Mainz to Basel. In case of a French attack, the two South German corps were to take positions as far forward as possible, and they were to be reinforced with all speed by the rest of the provisional army.[38]

Although no final operational plans were agreed upon, nor the commanders of the various armies chosen, Metternich told Emperor Francis that he believed much had been accomplished. He explained how the representatives of Bavaria and Württemberg had come to the conference intent on keeping their Seventh and Eighth Corps inseparable and independent in their own command. The degree of independence that that would have given them was unacceptable and had to be limited, but in such a manner that would not cause them to break up the conference. Metternich told Francis that, thanks to the cooperation of the other delegates at Berlin, the question of commands had been avoided, and it was seen to that in every order of battle Bavarian and Württemberg troops were to be placed with a majority of troops from one of the two great German powers. In the provisional army this would be the Austrians. In the final formation it would be the Prussians. In each case an Austrian or Prussian officer, as the representative of the state providing the most troops, could assume overall local command.[39]

Metternich emphasized that there were moral gains inherent in the Berlin protocol, too. First, the increased feeling of unity among the German powers and the support assured them by the Great Powers was to improve the posture of the German princes at home and abroad. Second, the Prussian neutrality system, called to life by General Rühle's mission to the South German capitals, was completely destroyed. Prussia now was in agreement with Austria on a federal defense system for all of Germany. Metternich praised the efforts of General Clam who had helped to make this possible. Not only was the Prussian-South German neutrality idea overcome and South German demands for independent action circumvented, but an agreement was reached that seemed to satisfy all of the participants.[40]

On 13 January 1833, Emperor Francis approved the Berlin protocol. Although he could have wished for more, he conceded that it represented the best that Austria could do.[41] As things turned out, even the emperor's moderate satisfaction was premature. The protocol was never ratified by the South German governments. Metternich had to be satisfied with the destruction of the plan for a Prussian-led South German neutrality system and the creation of a closer understanding between the two great German powers. The South German governments fell in behind Bavaria to insist on the fulfillment of their earlier demands for an effectively independent South German army.

King Ludwig decided that South Germany's demands would be appended as reservations to the ratifications they proposed to make to the Berlin protocol. The demands were reminiscent of the ideas that had been formulated by Armansperg and King William in the fall of 1830. The South German Seventh and Eighth Federal Corps were to be allowed to act together under their own commander and on their own initiative until they were joined by other federal troops. Even then, the South German forces were to form an independent army between the Prussian and Austrian forces. The number of troops that they would commit to such formations was not to be limited to the numbers specified in the protocol. Finally, the South Germans were to be assured that in the event of war their corps would be immediately reinforced by the remainder of the provisional army.[42]

That neither the Austrian nor Prussian ministers at Munich or Stuttgart would accept the South German ratifications with the appended reservations did not alter the position of the South German governments.[43] They did not waver, even when Metternich warned that Austria and Prussia would suspend their own ratifications if the protocol were not accepted as it stood. Foreign Minister Gise warned King Ludwig that, if he gave in to Metternich's wishes, the Seventh and Eighth Corps would lose their freedom to act in South Germany's best interest. They might be forced to retreat to rear positions and wait for a provisional army that would be formed only when the two great German powers pleased. Gise felt that, under such conditions, the king would have to consider Baden, Württemberg, and Bavaria's own Rhineland province as good as relinquished to France. Ludwig stood by his decision to insist on his reservations. With him stood the rulers of Württemberg and Baden.[44] Although the sovereigns of Württemberg and Baden would have preferred a compromise solution, they agreed to wait with Bavaria for Austria and Prussia to make the first offer in this regard.[45] It did not come—at least not until 1840, when a new French crisis threatened Germany.[46]

The outcome of Metternich's efforts to gain the acceptance of his military planning in South Germany was hardly impressive. It had the same negative character that was typical of the end product of most of his diplomatic efforts in the German Confederation. State sovereignty was always more attractive than federal duty: Metternich could not so much secure the cooperation of the German princes for his federalistic plans as he could ensure that it would be difficult for them to do otherwise. Metternich could not get the South Germans to agree to the Berlin defense protocol; but, because of his success in undermining the Bernstorff ministry and the resulting new attitude in official Berlin, it would be difficult for them to act independently if Germany were ever attacked.[47]

8
More Dangerous than Street Revolts, 1833

Metternich's German policy in 1833 consisted of turning to practical use the moral victories of the previous year. The enactment of the Six Articles by the Federal Diet was evidence of the most important of these. It was a sign of the continuing—although reluctant—acceptance of the Austrian solution to the German Question. Metternich's intention in 1833 was to make good use of the decline of progressive alternatives. He was convinced that the members of the German Confederation, for their own sake as well as that of the Habsburgs, had to act together against manifestations of revolution, whether in the form of parliamentary opposition or street radicalism. Metternich's efforts were aimed, therefore, at preparing the German rulers to stand firmly against both dangers. Parliamentary opposition was to be thwarted by adherence to both the legislation and the monarchic principles of the German Confederation. Open revolts were to be prevented by federal investigations to root out subversion or, if necessary, by federal arms. Finally, as in 1820, a German ministerial conference was to be called to ensure the further consolidation of the Confederation as the bulwark of the monarchic principle.

Metternich's first step toward the implementation of his policy in 1833 was to see that the diets of Württemberg and Baden were not allowed to intimidate their governments into noncompliance with the Six Articles. He knew from the sessions of the Hessian diet at Darmstadt in late 1832 that parliamentary oppositions would most certainly question the constitutionality and legality of recent federal legislation. The Six Articles could be used as an excuse to attack the Federal Diet and its conservative principles. Metternich urged the governments in Stuttgart and Karlsruhe to be firm in the face of such attacks. He proposed, moreover, that they discuss common principles and policies among themselves so that any alliance between the opposition parties in their two diets would be countered by the coordinated efforts of the two rulers. There was to be no successful parliamentary attack on a single German government that would encourage the opposition forces in neighboring states. Metternich particularly urged King William, as the most reliable of the constitutional princes, to initiate a common monarchic front made up, not only of the rulers of Württemberg and Baden, but of those of Grand Ducal Hesse, Electoral Hesse, Nassau and Saxony as well.[1]

Although King William expressed interest in Metternich's ideas, he was reluctant to take the initiative to organize the constitutional German governments against their diets. The minister president of Baden, Baron Sigismund von Reitzenstein, felt the same way. Nevertheless, each man assured Metternich of his government's willingness to cooperate in an understanding such as he proposed. They expressed their intention to see that in the meantime they would be firm in handling their own parliamentary bodies.[2] In fact, according to the Austrian minister in Stuttgart, Prince Schönburg, King William expressed regret that any German ruler had instituted a constitution since 1815. Such was the king's bleak mood that, when a diet deputy, Paul Pfizer, demanded that the Six Articles be either approved by the diet or suspended in Württemberg, Schönburg feared that the king might act too rashly against his own diet.[3] The conservativism of the South German governments grew with the vocal liberalism of their diets. By the time William dissolved his diet on 22 March— his reaction to the continuing dispute over the Pfizer motion— the governments of Württemberg, Baden and Ducal Hesse had agreed to support each other in a firm and common stand against the pressures of their diets.[4]

This growing conservative temper in the South German governments was one that Metternich could encourage and use. He had reports that the governments in Stuttgart and Karlsruhe were prepared to stand firmly against the liberals of their diets. At about the same time, he received word from Wrede that King Ludwig, disturbed by continuing unrest in his Rhineland province, looked to the two great German powers to "force" him to modify the liberal institutions there.[5] At this auspicious time, Metternich decided to reinforce and make use of the wary conservativism of the South German courts. One way to do this was to invite representatives of Württemberg and Bavaria to participate in Austro-Prussian investigations of German subversion. He was sure they would find some. He already had information on one Hanoverian-based secret society whose aim was the immediate liberation of the incarcerated leaders of the Hambach Festival, Philipp Siebenpfeiffer and Johann Wirth, and the eventual subversion and overthrow of the German governments. With the aid and assistance of French liberals and South German parliamentarians, they planned to turn southwest Germany into a republic.[6]

Through his conservative correspondent in Berlin, Prince Wittgenstein, Metternich first contacted the Prussian court with his plan for a joint investigating commission. However, he did not wait for the Prussian king's agreement. Even without it, he proceeded to approach the South German kings with the idea of creating a secret central investigating agency in Mainz. In a letter of 26 February to Field Marshall Wrede—a copy of which was sent to Schönburg for King William—Metternich detailed his proposal for such a joint Austrian, Prussian, Bavarian, and Württemberg institution. Its initial investigations were to be secret. It was better, Metternich explained, for things to have a small beginning and a big ending than the reverse. Metternich did not want to leave himself open to popular ridicule if nothing resulted from the investigations. He hoped, however, to be able to get at the German *comité directeur* and attack German subversion at its roots.[7]

The responses of the kings of Prussia, Württemberg, and Bavaria were encouraging. They all agreed in principle with Metternich's ideas, although King Ludwig was more hesitant than the rest.[8] The basis for further action was successfully laid. When Wittgenstein suggested that perhaps it would be better to forgo the participation of Bavaria and Württemberg to lessen the possibility of calling public attention to the investigations, Metternich revealed to the Prussian his full strategy. It was part of his plan that the South Germans take part in the investigations. He felt that both Bavaria and Württemberg were among those countries whose people were most involved in subversion. If South German commissioners participated in investigations of this subversion, their kings would see for themselves the reality of the dangers of which Metternich constantly warned. Their eyes opened, they might be ready for practical action.[9]

Before an investigating commission could be set up in Mainz, Metternich's desire to get practical action against German revolutionaries was brought a step closer to realization by the impact of the ill-fated Frankfurt putsch attempt of 3 April. That evening at 9:30 about fifty armed revolutionaries, mostly students, attacked the two city guard stations as the first move of a plan to capture the headquarters of the Federal Diet, its members, and its treasury. As a result of the ensuing fight between Frankfurt troops and the revolutionaries, six soldiers and one radical died. A total of twenty-four combatants were wounded. It was discovered in the days and weeks that followed that the putsch had been long planned and that its success was to have had widespread ramifications. A Lieutenant Ernst Ludwig Koseritz, stationed at Ludwigsburg had agreed to incite that Württemberg garrison to a coordinated attack on Stuttgart. Koseritz had been promised that several hundred Polish refugees in neighboring France would invade Baden and support the revolutionaries in Frankfurt and Stuttgart. In fact, several hundred Poles did leave France for Switzerland in preparation for such an attack. After the failure of the revolt in Frankfurt, it never came. Investigations revealed that the goal of the overall scheme was the creation of a federation of German republics, perhaps even a united republican Germany.[10]

As the complex background of the Frankfurt Putsch became known, the willingness of the German princes to see the dangers of the situation as Metternich did increased. The putsch attempt in itself was enough to give Metternich an excuse for federal action. He was glad that the attempt had not been prevented or suppressed by the Austrian and Prussian troops at nearby Mainz. These forces had been alerted when, on the afternoon of 3 April, the Bavarian federal deputy informed the Austrian minister resident in Frankfurt, Baron Paul von Handel, that he had been warned of an impending attack. As there were no signs of a forthcoming disturbance at the time, however, the troops at Mainz, like the city troops in Frankfurt, were merely placed on alert. When the revolt occurred it had to be suppressed by Frankfurt's own forces. Metternich felt that the absence of Austrian and Prussian soldiers put the revolutionary undertaking in a less heroic light. The whole affair, he told his emperor, was to have a happy ending. Just like the Hambach Festival, the Frankfurt Putsch would give added vigor to the efforts of the German governments to "uphold the right."[11]

Metternich felt that the time had come to have the Confederation act against the German revolutionaires. Three things he considered to be most important: the centralization of investigations into revolutionary activity, the preparation of sufficient military forces to deal with future revolts, and the resolution of all of the governments to stand firmly against factions at home.[12] Of these things, centralized federal investigations were Metternich's first objective. To get investigations underway, he advocated the immediate activation of the proposed four-power secret investigating commission at Mainz. He informed his conservative contacts in Prussia, Bavaria, and Württemberg that an Austrian agent was on his way and asked them to have their commissioners sent, too. Metternich explained that the secret agency that these officers were to form was to be only a filial of an official investigating body that he wanted the Federal Diet to create in Frankfurt. Until this official body could be formed, the agency at Mainz was to collect information for its official counterpart.[13]

Regarding this idea for an official federal investigating commission, Metternich was in contact with Prussia and the two South German kingdoms since the Frankfurt Putsch. The federal commission created back in June 1832 to prepare measures for the restoration of order in Germany had also, since mid-April, become the scene of debate on the proposed commission. Metternich wanted it to have more effective power than its predecessor of the 1820s, the Mainz Central Investigating Commission. The Mainz Commission had been given the authority to have suspects detained and to carry on its own investigations, but Bavarian obstructionism had limited its activity to collecting information sent in by state officials. Metternich wanted the new body to carry on its own interrogations or, at least, be able to direct the questioning of suspects by state officials.[14]

Such ideas were again vetoed by Bavaria. Although Prussia and Württemberg agreed with Metternich's proposals, and even wanted the establishment of a federal court to try revolutionaries, Bavaria was reluctant to risk any federal interference in its internal affairs. Her government set up its own investigating commission and was content to leave things at that.[15] Metternich's effort to change the Bavarian attitude, by trying to convince Wrede that a federal agency was needed to combat conspiracies aimed at the German Confederation, had little effect.[16] The federal agency that was finally approved by the Federal Diet on 20 June 1833 was designed to receive Bavarian approval. It was less powerful than its Mainz predecessor of the 1820s. Still, Metternich did secure the creation of a centralized agency that could requisition materials on state investigations and could coordinate the investigations throughout Germany.[17] The four-power secret commission at Mainz, slow to commence full operations because of the delay of the South Germans in naming their representatives, was dissolved in September as superfluous.[18]

Meanwhile, the Frankfurt Putsch attempt had frightened the

South German governments into military measures in preparation for other revolutionary outbreaks. The government of Baden placed sixteen hundred men on the Swiss border to prevent German revolutionaries from receiving help from the Polish refugees in that neighboring country.[19] The Bavarians doubled their contingent at the fortress of Landau and called furloughed soldiers back to the colors.[20] The King of Württemberg proposed to Austria that the Seventh and Eighth Federal Corps be mobilized so that they would be able to execute federal measures in case of further outbreaks.[21]

Metternich considered it wise for Austria to prepare to reinforce the South Germans should revolts occur. At the same time, he wanted to impress the South German governments with Austria's strong support. Through Wrede and the Austrian ministers in Stuttgart and Karlsruhe, Metternich informed the South German rulers that Austria was activating seventeen thousand men in Tyrol and Vorarlberg to provide emergency aid.[22]

When King William of Württemberg was notified of these measures, he indicated his continuing desire for formal federal action for the defense of South Germany. In fact, he expressed to the Austrian envoy his interest in commanding the federal military forces formed to combat German revolutionaries. To Schönburg this seemed a means by which the king hoped to have himself named commander of South Germany's federal forces in place of Field Marshall Wrede. The Austrian diplomat urged that, even if this were the case, Metternich would be wise to make use of William's offer. He felt that King William would lead a very effective anti-revolutionary effort in South Germany. At the same time, Austria could ensure the friendship of Württemberg and isolate anti-federalist Bavaria at a time when Bavaria was the main proponent of an independent South German defense system.[23] Metternich decided, however, that King William was more spirited than wise. The Austrian insisted that police measures, not military ones, were needed. Thus, when he sent Lieutenant Colonel Count Wilhelm Lichnowsky to Stuttgart and Karlsuhe in late May to discuss and encourage South German defense measures, he sent along several memoranda designed to steer King William away from his ideas of sweeping action and a powerful military command.[24]

The memoranda of 24 May that Metternich sent to King William—copies of which were also sent to Wrede for King Ludwig[25]—were designed first to impress the South German kings with their past mistakes. According to Metternich, their modern constitutions and past administrative errors had made their states most receptive to revolutionary contagion, while leaving them few means by which to defend themselves. "There exists," Metternich wrote, "between modern constitutions and the evil itself an analogy that one finds between a cause and its effects." The worst product of constitutional government, according to Metternich, was the "so-called constitutional opposition." The legislative revolts of this opposition—their constant demand for concessions—he described as more dangerous than actual street revolts. More difficult to combat than street revolts, legislative revolts could cause the downfall of a government just as effectively.[26]

Reforms, Metternich insisted, were urgently needed. It was up to the constitutional monarchs to make this possible. They had to stand firmly, but legally, against the incessant demands of their diets. The result of such firmness would be either the decline of parliamentary opposition or its development into open revolt. In the first case, the constitutional monarchs should make some obviously necessary reforms. Their civil service codes should be changed to prohibit officials from participating in parliamentary opposition. Diet debates should be kept from public knowledge, and there should be a limit put on the political items in the public press.[27]

If parliamentary opposition led to open revolt, then, Metternich noted, the monarch, alone or with federal assistance, would be justified in forceful repression. According to the Austrian foreign minister, it was Austria's federal policy to encourage the German princes to resist democratic principles, in accordance with the Six Articles and with confidence in federal support. There would be no federal intervention, however, unless the intrigues of demagogues made government impossible in individual states. Then alone would federal action be completely justified.[28]

The 24 May memorandum for Stuttgart and Munich indicated that Metternich felt the South German governments would not be safe from revolution until basic changes were made to minimize the dangers inherent in their representative constitutions. He had to be content for the moment to urge the constitutional rulers to act to mend their ways. He felt, however, that it would take more than Austrian diplomatic dispatches to give the South German rulers the confidence and feeling of federal duty required before they would act firmly against the anti-monarchic opposition within their own states. To achieve his goal Metternich would again need the support of Prussia.

To ensure Prussian support for the implementation of his plans, Metternich used both a negative and a positive approach. The negative took the form of trying to undermine the innovative influence of Johann Eichhorn, since May 1831, head of the Second Division (the German section) of the Prussian foreign ministry and advocate of the expanding Prussian Zollverein.[29] At the same time, Metternich tried to avoid open opposition to the entrance of Bavaria and Württemberg into the Prussian tariff system. He did not, however, hesitate to attempt to lure the South Germans by offers of more intimate commercial relations with Austria.[30] But he denied his real ill will toward the Zollverein and cautioned his diplomats to make no statements that could be taken as indicating open opposition to that institution.[31] Metternich viewed the Prussian-South German customs union treaty of 22 March 1833 as disruptive of the German Confederation—the work of the Eichhorn party in the Prussian ministry that aimed at Prussian leadership of a constitutional Germany. He recognized, however, that to antagonize Prussia would be to endanger the success of his broader German policies, as well as his European policies as a whole.[32] Therefore, through Wittgenstein, he attempted to limit Eichhorn's influence on Prussian policy. Wittgenstein was unable to have Eichhorn removed from office because of Foreign Minister Ancillon's sensitivity to the increasing leverage that Metternich had on Prussian policy. Wittgenstein did succeed, nevertheless, in having King Frederick William III curb Eichhorn's freedom of initiative in German affairs. On 19 June the King ordered that in the future instructions for the Prussian representative at the Federal Diet, communications to Vienna or to other German courts in regard to German affairs, and all ordinances regarding police affairs should be confidentially shared by Eichhorn with Prince Wittgenstein and Count Carl von Lottum before they were sent out.[33] With Bernstorff retired and Eichhorn so limited, there was little left of the "Bernstorff-Eichhorn party" and its alternatives to Metternich's solutions to the German Question.

Metternich's positive approach to winning Prussian support for his plans for German reforms took the form of meetings with King Frederick William and Foreign Minister Ancillon at Teplitz in August. It was the Austrian foreign minister's plan to make use of the king's usual summer visit to Bohemia to work out with the

Prussians a means to make Federal Diet more effective in its efforts to deal with German dangers.[34] The means Metternich proposed, and to which the Prussian king agreed, entailed the assembly of a German ministerial conference that was to establish concensus on how to handle the threats to all the German thrones. Frederick William's foreign minister agreed with his Austrian colleague that German demagogues could not be allowed to continue their excesses, nor could individual German governments be permitted to tolerate them. He and his king agreed with Metternich that a ministerial conference would be the most rapid and successful way to return to all the German governments the vigor they needed to act together against the troublemakers who plagued them. As Metternich explained to Emperor Francis, the conferences of 1819 and 1820 served him as a prototype for the conference that he proposed. To the Vienna Conference and the resulting Final Act of 1820 he attributed the peace that had reigned in Germany until the advent of the July Revolution.[35] He hoped that a similar peace could be assured again.

As a result of their agreement on the usefulness of a German ministerial conference, the Austrian and Prussian foreign ministers drew up a circular dispatch to be sent to their representatives at the key German capitals: Munich, Stuttgart, Karlsruhe, Dresden, Hanover, Cassel, and Darmstadt. The dispatch was designed to provide their diplomats with common instructions for joint overtures to the governments to which they were accredited. It stressed the common view of the two great German powers as to the dangers that faced Germany. This view was that the "spirit of movement," which had been abroad in Germany since the introduction of representative government in a portion of the German states, had been given a new and dangerous impetus by the July Revolution. Now the individual states and the German Confederation itself were imperiled. If something were not done both the federal organization and its component parts might be destroyed.[36]

The circular further declared that it was the view of the Austrian and Prussian governments that the Confederation and its individual members had to take simultaneous and cooperative action if the danger was to be met. Now, however, unlike in 1819 and 1820, no new federal laws were needed. Adequate laws already existed. They had only to be enforced. The Austrian and Prussian courts proposed a ministerial conference to prepare the ground for agreement on such enforcement. If the major German states were sympathetic to these ideas, a general invitation would be sent to all the German governments. For the moment, further plans depended on the response to these initial overtures.

The first of the secondary states to receive a copy of the joint circular was Bavaria. Prince Schönburg arrived there, directly from Teplitz, on 27 August. As King Ludwig was the most powerful and influential constitutional German ruler, his agreement to the proposed ministerial conference would almost certainly ensure that of the smaller courts. For that reason Meternich took special pains to influence the Bavarian king. First, he sent Ludwig's old friend and classmate, Prince Alfred von Schönburg, to convey the circular to the king. Second, in order that Ludwig be informed at once, Schönburg did not even wait for the Bavarian king to return to his capital; he sought him out at Nuremberg, where Ludwig was attending a festival.[37]

Metternich reinforced the impact of Schönburg's message by seeing to it that Field Marshal Wrede would support it. In a note that Schönburg presented to Wrede when he arrived in Nuremberg, Metternich asked that the marshal's influence be used in favor of the ideas expressed in the Austro-Prussian circular. The situation in Germany was such, Metternich declared, that the German states could not continue to exist if current trends were not stopped. Revolution was in progress under the guise of legislative legality. At the moment the "conspiracy between the German parliamentary chambers, the law courts, and the liberal press" was more dangerous than street revolts. If the German sovereigns wanted to continue to rule, they would have to preserve their power, both through their own efforts and those of the German Confederation. What means were to be used in each case should be agreed upon in an understanding between the German ministries. According to Metternich, the best means to achieve this understanding was through a German ministerial conference.[38]

From Stuttgart, on 1 September, Schönburg was able to report the success of his missions to the kings of both Bavaria and Württemberg. On 28 August he had written to Metternich of the favorable impression the circular had made on King Ludwig. Now he was able to give further details. The Bavarian king, he reported, had listened with interest to his overtures and had consulted with his adviser, Field Marshal Wrede. Wrede, at that point, made good use of the dispatch that he had received from Metternich. The result was that the Austro-Prussian proposals, which initially had surprised the king, were declared to have his full agreement. Wrede, convinced of the pressing need for the proposed conference, told Schönburg that he intended to stay close to Ludwig so that Foreign Minister Gise could not alter the king's good intentions.[39]

As for King William, Schönburg was pleased to report that he, too, had been persuaded to agree to the joint Austro-Prussian proposals. In his case, however, Schönburg had had to overcome the king's fear that any measures agreed upon by a German ministerial conference would be weak and ineffective. In addition, it worried William that the two great German powers aimed only at securing the enforcement of already existing legislation. He felt that existing legislation had already shown itself insufficient. Schönburg also had to convince him that the conference would be worth the popular agitation that its convocation would inevitably provoke.[40]

While at Münchengrätz in September 1833 preparing his long-sought agreement with Tsar Nicholas for a continental entente and joint declaration against the French principle of nonintervention, Metternich was able to report to Emperor Francis the progress he was making in the realization of his German policies as well. Presenting Schönburg's reports of his meetings with the kings of Bavaria and Württemberg, he explained the satisfactory results of his agent's mission. Both South German monarchs, Metternich concluded, were in a good mood for the forthcoming agreements.[41]

Metternich admitted to Münch at Frankfurt that there were still some problems. The Prussian government had agreed that the two great German powers would make no preliminary statement regarding the matters to be discussed at the ministerial conference. The subjects to be dealt with were to be chosen by the constitutional governments. Bavaria, however, insisted on learning what Austria and Prussia had in mind. In this situation, Metternich considered it fortunate that King Ludwig was planning a family visit with his brother-in-law, the Austrian emperor, at Linz in early October. The Austrian foreign minister planned to use the opportunity to convince the king of the inappropriateness of his demand.[42] It was an important Metternichian tactic to have the South Germans propose the measures for their own salvation. By withholding his own proposals, Metternich could avoid early alienation of the particularists and make it difficult for them to criticize later the measures that they themselves proposed.

In his meetings with King Ludwig in Linz in mid-October,

Metternich tried to persuade the Bavarian monarch that it was up to the constitutional governments to decide what was to be discussed at a German ministerial conference. According to the report of the interviews that Metternich sent to his minister in Stuttgart—in a dispatch that was to be shared with the King of Württemberg—he was, in fact, able to convince Ludwig of the practicality of this view. It was up to the states most endangered by the current evils to present their ideas on how to stop them, he told the Bavarian monarch. Counsel and support were all that could be expected from Austria and Prussia.[43]

The ideas expressed to King Ludwig at Linz were the basis for Metternich's language to all of the German diplomatic corps at Vienna in the next few weeks. He let it be known that he wanted each government to prepare a list of the subjects that it wanted dealt with at a ministerial conference. He assured the South Germans that it lay in the intentions of Austria and Prussia neither to infringe on the independence of their German confederates nor to change their constitutions. In fact, Austria and Prussia wanted to hear the views of all of the German regents before supporting any action. The views of the other German courts would serve as the basis for the discussions at the conference. Metternich reminded the South German diplomats, however, that in preparing their views, their governments should remember that the purpose of the measures that were to come out of the ministerial meetings should be the preservation of the monarchic principle. An end had to be put to subversion within each government, as well as to the obnoxious propaganda that attacked from without. This was to be accomplished, Metternich said, through the cooperation of all of the German governments and their enforcement of existing federal laws.[44]

The reaction of the South German governments to Metternich's generalities was a mixture of caution and suspicion. King William was wary of the development of abstract principles that might be used in the future to limit his own sovereignty. He felt that the Six Articles were dangerously abstract, and he feared that a German ministerial conference would dole out similar medicine. In Stuttgart and Karlsruhe the desire was for measures of practical import. Precisely how could monarchs limit the power of their diets in military questions? If endangered, how could they be assured that federal troops would act quickly to protect them?[45] When it came right down to it, however, Baden's minister president, Baron Sigismund von Reitzenstein, was not even sure that he wanted to risk a federal attempt to solve South

Germany's problems. He considered it up to each government to handle its own affairs.[46]

The Bavarian foreign mnister, Baron August von Gise, was even more suspicious of the possible results of a ministerial conference than the leading statesmen of Württemberg and Baden. He told King Ludwig that the real aim of the great German powers was to attack Bavarian sovereignty and to end her independence within Germany. He warned that the present moment was favorable for such an effort, because the Bavarian government obviously had to retreat from its strict constitutional position. Her liberals made government impossible on that basis. Gise felt that Austria and Prussia would try to use this opportunity to urge upon Ludwig policies that would not be in keeping with his sovereign rights. Such, he told his king, had been the aim of the great German powers in the enactment of the Six Articles.[47]

According to the Bavarian foreign minister, the Six Articles and the 2 March 1832 federal press rulings were both based on Metternich's principle that state laws were subordinate to federal laws. Gise warned that Metternich might try to use this principle at the coming conference. Bavaria, he said, had to be ready to defend her laws against a potential reactionary attack. He urged that her government act in accordance with monarchic principles in a cooperative effort to put state administrations in conformity with the demands of the German Confederation. Nevertheless, he proposed that Bavaria place herself at the head of the constitutional states and see to it that any reforms be made in a constitutional manner. Through such leadership, Bavaria would protect her own sovereignty and, at the same time, raise herself to the status of a third great power in Germany. King Ludwig agreed. German patriot that he was, however, he demanded that Gise's plan be implemented only insofar as an increase of Bavarian power did not decrease that of Germany as a whole.[48]

At Linz, Metternich had suggested to Gise that Bavaria and Württemberg jointly consider proposals for the work of the ministerial conference. Here lay an opportunity for the Bavarian foreign minister to develop his own plans. When the Saxon minister, Bernard von Lindenau, visited Munich to discuss tariff matters in November, Gise invited Württemberg's foreign minister, Count Joseph von Beroldingen, to join them to discuss the German conference.[49]

As a result of Gise's invitation, the three ministers met in Munich on 11 November. An official resumé of their discussions was drawn up to indicate the general principles upon which they were sure that their courts could agree to cooperate at the forthcoming ministerial conference. It was decided that there should be no new federal laws. The execution of existing laws was to be considered primarily a function of the states and not that of the federal government. Any coercive measures against state diets were to be left to the states themselves, although federal support had to be guaranteed. Finally, the German Confederation should reassure the German people that their diets would continue to meet, but that these bodies would be expected to behave in accordance with their legal rights and obligations. In short, Bavaria, Württemberg, and Saxony agreed to cooperate with the other members of the Confederation in a monarchic and federative manner, but they also agreed to insist on the preservation of their state sovereignty as guaranteed by the Federal Act.[50]

In September, Metternich had responded favorably to the request of several governments that the ministerial meetings be held off until the end of the current sessions of their diets.[51] On the other hand, Metternich wanted to favor the Bavarian plea that the conference be held before the opening of its diet in January 1834.[52] By mid-November, therefore, the Austrian foreign minister felt that it was finally time for Austria and Prussia to agree on a time and place for the conference. Further delay might only give agitators inside and outside Germany the opportunity to question whether the conference would ever be held. Troublemakers would also have time to impune the intentions of the great German powers and to discourage the cooperation of the other German governments.[53]

On 18 November Metternich sent to Berlin Austria's invitations to the German princes. He left space open for the date so that the Prussian government could fill that in and send out the Austrian invitations along with their own. Though Metternich knew that the Prussian foreign minister wanted to see the course of international events—especially regarding the Spanish succession question[54]—before turning his full attention to German affairs, the Austrian expressed the hope that the German ministerial conference might begin at the end of November or in early December. If Ancillon insisted on a date no earlier than 1 January 1834, Metternich indicated that that exact date would be acceptable. In any case, because the Prussian had left the place of the meetings up to the Austrian goverment, but had suggested either Prague or Vienna, Emperor Francis chose Vienna.[53]

In his report from Berlin on 28 November, Trauttmansdorff informed Metternich that the Prussian government had chosen 1 January as the opening date and was about to issue the joint invitations the next day.[56] Soon thereafter acceptances arrived in Vienna. On 4 December Buol reported from Karlsruhe that the invitation had been received the day before. He and the Prussian envoy had met that evening with Minister President Reitzenstein, who told them that he would attend the conference himself.[57] On 11 December, Speigel reported that King Ludwig, reluctant though he was even to have the conference agreed to send his foreign minister, Baron August von Gise.[58] The King of Württemberg also quickly agreed to send his foreign minister. In his dispatch of 14 December, Schönberg spoke of Beroldingen's mission as having already been decided upon.[59]

The South German states had agreed again to participate in a ministerial conference such as those by which Metternich had maneuvered them into the acceptance of his conservative federal policies in 1819 and 1820. The question remained whether he could successfully repeat his strategy in 1834. King William, in conversation with Prince Schönburg, stated precisely what problems were involved. He said that he was concerned that the conference in Vienna would have no practical results; it could end in mere double-entendre phraseology. He saw, in any case, two great obstacles to substantial results. The first he described as the impractical character of Prussia's foreign minister, Ancillon, and the whole "seesaw system" of Prussian politics in recent years. The second, he believed, was the ambiguous position of the Bavarian government on all federal questions.[60] Indeed, King William was prophetic: the success of Metternich's German policies in 1834 would depend on his adeptness at handling both of these problems.

9

The Act of Unity That Almost Failed: The Vienna Conference of 1834

The ministerial conference was Metternich's favorite mode of diplomacy. It was a form in which he personally excelled and through which he had achieved the major successes of his German policy. In 1815 he saw to the foundation of the German Confederation as a major European power and a bulwark for Austria. In 1820 he consolidated the bulwark through a definition of the Confederation's fundamental laws in a most conservative and federalistic sense. In 1834 he planned to reunite the German governments in firm adherence to the letter and spirit of these fundamental laws.

The attitude of the South German governments was the chief obstacle that confronted Metternich's efforts at the Vienna Conference of 1834, as at the Vienna Conference of 1820. Their attitude was, at the same time, the reason why Metternich felt the conference so necessary. The South German governments still elevated state sovereignty over federal duty in their relations with the German Confederation. This led them to resist the decisions of the Federal Diet, and to assert their own interpretations of federal law in the interest of particularism. Such particularism, when it encouraged liberalism, and thus revolution, among their subjects, threatened the maintenance of the German Confederation as a monarchic stronghold. Metternich hoped through a major German ministerial conference in 1834, as in 1820, to revive among the German princes a federalistic, as well as monarchic, concensus.[1] He planned to overcome the resistance of the South German monarchs, not to his goal of protecting monarchic institutions—which they thoroughly endorsed—but to the means for such a preservation. This means was the strengthening of the German Confederation as a bulwark against popular sovereignty. King Ludwig of Bavaria and his foreign minister, August von Gise, suspected that the Austrian foreign minister had other intentions as well. The Bavarians did not want the institutions of the German Confederation to be the instruments of Austrian domination in Germany.[2] The resulting Bavarian attitude at the Vienna Conference nearly destroyed the spirit of monarchic solidarity upon which Metternich counted for the success of the conference. German monarchic solidarity, created through a successful conference, was—after all—the Austrian's most important goal.

Metternich's opening speech to the Vienna conference on 13 January 1834 defined the Austrian view of the problems that were to concern the conference and the goal that it was to achieve. The basic problem of the day, as Metternich saw it, was the attempt of a "faction" to transfer the sovereign authority of the German rulers to the diets of their respective states. First, through abuse of the legal forms of the modern German constitutions, this faction created a schism between the federal constitution—devoted to the maintenance of the monarchic principle— and the constitutions of the particular states. Then, into these state constitutions, the faction sought to implant the principle of popular sovereignty. According to Metternich, all of the current symptoms of popular unrest in Germany were the inevitable result of the increasing influence of this dangerous principle. In states in which the representative system favored its growth, subversives propagated it further through the political press and the published debates of the state diets. They appealed most effectively to the immaturity of youth and the greed of the lower classes to gain supporters for their attacks upon all existing laws and institutions.[3]

It was the view of the Emperor of Austria, Metternich said, that all of these terrible symptoms would vanish as soon as their principle causes were eliminated. It was necessary, therefore, that the German sovereigns see through the "sophisms" of the "subversive faction" and act to preserve their sovereignty. The dangers that they faced were faced both as independent sovereigns and as members of a confederation designed to protect the external and internal peace of Germany. Help was to be sought on both levels. The work of the German ministers at Vienna was to decide what, in connection with the present dangers, the German Confederation could expect of the German governments and what the German governments could expect of the German Confederation.

At Metternich's suggestion, it was decided that the preliminary work of the conference would be divided among five commissions that could deal individually with the problems that seemed of most pressing concern. These included the question of the degree of power that a state diet should share with its monarch; the degree of publicity to be granted the debates of a state diet; the means of ending the irregularities at German schools and universities with regard to the federal decrees of 1819, 1824, and 1832; the just limits of freedom of the press; and the relation of state legislation to that of the Federal Diet. To simplify the selection of the members of each commission, the conference also accepted Metternich's proposal that he suggest the membership. At the same time, however, it was decided that attendance and participation at the meetings of each of the commissions would be left open to any members of the conference.[4]

The work of the individual commissions was to be the real center of the work of the Vienna conference, and Metternich did not propose the membership of the most important commissions without a definite plan. As he revealed to Emperor Francis and to the Prussian foreign minister, Ancillon, he arranged the membership of the First Commission—the one dealing with the respective powers of the German princes and their diets—so that neither Austria nor Prussia were represented. On this important question, he wanted to avoid the appearance that the two great German powers exerted an undue influence. He saw to it, however, that the membership of the commission contained ministers from states whose rulers had already granted their diets a share of their power—Bavaria, Saxony, and Electoral Hesse—and those whose rulers had not—Grand Ducal Hesse, the Mecklenburgs, and Oldenburg. Because these two groups would be most interested in the question of the division of princely and parliamentary power, yet most opposed because of their respective constitutions, Metternich doubted that their discussions would come to anything. If that were the case, the need for the help of the two Great Powers would be clearly demonstrated. In any case, Austria and Prussia were represented in the Fifth Commission— the one dealing with the relationship of state to federal legislation. That commission Metternich considered to be the most important—the real "key to the vault." Through it he could control the final influence of the work of the First Commission.[5]

During the first few weeks of the conference, Metternich was generally hopeful concerning its final results. He felt that compared to the delegates at the Carlsbad and Vienna conferences of 1819 and 1820, the current conferees seemed basically free from prejudice against the federal system and aware, through experience, of the dangers inherent in modern governmental theories. He was convinced that all of the participants thought as one as to the purpose of the meetings and their necessity. Nevertheless, he saw in the conduct of the German ministers the differing policies of the states that they represented. Baden, for instance, seemed to want help, but showed little willingness to make use of it. Württemberg was restrained and waited to see what would happen. Bavaria appeared unopposed to federative action, but wanted it to meet Bavarian specifications.[6]

The attempts of the Bavarian delegate to ensure the sovereignty of his monarch against the attacks of his diet, while limiting interference by the Confederation, soon became the major obstacle to the federative goal that Metternich wanted to achieve at the conference. Baron August von Gise, the Bavarian foreign minister, and chairman of the First Commission, came to Vienna with high hopes of placing Bavaria at the head of a group of constitutional German states that would help him achieve King Ludwig's goals.[7] Upon Gise's arrival, he proposed a treaty between the constitutional states by which they would agree to common means for controlling their separate diets. Gise even approached Metternich with his idea. In exchange for Austrian support for such a treaty, he offered increased economic ties between the constitutional states and Austria. He told Metternich that Bavaria's tariff union with Prussia put her in need of a counterweight to Prussian influence. If an Austrian-South German economic arrangement were developed, balance could be restored.[8]

Metternich had no intention of antagonizing his Prussian ally by discussing a politically motivated economic agreement with the South Germans. Neither had he a desire to support a constitutional *Bund im Bund* (confederation within the Confederation). He told Gise and, through Wrede, King Ludwig that there already existed one federal treaty. New treaties would only weaken the existing guarantees of monarchic security while adding little of real value themselves.[9] In fact, Metternich's attitude discouraged Gise so much that, as early as 21 January, he requested that King Ludwig recall him. He felt that his project had angered the Austrian foreign minister to the point that his continued presence in Vienna would be useless.[10] Until he was replaced by Arnold von Mieg in March, however, Gise continued to organize the constitutional states to resist federal action that might endanger their constitutions. Each day, the representatives of the constitutional states held meetings in his quarters to discuss their common interests and policies.[11]

The Bavarian delegate took the lead in organizing the constitutional ministers to moderate the influence of their more conservative colleagues in Vienna. Still, although Gise was Metternich's chief focus of complaint, he was not alone. Minister President Sigismund von Reitzenstien of Baden was another of the South Germans whose views Metternich considered ill-conceived, if not reprehensible. Metternich decribed him as a "liberal doctrinaire"—one who, even with the best of intentions, spoiled the projects of wiser men through an insistence on impractical solutions.[12] Together Gise and Reitzenstein displayed an interest in preserving state constitutionalism and in limiting federal powers, thereby greatly irritating Metternich and his conservative allies. Worst of all, the two South Germans declared that they had come to the conference only because they had been called. According to them, their respective states were not particularly in need of help, and they would protest any that was forced upon them by the German Confederation.[13]

Such an attitude was inimical to Metternich's goals. Especially Bavaria, the most influential of the constitutional German states, had to be convinced of the necessity of a more cooperative attitude if the unity of the conference was to be maintained. Through Wrede, Metternich tried to produce the desired change in the Bavarian position. He characterized Gise's strict attention to constitutional legality as a complete waste of time. One might think, he accused, that the Bavarian delegate was trying to ensure that the conference came to nothing. Metternich argued that the goal of the meetings was the salvation and protection of the rights of the German sovereigns. Gise acted as if their purpose was the limitation of these rights.[14]

Wrede warned Metternich that the opposition of the Bavarian delegate was not without the sympathy of King Ludwig. The king's principle complaint against his diet in 1831 was its resistance to his civil list. He was having a much better time with the more moderate diet that was just beginning its meetings in Munich. As Ludwig hoped that the new diet would approve his monetary requests, he felt less in need of the regulations that were to have been designed in Vienna.[15]

The King of Bavaria not only felt no need for federal action, he also feared that such action would disturb the currently happy situation in his country. The amicable relationship between his government and diet was not to be spoiled. He intended to cultivate that amity, at least until his civil list was approved. Any news of the Vienna meetings, he felt, would sabotage his efforts. He was sure that this would be true in view of Gise's reports of the discussions of the First Commission and the narrow limits to which that Commission wished to confine the authority of the German diets. Ludwig insisted that he could not agree to proposals that would be in conflict with the articles of his constitution, nor would he agree to things that would only provoke his diet.[16]

Metternich hastened to reassure King Ludwig. Through Wrede, he informed the particularistic monarch that the results of the Vienna conference were not to be incorporated in the form of a treaty or federal decree—thus to become known to the public. Instead, Metternich proposed that the results of the conference take the form of agreement to a protocol to be placed in the secret archives of the Federal Diet. In that form, while not provoking the public, the agreement would serve the Federal Diet as the officially sanctioned interpretation of existing federal laws in relation to state constitutional systems. The secret protocol would define the defense that federal laws were to provide the sovereign rights of the princes against attacks growing out of their constitutional systems. There would be no public proclamations that radicals could picture as the result of a conspiracy of the princes against the rights of their diets or the "so-called freedom of the peoples."[17]

But secrecy was not enough to satisfy the King of Bavaria. On 21 March, the Bavarian diet approved his civil list. That gave him new confidence in the loyalty of his subjects and the feeling that he could do without the aid and interference of the Confederation. He decided that he could rely on popular support at home, if he maintained his constitutional system intact. Gise's replacement at the Vienna Conference, Arnold von Mieg, normally the Bavarian delegate to the Federal Diet, was instructed to continue to oppose any agreement that would conflict with the Bavarian constitution. He was to consider with particular caution any proposal for limitation of the press or for the curtailment of open meetings of the state diets.[18]

As Metternich hoped to end the conference by about mid-April, he put to use all of his standard tactics to keep Bavaria from destroying the conservative solidarity that was to be the result of the Vienna reunion. One of the most important tactics was to confront the South Germans with Austro-Prussian unity and cooperation. From the beginning of the conference, Metternich worked to ensure this unity. In January, he catered to the Prussian ministry by his proposal that no opening statement be made to the conference until it had been agreed upon by the representatives of the two governments.[19] Similar consideration caused Metternich to postpone the second plenary session of the conference until 26 March. Foreign Minister Ancillon arrived only on 17 March. He had been delayed by illness and was represented until then by a lesser Prussian official, Count Albrecht von Alvensleben.[20] Finally, Metternich ensured Prussian good will by his neutral stand on a Hanoverian proposition that the conference consider means to develop a common German tariff system.[21] As with Gise's earlier economic proposal, Metternich avoided antagonizing his Prussian ally by not involving Austria in a program in competition with the Prussian Zollverein.

While confronting the South Germans with Austro-Prussian unity, Metternich continued to write to Field Marshal Wrede. He hoped to use the influence of Ludwig's conservative advisor to convince the Bavarian ruler of the need to see the Vienna conference through to a practical conclusion. The Austrian foreign minister's tone in this correspondence was plaintive and pedantic. He exclaimed how different things would have been in Germany and Europe if, in 1817, the chief German ministers had assembled to discuss the proper form for the constitutions of their various states. Now the German ministers had to agree on a means to control the evils that had developed out of the constitutions that were introduced. According to Metternich, the situation would have been quite different if an early understanding had not been thwarted by the competition of the German governments for popular favor. He insisted that recognition of the evils that resulted from those attempts to curry popular favor was the basis upon which the German rulers now had to determine their future policies. Metternich made it his task, he told Wrede, to make that basis as solid as possible.[22]

Metternich's dispatch of 21 April to Wrede is one example of how he tried to bring King Ludwig to recognize the manner in which the king was being repaid for his efforts to win popular favor. Metternich let it be known that Austrian authorities had uncovered a revolutionary conspiracy that aimed at provoking simultaneous revolts on 4 May in Galicia, Posen, the Kingdom of Poland, the Polish-Russian provinces, and St. Petersburg. According to the testimony of one of the conspirators, there was also to be a revolt on 4 May in Germany. Planning for this uprising included a plot for the assassination of King Ludwig of Bavaria. In order that the neighboring governments of Bavaria and Württemberg be prepared for any eventuality, Metternich suggested that they concert on appropriate defensive measures.

As it turned out, however, their troop mobilizations and investigations proved unnecessary. No revolt occurred in South Germany or elsewhere.[23]

While employing all of these tactics—the example of Austro-Prussian unity, the influence of conservative advisors, and the stimulus of suspicion and fear—Metternich pushed for a proper end to the prolonged Vienna conference. In the seventh plenary meeting on 30 April, he noted that most of the proposals of the individual commissions had been discussed and had received preliminary acceptance. He proposed, therefore, that they be prepared in final draft form. He also proposed that the Fifth Commission—in which Austria and Prussia were both represented—should be empowered to consider which sections of the Vienna agreements were appropriate to turn into federal decrees and which sections should remain hidden from public view. These latter, he told the next plenary meeting, should be regarded by the German governments as having the power of federal decrees, but should be kept secret in the federal archives in Frankfurt.[24]

The most important agreements of the Vienna Conference concerned the creation of a federal court of arbitration to settle disputes between state governments and their diets, the limitation of the power of the state diets, the enforcement of press censorship, and the surveillance of the German universities.[25] According to Metternich's report to the plenary session of the conference on 5 May, the Fifth Commission proposed that only the details of the federal court and parts of the university regulations should be turned into federal decrees. It was agreed in the plenum that the rest of the articles, of the sixty that were to make up the final protocol, were to remain secret.[26]

The German people were to learn that their governments—and their governments alone—could demand an arbitral court decision on the limits of the power of their diets.[27] They were also to learn that a student's participation in a forbidden political organization could permanently exclude him from civil service or a profession in law, teaching, or the church.[28] They were not to know that the German governments were carefully to control what they learned of the debates of the state diets;[29] that these diets were to be prevented from debating federal law;[30] or that the German governments were to dissolve their diets and continue to collect taxes in case of parliamentary resistance to proposed governmental budgets.[31] Nor were the German people to learn that their governments had agreed to censor carefully all newspaper accounts of trials and diet debates[32] and to take steps to decrease the number of political papers by requiring that each operate only through governmental concession.[33] Finally, they were not to know that it was agreed that no German government would allow its armed forces to take an oath to uphold a constitution.[34]

The fate of all of these agreements seemed uncertain in May 1834. Metternich asked at the beginning of that month that all of the delegates obtain the approval of their governments to sign the final protocol of the conference.[35] At that point, however, the hesitancy of the Bavarian government threatened to spoil the work of the entire conference.[36] Metternich feared that the unity of the German princes, so important for intimidating the revolutionary party, would be lost.[37] The work of the conference came to a standstill. Even Reitzenstein of Baden complained that this result of Bavarian delay put all of the delegates in despair.[38] From Berlin, Trauttmansdorff reported that the Prussian government was exasperated. It felt that, if necessary, the other states should accept and then keep secret the conditions by which the Bavarian government might alone adhere to the protocol. Better that great concession than to have the work of the conference completely ruined.[39]

Through Wrede's letter of 30 May, Metternich learned that Bavarian reluctance to agree to the conference protocol was the result of the influence of the Bavarian minister of interior, Prince Ludwig von Wallerstein. According to Wrede, Wallerstein convinced Ludwig that a federal court of arbitration would be inconsistent with the princples of the Bavarian constitution, and its activity could potentially infringe on the king's sovereign rights. Wrede assured Metternich, however, that Wallerstein's view isolated him from the rest of the Bavarian ministry. The field marshal was personally mounting a concentrated ministerial effort against the minister of the interior, and he felt sure that Ludwig could be persuaded to give up his suspicions and resistance.[40]

On 2 June, Wrede wrote that his efforts against Wallerstein were successful. In the course of a four-hour ministerial council meeting, the king was won over. Mieg was to receive more satisfactory instructions. According to Wrede, the Bavarian government would now merely insist on some minor editorial changes in the final protocol. As that was the case, he urged Metternich to be cooperative.[41]

In fact, the editorial changes that King Ludwig insisted upon were far from limited in importance. One of these changes was that the provision concerning press censorship and regulation of the German universities was to be made applicable for only six years initially.[42] More important was Ludwig's insistence that the referral of government-diet disputes to the court of arbitration not be obligatory, but the result of an agreement between the government and its diet in each case.[43] Most important was the Bavarian demand for the inclusion of a general constitutional reservation regarding numerous articles of the protocol. On this question, unlike the others, it took several days of strenuous negotiations before a compromise could be achieved.

The compromise with Bavaria took the form of a confidential exchange of declaration between the Bavarian delegate and the other members of the conference. Its subject was protocol Article 59. That article required each state to change its laws so as to bring them into conformity with the decisions of the conference. The Bavarian plenipotentiary finally declared that his government agreed to work to change its laws and constitutional provisions to implement Article 23, 24, 30, 32, and 33. These articles required royal permission for civil servants to serve in state diets, prohibited the requirement of a constitutional oath for the military, introduced a system of governmental sanction for only a limited number of political papers, required careful censorship of German publications printed outside Germany, and limited press coverage of diet debates. However, the Bavarian declaration asserted that as these provisions conflicted with the Bavarian constitution, the changes required would be undertaken only by constitutional means. The agreement of the other German ministers to accept this apparent declaration of Bavarian constitutional sovereignty preceded the Bavarian delegate's signature of the final protocol.[44]

But reality does not always lie in appearances. Now, as in 1820 at the earlier Vienna Conference, Metternich accepted the assertion that existing constitutions could only be changed by constitutional means in order to receive agreement that Bavaria—and all the German states—would work within the Confederation to preserve the monarchic character of their states. Articles 56 and 57 of the Vienna Final Act of 1820 stated exactly the same things and in this very order: constitutional changes by constitutional means, but the supremacy of the monarchic principle in each constitution.[45] In the interest of preserving the unity of the Confederation for the maintenance of the status quo, a status quo in which the monarchic principle was to remain supreme, federal duties were declared to be consistent with the state's rights. That was, of course, because in 1834 (as in 1820) neither the Bavarian government nor any other dreamed of states' rights for any other purpose but to maintain the sovereignty of their monarchs. Metternich's seeming concessions to constitutionalism were, in fact, assertions of the German Confederation's identification with the monarchic principle and with the maintenance of the status quo.

This established, the Vienna Conference was brought to an end with the signature of the final protocol on 12 June. Metternich felt that the agreement that it signified opened the path for an escape from current German dangers. If adhered to, this agreement offered a means to order, a true freedom, and justice. This hope, Metternich told the German ministers, rested on his belief in the benefit of the two arrangements that he considered the core of the work of the conference: the federal court of arbitration and the related provision by which the governments would have their finances ensured against the threats of "anarchists" in their diets.[46]

Metternich believed that, because of the federal court of arbitration, state diets would no longer be able to take it upon themselves to interpret constitutions as they pleased. They could not set themselves up as the final authority in disputes between themselves and their sovereigns. Thus, the tendency of the representative system to turn sovereign power over to democratic assemblies of representatives of the people would be curtailed. Henceforth, a high judicial authority would alone decide the outcome of conflicts between state governments and their diets. Nevertheless, the future of Germany was placed in the hands of the German governments. To their wisdom was entrusted the selection of the pool of disinterested judges.[47]

The second product of the conference that Metternich particularly acclaimed was another arrangement by which a government could limit the influence of its parliamentary opposition. It was a legal provision that ended one of the chief menaces to the monarchic system inherent in the theory of representative government—the idea that a diet could influence state policies by threatening to withhold its approval from government budgets. By Article 21 of the final protocol, the German governments were empowered to send before the federal court of arbitration budget cases in which they and their diets could not agree. If a diet refused to grant sufficient funds for government operations until the court decision was reached, or if it refused to submit to the decision of the court, the government concerned was free to collect previously approved taxes without renewed diet approval. If necessary, the Federal Diet was to see that federal troops intervened to support such government action. Hereafter, Metternich said, the German governments could defend "the cause of justice and order" without fear of parliamentary obstructionism.[48]

Finally, of course, Metternich saw the benefits of the Vienna Conference in more than just its written results—the final protocol with its provision for a court of arbitration and rules for the control of state diets, the press, and the German universities. He considered that the personal contact between the chief German ministers would in itself have a good effect. No one, he felt, left the meetings without feeling reassured and strengthened, ready to fight the good fight when he returned to his home state.[49] That was Metternich's reason for calling the conference in the first place and the reason why he worked so hard to prevent Bavaria from destroying the spirit of the conference by a last minute rejection of its accomplishments.[50]

Although the protocol that was signed in Vienna on 12 June still had to be officially ratified by each of the German governments, that proved to be no great problem. The South Germans were not uncooperative. Bavaria was not tardy in its acceptance of the protocol that had been modified according to her wishes. The Bavarian ratification, dated 1 July, was sent to Vienna on 9 July.[51] Württemberg's instrument of ratification was dated 24 June and Baden's was dated 2 July. Both ratifications, however, seem to have been decided upon really only in mid-July.[52]

The cooperation of the South German courts in the rapid ratification of the final protocol seems to have been motivated by different reasons in each case. Metternich would not have approved of all of them. The King of Württemberg was moved by the hope of vigorous action against the "evils" of the day.[53] In Karlsruhe, however, Reitzenstein urged the grand duke to action to end Baden's reputation for liberalism and return her to the good graces of Austria and Prussia. In any case, his colleagues in the ministry told Grand Duke Leopold that the results of the conference did not really affect Baden's constitution or the principles of the German Confederation.[54] Finally, in Bavaria, Foreign Minister Gise urged Ludwig to quick ratification for the same reason that he had advocated an independent Bavarian program at the conference in Vienna.

The Bavarian foreign minister wanted to protect the sovereignty and prestige of his state. He told King Ludwig that, as he had warned, the Vienna Conference had been aimed at Bavaria.

Her delegates had had to defend her independence and her constitution. Because of their fortitude, however, important concessions had been won and Bavarian political influence increased. Unfortunately, the last-minute resistance to the idea of the court of arbitration made it seem that the Bavarian government intended to sabotage the conference. To regain the lost trust of his neighbors and to assure Bavaria's prominence, Gise recommended that the king act quickly to ratify the final protocol. Moreover, Metternich was preparing a ratification formula to be suggested to the German courts, and Gise urged Ludwig to act on his own initiative before he received the formula from Vienna.[55]

Thus, while Metternich's Vienna Conference of 1834 did bring a certain conservative and federalistic consensus to German politics, the Austrian foreign minister had to become inured to the particularism of the German states—especially Bavaria. Bavaria continued to try to exercise the independence of a great European state. Even after gaining extensive concessions in Vienna— achieving the means of securing federal protection for Ludwig's monarchic sovereignty while escaping the imposition of unwanted federal duties—the Bavarian government continued to examine each bit of potential federal legislation with suspicion and care. When the articles of the final protocol concerning universities were turned into federal decrees on 13 November 1834, the Bavarian delegate at Frankfurt had still not been instructed to vote affirmatively. The protocol had to be left open until 18 November, when he received final instructions from Munich.[56]

He, like his South German colleagues, did vote on 30 October to establish the federal court of arbitration.[57] Bavaria, like Württemberg and Baden, was basically in agreement with Metternich regarding the dangers inherent in representative government. When Foreign Minister Gise was unable to organize a special constitutional confederation within the Confederation to protect the Bavarian government from the dangers of its diet, King Ludwig chose safety within the context of the existing German Confederation.

Ludwig had little choice. Württemberg and Baden, not to mention Prussia, were not prepared to give his government the consistent backing it needed to initiate a truly independent "third German" policy. King William of Württemberg, the original propounder of *Triaspolitik*, had become increasingly convinced that the only defense against the dangers of representative government was joint action by all the German states through the institutions of the German Confederation.[58] Grand Duke Leopold of Baden came to the same conclusion. In the past his government, more than that of Württemberg, suffered the verbal attacks of both the great German powers and its own diet, because of its attempt to steer a course between the extremes. His minister president, like many other South German statesmen, wished to hold federal interference in internal South German affairs to a minimum. Reitzenstein concluded, however, that Baden could not continue to alienate her guardians, Austria and Prussia.[59]

The importance of the Vienna Conference of 1834 lay ultimately not in what was done there, but in what was not done. The resistance of the South German states—especially Bavaria—kept the conference from achieving little more than a series of unenforceable agreements for the maintenance of monarchic government in Germany. Not even the use of the new federal court of arbitration was obligatory.[60] Yet despite the initial attempt of the Bavarian foreign minister to create a constitutional and progressive alliance within the German Confederation, there was no change from the conservative, federalistic, and defensive characteristics of the Confederation that Metternich offered as the Austrian answer to the German Question[61]

Two factors were chiefly responsible for this situation: the conservatism of the German rulers and their conclusion that they could not afford to alienate their two great German protectors, Austria and Prussia. Austro-Prussian cooperation and the basic conservatism of the German princes—both purposefully reinforced by Metternich through and at the Vienna Conference of 1834—ensured again the relative and temporary success of Metternich's German policies for the rest of the decade. Remnants of these influences would continue to hinder the advance of the principle of popular sovereignty in Germany and to limit the development of democratic institutions for many years to come.

10

Metternich's School of Nationalism for the German Princes

The aim of the present study has been to examine the nature of Metternich's solution to the German Question and the degree to which its implementation could be considered a success during the period between 1820 and 1834. That solution involved the propagation of Metternich's special brand of German federalism. It was a federalism that combined a healthy regard for the rights of the individual German monarchs with a call for the fulfillment of their federal duties. The success of Metternich's policy, to the extent to which his policies could be said to have been successful—even in the short run—is attributable to the fact that he repeatedly was able to convince the German princes that the best security for their monarchic sovereignty was to be found in their corporate loyalty to the purposes and statutes of the German Confederation. Metternich thereby stimulated a new vision of German nationalism: a federalistic, monarchistic, and pacific *grossdeutsch* nationalism that would serve both the particularistic interests of the German princes and the larger German and European interests of Austria. "Professor" Metternich sought to make the German Confederation "a school of nationalism for the German princes."

Of course, to even associate Metternich's name with the concept of German nationalism seems ironic, inappropriate, or even preposterous. That it does is an indication of the tyranny of Prussian-German historiography since Treitschke. The Prussian *kleindeutsch* concept of German nationalism has captured the minds of historians and of most German nationals since Bismarck's *Reichsgründung*.[1] This tyranny, which has been increasingly scrutinized by German and American historians,[2] did not exist in the *Vormärz* period. At that time it was only one of the competing interpretations of the proper concept of German nationalism. In 1832, Leopold von Ranke still remained pessi-

171

172 METTERNICH AND THE GERMAN QUESTION

mistic that an answer could be found to the question as to what
was Germany. "Who will be able to grasp in a word or concept
what is German? Who will call it by name, the genius of our
country, of the past and future? It would only be another phan-
tom to lure us on one more false road."[3] The foundation of the
Second Empire in 1871 and Heinrich von Treitschke's *History of
Germany in the Nineteenth Century*, published between 1879
and 1894, put their stamp of identification on German nationalism, leading Germans up "one more false road." These
events also established a tyranny of persuasive rhetoric regarding
the proper connotations of "German nationalism" that still en-
snare students of German nationalism today.

That tyranny of the *kleindeutsch* interpretation of German
nationalism was not established in *Vormärz*. In fact, to prevent it,
Metternich sought to establish another concept of German nationalism. It is useful to remember, as Robert Berdahl has pointed
out, that one must distinguish between the "idea" of a nation and
the "ideology" of nationalism. "The idea of nationality implies
something unique about a people because of culture, language,
race, or historical development; such a view may be seen, for
example in the writings of Herder. Nationalism as an ideology is
functional. It serves a definite purpose of elites, as, for example,
furthering economic development or binding a community together during a period of social upheaval."[4] Thus Prusso-centric
German nationalism could be—and was—used to implement the
Zollverein and ultimately to achieve "national" unity under
Prussia. But, in Metternich's monarchistic, federalistic, and pacific *grossdeutsch* version, it could and did manifest itself in an
Austrian attempt to preserve the German monarchs, in the face of
foreign and domestic dangers, through German unity without
unification.

Metternich's was an ideology of German nationalism designed
to maintain international peace and monarchic sovereignty in
central Europe through the protection of monarchic sovereignty
in the individual German states. It was an ideology of nationalism that was not so different from that which flourished
among the aristocrats of the American South during the same
period. The American nationalism of the Southern aristocrat was
a nationalism characterized by a love of the United States that
was made possible by a national government that was identified
with the perpetuation of states' rights and thus of each state's
"peculiar institutions." This kind of American nationalism was
also a form of nationalism, which like the German nationalism

envisioned by Metternich, was made outmoded by the trauma of civil war and domination by a different elite with its own ideology of nationalism. Between 1815 and 1871 in Germany, as between 1776 and 1865 in the United States, the definition of nationalism was still unsettled. A variety of ideologies of German nationalism were in competition. Through the benefits of the German Confederation with its protection of states' rights, "Professor" Metternich hoped throughout his career—and even in his retirement[5]—to lead the German princes to instinctively accept his ideology of German nationalism. Thus Metternich tried to make the German Confederation his "school of nationalism for the German princes."

But the German Confederation, if a school, had competing groups of tutors. Each pursued its own tuition, although sometimes lesson plans overlapped. Metternich's most important competition—as well as frequent support—came from Prussia. Prussia was the only German state powerful enough to offer alternative leadership to the German princes in a period when France was too revolutionary and Russia was both too far away and too reactionary. The Prussian state, although led by a well-meaning and conservative king, threatened Metternich's German policy because of progressive ministers like Motz, Bernstorff, and Eichhorn. They sought reforms from above to satisfy the economic and nationalistic desires of the German people and, thus, to take steps toward turning the German Confederation into a unified nation under Prussian leadership.

After Prussia, the South Germans—particularly the Kings of Württemberg and Bavaria—were Metternich's competitors and sometime students in the German school of nationalism. As we have seen, it was these two South German princes, leaders of constitutional Germany and competing rivals for leadership of a Third Germany, who most immediately threatened Metternich's German solutions. King William and King Ludwig, who had received their extended territories and monarchic sovereignty through the quirks of the Napoleonic period, saw constitutionalism as a tool by which to integrate states and defend them against foreign intrusion. Constitutionalism was designed to prevent intrusions by the German Confederation as well. Although self-proclaimed German patriots and defenders of the German Confederation as the guarantor of their sovereignty in the world of post-Napoleonic Europe, the South German rulers were adamant defenders of a states' rights tradition that would have made American Southerners of the same era proud. For them, as for their brethern in the American South, the attraction of a greater nationalism beyond their particular state boundaries resided precisely in the fact that nationalism—as they interpreted it—guaranteed their sovereign rights to do as they pleased. The results, of course, in both the United States and Germany was a major clash over the proper interpretation of the meaning of nationalism, particularly over the proper balance between states' rights and federal duties.

Complicating these issues was the general state of European affairs in the 1820s and 1830s. A shifting balance of power and threats of war and revolution provided the context for the debates that went on in monarchic circles in Germany about the proper solution to the German Question. For Metternich, the German Question never stood alone but was always part of the larger European one. What Metternich really wanted of the German princes was moral and, if necessary, diplomatic and military support for the European policies of the Habsburgs. Financially stricken and constantly troubled by the administrative problems of a conglomerate empire, Emperor Francis needed to maintain the status quo in Europe. It was up to Metternich to do so by primarily diplomatic means. Only when and where immediate injury to Habsburg territories threatened was Francis ready to use military force. Only in Austrian Italy did the Hofburg feel immediately endangered by revolutionary excesses during this period. Only in Italy did Austrian troops intervene in the 1820s and again in 1831. For such interventions Metternich wanted to guarantee the protection of the European powers, one of which he considered to be the German Confederation. It was the German Confederation that Austria expected to secure Austria's northwestern flank against both French threats and possible military intervention. And it was against what often seemed such a purely Austrian use of the German Confederation that the other German states protested. They did so through opposition at the Federal Diet and through assertions of sovereign particularism when outvoted or outmaneuvered by Metternich.

Metternich's concerns were not chiefly military. His most frequent concern for the German Confederation during the period 1820 to 1834 was not its submission to French armies but its members' acquiescence to the French doctrine of popular sovereignty. In Metternich's eyes such a doctrine threatened to undermine the monarchic structure of Germany and the stability of the German Confederation, which Metternich wanted to serve as the keystone of European peace and stability.

The danger was not only one for the long run. Metternich could not tolerate the acceptance of the principle of popular sovereignty by the German rulers because, even before its triumph, the doctrine influenced monarchs to attempt to harness popular opinions to their own ends. The results immediately endangered Austrian security by encouraging Franco-South German sympathies, South German-Prussian alignments, and the end of German monarchic unity in the defense of the status quo.

Metternich considered himself a realist. Of course, he sought to have the German governments defend themselves against the doctrine of popular sovereignty and its propagators—whether armed revolutionaries or the more insidiously dangerous parliaments and press. Only then could they defend Austria from that doctrine in both the short and long run. But Metternich's German policy was, in his own mind, not based merely on Austrian self-interest. He was convinced that his efforts were in the best interest of all the German princes. Underlying his reactionary exhortations was his assumption that the end of monarchic power, whether through war, street violence, or legislative evolution, meant chaos. The stated goal of German revolutionaries might be a peaceful, united German republic, the goal of liberals a constitutional federation, but in either case the transition period would be one of European chaos. The key to understanding Metternich's solution for the German Question is neither the principle of legitimacy nor the unscrupulous pursuit of raison d'état. The key is Metternich's socially conservative world view. Metternich's world was one of monarchs and aristocrats. They, in his view, alone preserved sanity in the world and provided the peace and security that the average man sought and required. Metternich was particularly concerned for the peace and security of Austria, but he felt that his ideas had general applicability.

The force of Metternich's arguments to contemporary statesmen is attributable to both his conservative convictions and to those of his auditors. They shared the same assumptions as he did. Metternich's policies for the defense of the monarchic system in Austria seemed applicable throughout Germany as well. The South German monarchs were, of course, most susceptible to Metternich's views when their own policies were threatened by foreign invasion or domestic distress. It was easy to resist Metternich's deliniation of federal duties in the name of state sovereignty when things went well. Federal duties were like a suit of armor: confining in times of peace; a recognized necessity in times of turmoil. And, of course, Metternich convinced others of the benefits of the federal armor because he was convinced himself. He viewed the implementation of federal policies in the German states as no less in their interest than in his own. He was convinced that the Prussian and South German factions that opposed him were not evil but simply wrongheaded: the end of Austria's conservative influence in Germany would bring with it the collapse of the governmental and social order as well.

Their security, Metternich told the German princes, lay in strict adherence to the German Confederation and the duties that it prescribed. Foremost of these duties was to use the provisions of the Federal Constitution and the Final Act to ensure that their own governments were conducted in a strictly monarchic sense. Metternich insisted that revolution through legislative means was more dangerous than street revolts. In either case, however, it was adherence to the laws of the German Confederation that would save its princes. Whether hard pressed by their constitutional diets or by mobs they could find both excuse and backing for their resolves by appealing to the principles and provisions of the German Confederation. If that were not enough they could count on both the diplomatic and military backing of their confederates to give strength to their resolve. The key to security within the Confederation, however, was the acceptance by the German princes of the principle that federal law had supremacy over state law, federal duty over state sovereignty.

Herein, of course, lies the problem of every federal state: the paradox and imprecision involved in determining to what degree a state must surrender its sovereignty to preserve it. The German princes joined Metternich's German Confederation in 1815 to protect themselves in a Europe of great states whose immense power threatened them if they stood alone. The South German monarchs then instituted constitutions, in part, to protect themseles from their new protector. But constitutions introduced their own threat: the threat of the decline of monarchic sovereignty in the face of expanding legislative demands and assertions. Alternately sheltered and trapped by the competing demands and duties of the German Confederation and their state constitutions, the South German monarchs steered a perilous course between extremes.

In their navigation the German monarchs were dependent on the advice of their advisors. It was, therefore, a tactical policy of Metternich to enlist the influence of men with direct access to the German princes to encourage them to a "correct" course. Bypassing and undermining dissonant voices like those of

Bernstorff and Armansperg, Metternich sought acceptance for his views through influential conservatives within the major courts. In Prussia it was Prince Wittgenstein. In Bavaria his mouthpiece was Field Marshal Wrede. In Württemberg, Metternich relied on the persuasive powers of the Austrian envoy, Prince von Schönburg. Through the influence of these men, Metternich was repeatedly able to separate the monarchs from the advice of their own ministers. This could be done only because the German monarchs of the period did not insist that diplomatic communications follow official channels. As a rule, they did not even consider ministerial unity necessary or even desirable. In an age of monarchs, and before ministerial responsibility, the decision making processes of individual monarchs was as erratic as their own personalities. And in an age of personal diplomacy, Metternich was still master.

Yet as we have seen, mastery was not assured, easy, or lasting. Agreements of one day were often forgotten the next or modified out of existence by post facto reservations. Such was the case with Metternich's "triumphs" from the Vienna Conferences of 1820 through the Vienna Conference of 1834. The rulers of constitutional Germany, especially King William of Württemberg and King Ludwig of Bavaria, vied with each other to extend their influence within the German Confederation by the assertion of their sovereign and constitutional rights. Metternich could rely in the short run on their innate conservatism overriding their particularism when faced with severe threats at home or abroad; he could never count on their total acquiescence to an Austrian answer to the German Question. Fiercely proud of the new lands and titles with which they had emerged from the Napoleonic Wars, the South German kings were undaunted in their efforts to increase their political importance. They were justly suspicious that Metternich, like Napoleon, dealt with them as pawns in his European politics. They were also skeptical of the future of the Habsburg Monarchy. Soon, they felt, its internal problems and non-German interests would bring its end as the guarantor of German security; the Monarchy itself would need the protection of the German Confederation. With an eye to the future, the German princes repeatedly sought protection for their own interests through unity among themselves and in alliance with Prussia. They were checked, however, through most of the period between 1820 and 1834 by the recurrence of both Austro-Prussian unity and their own fears of revolution.

The factors that caused the relative success of Metternich's solution to the German Question between 1820 and 1834—the basic conservatism of the German monarchs and their inability to find a satisfactory alternative to Austrian protection—would prolong that success until the revolutions of 1848. The basic conservatism of the constitutional German monarchs, reinforced by their reaction to the Hambach Festival and the Frankfurt Putsch, and rationalized through the new federal decrees and secret agreements resulting from the Vienna Conference of 1834, gave a definitely conservative and Austrian-inspired coloration to the politics of these states after 1834. An important exception was the Bavarian-led attempt of the constitutional states to have the Confederation save the Hanoverian constitution in 1837–1840. The war scare of 1840 and the accompanying threat of a Prussian-led reform of federal military institutions would further threaten to undermine Metternich's efforts to preserve his design and purpose for the German Confederation. It would be increasingly difficult for him to find for the German princes the proper balance between states' rights and federal duties.

Notes

Preface

1. Heinrich von Treitschke, *Deutsche Geschichte im neunzehnten Jahrhundert*, 5 vols. (Leipzig, 1879–94).
2. Heinrich Ritter von Srbik, *Metternich der Staatsmann und der Mensch*, 3 vols. (Munich, 1925–54).
3. Peter Viereck, *Conservatism Revisited* (New York, 1949).
4. Henry Kissinger, *A World Restored* (New York, 1957); Paul W. Schroeder, *Metternich's Diplomacy at Its Zenith, 1820–1823* (Austin, 1962); and Enno E. Kraehe, *Metternich's German Policy*: vol. 1: *The Contest with Napoleon, 1799–1814* (Princeton, 1963) and vol. 2: *The Congress of Vienna, 1814–1815* (Princeton, 1983).
5. See George S. Werner, *Bavaria in the German Confederation, 1820–1848* (Rutherford, N.J., 1977); Robert D. Billinger, Jr., "The German Confederation: Metternich's School of Nationalism for the German Princes, 1815–1834," *Proceedings of the Consortium on Revolutionary Europe*, 2 vols. (Athens, Ga., 1980), 1: 174–82; Michael Derndarsky, "Österreich und der Deutsche Bund 1815–1866," in *Österreich und die deutsche Frage im 19. und 20. Jahrhundert* (Wiener Beiträge zur Geschichte der Neuzeit, vol. 9; Munich, 1982), 92–116; Wolf D. Gruner, "Der Deutsche Bund—Modell für eine Zwischenlösung? *Politik und Kultur* (1982, Heft 5): 22–42; Gruner, "Europa, Deutschland und die internationale Ordnung im 19. Jahrhundert," *Politik und Kultur* (1984, Heft 2): 24–53; and Gruner, *Die deutsche Frage: Ein Problem der europäischen Geschichte seit 1800* (Munich, 1985). For an amateur's attempt, see Ludwig Bentfeldt, *Der Deutsche Bund als nationales Band, 1815–1866* (Göttingen, 1985).
6. See Kraehe in n. 4.
7. See Billinger, "The German Confederation."
8. See Lawrence J. Baack, *Christian Bernstorff and Prussia: Diplomacy and Reform Conservatism, 1818–1832* (New Brunswick, N.J., 1980).
9. For insights in this regard, I am indebted to Roy Austensen, "Einheit oder Einigkeit? Another Look at Metternich's View of the German Dilemma," *German Studies Review*, 6 (February 1983): 41–57.
10. An insight stressed by Austensen, "The Making of Austria's Prussian Policy, 1848–1852," *The Historical Journal*, 27, no. 4 (1984): 861.
11. Peter Burg, *Der Wiener Kongress: Der Deutsche Bund im europäischen Staatensystem* (Munich, 1984), 182–83, comments that the limits to Metternich's ability to confine the German Confederation within the Metternich System is the chief focus of Robert D. Billinger, Jr., "Metternich's Policy Toward the South German States, 1830–1834," (Ph.D. dissertation, University of North Carolina at Chapel Hill, 1973). For the story of Bavarian resistance to Austrian-inspired federal duties see Werner, *Bavaria in the German Confederation*.

Chapter 1. Federal Duties and the Metternich System, 1815–1824

1. Explained by Kraehe, *Metternich's German Policy*, 2: 396–397. See Articles 1 and 2 of the Federal Act in Ernst Rudolf Huber, ed., *Dokumente zur deutschen Verfassungsgeschichte*, 3 vols. (Stuttgart, 1961–1966), 1: 75–76.

2. Kraehe, *Metternich's German Policy*, 2: 392–93.

3. For an insightful discussion of the Confederation of the Rhine see Hans A. Schmitt, "Germany Without Prussia: A Closer Look at the Confederation of the Rhine," *German Studies Review*, 6, no. 1 (February 1983): 9–39.

4. Kraehe, *Metternich's German Policy*, 1: 46; 2: 396–97.

5. Ibid., 1: 277–78. See also Ulrike Eich, *Russland und Europa: Studien zur russischen Deutschlandspolitik in der Zeit des Wiener Kongresses* (Passauer Historische Forschungen, Bd. I; Cologne, 1986), 280–85, for the Stein-Alexander connection as late as the Congress of Vienna.

6. For a review of Hardenberg's role, see Kraehe, *Metternich's German Policy*, 2: 393–96.

7. Metternich to Emperor Francis, 1 August 1819, NP, 3: 261–68.

8. Metternich to Gentz, 9, 23, 30 April; 7 May; and 17 June 1819, in Friedrich von Gentz, *Briefe von und an Friedrich von Gentz*, ed., Friedrich Carl Wittichen and Ernst Salzer, 3 vols., (Munich, 1913), 3: pt.1. 389, 408–09, 419–20, 425–27, 465–69.

9. Enno E. Kraehe, "Raison d'état et idéologie dans la politique allemande de Metternich (1809–1820)," *Revue d'histoire moderne et contemporaine* (July–September 1966): 119; Eberhard Büssem, *Die Karlsbader Beschlüsse von 1819* (Hildesheim, 1974), 102–03.

10. Charles K. Webster, *The Foreign Policy of Castlereagh, 1815–1822: Britain and the European Alliance* (London, 1939 [1925]), 188–89.

11. Baack, *Bernstorff*, 59.

12. On the Teplitz and Carlsbad meetings see Büssem, *Karlsbader Beschlüsse*, 263–89; 290–473; Baack, *Bernstorff*, 65–68; and Robert D. Billinger, Jr., "The Austro-Russian Struggle for Germany and the Carlsbad Decrees, 1815–20" (Masters thesis, University of North Carolina at Chapel Hill, 1968), chap. 3. Metternich's planning for the Carlsbad Conference can be followed in NP, 3, passim, and in Wittichen, ed., *Briefe von und an Gentz*, 3, passim. The protocols of the conference are in Carl Theodor Welcker, *Wichtige Urkunden für den Rechtszustand der deutschen Nation* (Mannheim, 1844).

13. Metternich noted this when it came time for the Carlsbad Decrees to be renewed. See Metternich to Emperor Francis, 29 July 1824, NP, 4: 117.

14. For the text of the Carlsbad Decrees see Huber, *Dokumente*, 1: 90–95.

15. The limitation of the sovereignty of the confederate states through the Carlsbad Decrees is noted by Paul W. Schroeder, *Metternich's Diplomacy at Its Zenith*, 18. The effect of the executive order is elaborated on by Ernst Rudolf Huber, *Deutsche Verfassungsgeschichte seit 1789*, 7 vols. (Stuttgart, 1957–1984), 1: 635, 749.

16. Treitschke, *Deutsche Geschichte*, 2: 295; Carl von Kaltenborn, *Geschichte der deutschen Bundesverhältnisse und Einheitsbestrebungen von 1806 bis 1850*, 2 vols. (Berlin, 1852), 1: 338–39.

17. Kraehe, "Raison d'état," 191; Willy Andreas, *Der Aufbau des Staates im*

Zusammenhang der allgemeinen Politik, vol. 1 of Geschichte der Badischen Verwaltungsorganization und Verfassung in den Jahren 1802–1818, ed. Badische Historische Kommission (Leipzig, 1913), 472.

18. Actually Bavaria published the Decrees as the "common disposition of the member states" rather than as federal decrees and stated that they were to be followed only as far as "the sovereignty, the constitution and the standing laws [of Bavaria] are not contravened." See Werner, Bavaria and the German Confederation, 19.

19. "The Carlsbad Decrees marked the zenith of Metternich's domination of Germany," according to Baack, Bernstorff, 68. "Carlsbad marked the greatest height that he reached in his European and German politics in the period after 1815." "In Carlsbad he was the leader; here he forced his spirit on Germany and achieved for Austria a leading role, like to which this state had never attained under the old Holy Roman Empire." So Srbik, Metternich, 1: 595. For a similar evaluation see Büssem, Karlsbader Beschlüsse, 466–71.

20. For the existence of Russian attempts to persuade Great Britain to join a protest against the Carlsbad Decrees see Billinger, "The Austro-Russian Struggle for Germany," 66–70; Karl Hammer, Die Französische Diplomatie der Restauration und Duetschland, 1814–1830 (vol. 1 of Pariser Studien; Stuttgart, 1963), 77–78; and Webster, Castlereagh, 193. Capodistria told the ambassador from Württemberg that the Carlsbad Decrees were not compatible with the sovereignty of the individual German states. He added that if Austria and Prussia were so concerned about the growth of constitutions in Germany they should have set an example by granting model constitutions so that their fellow sovereigns would have known how best to proceed before demagogues demanded concessions. See Beroldingen to King William, 21 November 1819, WHSA, E 71, Verz. 30, Carton VIII-2, 1819, Fasc. 3.

21. Metternich to Emperor Francis, 1 August 1819, NP, 3: 267.

22. Beroldingen to King William, 8 and 14 February, 16 May, and 9 June 1820, WHSA, E 71, Verz. 30, Carton VIII-2, 1820, Fasc.1.

23. Article 57 of the Final Act. For the text of the Final Act see Huber, ed., Dokumente, 1: 81–90. For information on the Vienna Conference of 1820, see Ludwig Karl Aegidi, Die Schluss-Acte der Wiener Ministerial-Conferenzen: Abteilung 1: Urkunden (Berlin, 1860), and Abteilung 2: Geschichte der Wiener Schluss-Acte (Berlin, 1869); Friedrich Otto Aristides von Weech, Correspondenzen und Actenstücke zur Geschichte der Ministerial-Conferenzen von Carlsbad und Wien in den Jahren 1819, 1820 und 1834 (Leipzig, 1865); and Treitschke, Deutsche Geschichte, 3: 3–29. For more details on the Vienna Conferences, see L. Fr. Ilse, Geschichte der deutschen Bundesversammlung insbesondere ihres Verhalten zu den deutschen National-Interessen, 3 vols. (Marburg, 1861–162; repro. Verlag Dr. H. A. Gerstenberg, Hildesheim in 1972), 2: 387–567. For a perspective from Hesse-Darmstadt, see Karl Wilhelm Heinrich du Bos du Thil, Denkwürdigkeiten aus dem Dienstleben des Hessen-Darmstädtischen Staatsminister Freiherrn du Thil, 1803–1848, ed. Heinrich Ulmann (1921), repr. vol. 3 of Deutsche Geschichtsquellen de 19. Jahrhundert (Historische Kommission bei der Bayerischen Akademie der Wissenschaften, Osnabrück, 1967), 246–75.

24. Articles 25 and 26 of the Final Act.

25. Wolfgang von Hippel, Friedrich Landolin Karl von Blittersdorff 1792–1861: Ein Beitrag zur badischen Landtags-und Bundespolitik im Vormärz (Veröffentlichungen der Kommission für Geschichtliche Landeskunde in Baden-

Württemberg, Reihe B: Forschungen, vol. 38: Stuttgart, 1967), 24; Aegidi, *Die Urkunden*, 153–55; Alexander Winter, *Karl Philipp Fürst von Wrede als Berater des Königs Max Joseph und der Kronprinzen Ludwig von Bayern (1813–1825)* (Miscellanea Bavarica Monacensia, no. 7; Munich, 1968), 315–16.

26. For the provisions of the Federal Act, see Huber, ed. *Dokumente*, 1: 75–81.

27. Baack, *Bernstorff*, 93–94. For the position taken by Württemberg, see twentieth session at Vienna, 29 March 1820, in Aegidi, *Urkunden*, 153–55. Metternich tried to convince the tsar of the danger to which Württemberg exposed Germany because of her independent position. See Metternich to Lebzeltern, 25 April 1820, Ludwig von Lebzeltern, *Les rapports diplomatique de Lebzeltern*, ed. Grand Duc Nicolas Mikhailowitch (St. Petersburg, 1913), 221–22. Yet Capodistria, the Russian foreign secretary, seemed to encourage Württemberg's protest by his statements of approval to her ambassador in St. Petersburg. See Beroldingen to King William, 16 May 1820, WHSA, E 71, Verz. 30, Carton VIII-2, Fasc.1.

28. Metternich to Emperor Francis, 14 May 1820, NP, 3: 518. Such was the ambivalence of the official Russian position—often formally in support of Prussia and Austria—that, as 1820 ended, the governments of both Württemberg and Bavaria felt it necessary to assure the tsar that, contrary to rumors, they had no plans to form a separate confederation within the Confederation to protect their interests. See Beroldingen to King William, 10 December 1820, WHSA, E 71, Verz. 30, Carton VIII-2, 1820, Fasc.1.

29. Schroeder, *Metternich's Diplomacy*.

30. Ibid., 237–38.

31. Ibid., 254.

32. Hammer, *Französische Diplomatie*, 135, 195.

33. The information in this and the following paragraph can be found in Karl-Johannes Grauer, *Wilhelm I. König von Württemberg: Ein Bild seines Lebens un seiner Zeit* (Stuttgart, 1960), 179–87; Huber, *Deutsche Verfassungsgeschichte*, 1: 755–56; Alfred Stern, *Geschichte Europas seit den Verträgen von 1815 bis zum Frankfurter Frieden von 1871*, 10 vols. (Berlin, 1913–1924), 2: 144.

34. Curt Albrecht, *Die Triaspolitik des Frhr. [Freiherr] K.[arl] Aug.[ust] v.[on] Wangenheim* (Darstellungen aus der Württembergischen Geschichte, vol. 12) (Stuttgart, 1914), 143.

35. Ibid., 88–89.

36. The description "reform conservative" is used by Baack to describe the foreign minister of Prussia. See Baack, *Bernstorff*, xi.

37. Albrecht, *Triaspolitik*, 160–61.

38. Wangenheim's opposition to Austria on these questions is dealt with in Stern, *Geschichte Europas*, 2: 390–96. Wangenheim's role in all of these questions is the substance of Albrecht, *Triaspolitik*.

39. Schroeder, *Metternich's Diplomacy*, 80f.

40. Hippel, *Blittersdorff*, 31–32; Wolff to Metternich, 30 March 1821, BOG, 1: 337–38. King William also thanked the British government for its note condemning the Troppau Conference and circularized the envoys of Württemberg to the German courts with the view that while the intentions of the Great Powers were to be commended, any generalized right of intervention in the affairs of neighboring states was incompatible with the sovereignty of those states. See

response to Ambassador Cockburn, 31 January 1821, and circular to legations, 7 February 1821, WHSA, E 36–38, Verz. 13 II, Bü. 2.

41. See Robert D. Billinger, Jr., "The War Scare of 1831 and the Prussian-South German Attempt to End Austrian Dominance in Germany," *Central European History*, 9 (September 1976): 203–219; Billinger, "They Sing the Best Songs Badly: Metternich, Frederick William IV, and the German Confederation during the War Scare of 1840–41," *Deutscher Bund und deutsche Frage, 1815–1866* (Wiener Beiträge zur Geschichte der Neuzeit, vol. 16/17. Vienna, 1990); and Irmline Veit-Brause, "Die deutsche-französische Krise von 1840: Studien zur deutschen Einheitsbewegung" (Ph.D. diss., Cologne, 1967).

42. Schroeder, *Metternich's Diplomacy*, 173.

43. Treitschke, *Deutsche Geschichte*, 3: 195, 259–60.

44. Ibid., 290–91; Trauttmansdorff to Metternich, 15 September 1821, BOG, 1: 384; Metternich to Lebzeltern, 31 March 1822, in Lebzeltern, *Rapports*, 358–59.

45. For a treatment of Wangenheim's career at the Federal Diet, see Albrecht, *Triaspolitik*.

46. Huber, *Deutsche Verfassungsgeschichte*, 1: 757.

47. Trauttmansdorff to Metternich, 17 July 1822, BOG, 1: 464–65.

48. Le Moussaye to Montmorency, 5 April 1822, BFG, 1: 174.

49. Stern, *Geschichte Europas*, 2: 310. The full text of the circular dispatch of 14 December 1822 can be found in NP, 3: 578–86.

50. Eich, *Russland und Europa*, 412, notes this major change but maintains the problematic thesis that the tsar really supported Metternich's views since at least 1818. The envoy from Württemberg to Russia noted the difference in attitudes toward Württemberg and her constitution expressed by Capodistria and Nesselrode and the influence of the Austrian ambassador on the latter. See Beroldingen to King William, 21 November 1819, WHSA, E 71, Verz. 30, Carton VIII-2, 1819, Fasc. 3.

51. Copies of the various drafts of the Württemberg circular and its final version are in WHSA, E 36–38, Verz. 13 II, Bü. 5. The text and Metternich's comments can also be found in NP, 4: 28–32. Regarding Wangenheim's action see Huber, *Deutsche Verfassungsgeschichte*, 1: 757. That Wangenheim was acting on the instructions and with the approval of the Stuttgart government can be seen in his correspondence with the foreign minister. See Wangenheim to Wintzingerode, 7, 20, and 21 February 1823, WHSA, E 36–38, Verz. 57, Fasc. 173.

52. Lebzeltern, *Les rapports diplomatique*, 109. Baack, *Bernstorff*, 96, suggests that the withdrawal of the ministers from Stuttgart was primarily the result of Bernstorff's initiative.

53. See Treitschke, *Deutsche Geschichte*, 3: 320. Copies of the notes of recall can be found in WHSA, E 36–38, Verz. 13 II, Bü. 5, Fasc. 15. Metternich's explanation of the Great Power's severance of diplomatic relations with Stuttgart can be found in his dispatch to Vincent in Paris, 19 April 1823, NP, 4: 32–33.

54. Bavarian newspapers were forbidden to note the recall of the ambassadors of the Great Powers from Stuttgart, and the vacationing Bavarian ambassador was ordered back to his post. See Ségur to Chateaubriand, 15 June 1823, BFG, 1: 206. King William forbade the reporting of the diplomatic recall by the Württemberg press. See King William's note to his minister of foreign affairs, 12

June 1823, WHSA, E 36–38, Verz. 13 II, Bü. 5, Fasc. 15. Reports from St. Petersburg had earlier indicated that King William could expect no sympathy from the tsar unless Wangenheim was replaced. See reports from Beroldingen, 11, 22, and 26 March, 19 April, and 6 and 15 May 1823, WHSA, E 71, Verz. 30, Carton VIII-3, 1823, Fasc. 1. See also Eich, *Russland und Europa*, 414.

55. Beroldingen to Fleischmann, 19 August, 27 September and 30 October 1824, WHSA, E 72, Bü. 141. These instructions from the minister of foreign affairs to his envoy in St. Petersburg contain copies of King William's pleas for the resumption of good relations based on his support for the renewal of the Carlsbad Decrees and copies of notes of acceptance on that score from the emperor of Austria and the king of Prussia.

56. Huber, *Deutsche Verfassungsgeschichte*, 1: 765.

57. Metternich to Trauttmansdorff, 8 September 1821, BOG, 1: 376–77; Stern, *Geschichte Europas*, 2: 398.

58. Hippel, *Blittersdorff*, 41–42.

59. Treitschke, *Deutsche Geschichte*, 3: 270–71; Ségur to Montmorency, 29 September 1822, BFG, 1: 190–91; Hippel, *Blittersdorff*, 42–43; Winter, *Wrede*, 322–24. Regarding those eventually participating, see Treitschke, *Deutsche Geschichte*, 3: 314. Württemberg was invited to send a representative but King William declined, insisting that reforms should only come as a result of discussion at the Federal Diet. See William's instructions to his foreign minister as to how to respond to Metternich's invitation, 18 January 1823, WHSA, E 36–38, Verz. 57, Fasc. 173.

60. For the Vienna meetings of January 1823, see Werner, *Bavaria in the German Confederation*, 54–59; Ilse, *Geschichte der deutschen Bundesversammlung*, 2: 576–97; Stern, *Geschichte Europas*, 2: 399–401; Treitschke, *Deutsche Geschichte*, 3: 314–18; Hippel, *Blittersdorff*, 50–51.

61. Federal action did not come until July and August 1824. See Huber, *Deutsche Verfassungsgeschichte*, 1: 764–65.

62. Treitschke, *Deutsche Geschichte*, 3: 317; Stern, *Geschichte Europas*, 2: 401; Winter, *Wrede*, 324–25; Hippel, *Blittersdorff*, 50–51.

63. These changes are listed and explained in Huber, *Deutsche Verfassungsgeschichte*, 1: 764, and Treitschke, *Deutsche Geschichte*, 3: 328–30.

64. Stern, *Geschichte Europas*, 2: 408–9; Trauttmansdorff to Metternich, 21 February 1824, BOG, 1: 525.

65. Hippel, *Blittersdorff*, 54; Trauttmansdorff to Metternich, 12 April 1824, BOG, 1: 533; Küster to King Frederick William III, 31 March, 11 April 1824, BPG, 1: 335–37.

66. Metternich to Lebzeltern, 7 February 1824, and Lebzeltern to Metternich, 31 March and 17 April 1824, in Lebzeltern, *Rapports*, 135, 137–38, 272–77; Treitschke, *Deutsche Geschichte*, 3: 333.

67. See Metternich's private correspondence of 23 April 1824, NP, 4: 94.

68. Metternich described his meetings with the Bavarian ministers at Tegernsee and the resulting Zentner memorandum to Gentz in letters of 7 and 30 June 1824, and to Emperor Francis on 29 July 1824. See NP, 4: 95–96, 103–4, 118–19. See also Winter, *Wrede*, 330–32; Stern, *Geschichte Europas*, 2: 412; Treitschke, *Deutsche Geschichte*, 3: 335–36.

69. The diplomats were Baron Johann von Anstett from Frankfurt and Count Demetri Tatischev from Vienna. For these prearrangements with St. Petersburg, see Metternich to Lebzeltern, 31 March and 13 May 1824, Lebzeltern, *Rapports*, 135, 142–43, 272–277.

70. Beroldingen to Fleischmann, 23 June and 15 July 1824, WHSA, E 72, Bü. 141. These dispatches show the great interest that Württemberg had in informing the tsar of Württemberg's active participation in planning for the renewal of the Carlsbad Decrees, and thus its good intentions.

71. Metternich's report to Emperor Francis, 29 July 1824, NP, 4: 119. For more information on the conferences, see Treitschke, *Deutsche Geschichte*, 3: 337, and Hippel, Blittersdorff, 53.

72. The notation on Metternich's report of 29 July 1824 can be seen in NP, 4: 120.

73. These federal laws can be found in Huber, ed., *Dokumente*, 1: 117. They are explained in Huber, *Deutsche Verfassungsgeschichte*, 1: 765, 766; and in Treitschke, *Deutsche Geschichte*, 3: 338. Parenthetically, it is interesting to note that Bavaria had wished to change the wording of the decrees from federal "laws" to "measures," because Bavaria did not wish to grant the Federal Assembly legislative powers. The Bavarian ministerial council also questioned the proposed indefinite term of the press law and insisted on "as formerly" thereby extending limits that Bavaria placed on the press decree in 1819. But the Bavarian ambassador in Frankfurt did not insist on these changes. See Werner, *Bavaria and the German Confederation*, 62.

74. Treitschke, *Deutsche Geschichte*, 3: 338.

Chapter 2. States' Rights and the European Balance, 1824–1830

1. General information on the Mainz Central Investigating Commission can be found in Huber, *Deutsche Verfassungsgeschichte*, 1: 747; Stern, *Geschichte Europas*, 2: 395–97, 422; and Karl Biedermann, *Fünfundzwanzig Jahre Deutsche Geschichte*, 2 vols. (Breslau, 1890), 2: 121–36. More extensive studies are A. Petzold, "Die Zentral-Untersuchungs-Kommission in Mainz," *Quellen und Darstellungen zur Geschichte der Burschenschaft und der deutschen Einheitsbewegung*, 5 (1920): 171–258; and L.[eopold] Fr.[iedrich] Ilse, *Geschichte der politische Untersuchungen welche durch die neben der Bundesversammlung errichteten Commission, der Central-Untersuchungs-Commission zu Mainz und der Bundes-Central-Behörde zu Frankfurt in den Jahren 1819 bis 1827 und 1833 bis 1842 geführt sind* (Frankfurt a.M., 1860).

2. On 14 February 1826, the Austrian minister in Munich reported that Bavaria felt free of Austrian power over Germany because of the dissolution of good Austro-Russian relations. See BOG, 2: 69.

3. Stern, *Geschichte Europas*, 3: 81–83.

4. Baack, *Bernstorff*, 150–53.

5. The story is traced with special emphasis on Metternich in Srbik, *Metternich*, 1: 624–36. See also Treitschke, *Deutsche Geschichte*, 3: 729–41.

6. Baack, *Bernstorff*, 161. Treitschke portrays the King of Prussia's efforts to bring peace between Russia and Turkey as the result of his desire to save the German Confederation from collapse and Germany from civil war. See Treitschke, *Deutsche Geschichte*, 3: 739, 746. French diplomats in Germany reported the possibility of a European war in which Prussia would take over the leadership of Germany, according to Hammer, *Französische Diplomatie*, 135.

Similar reports are also found in Bavarian sources as shown in Maximilian Freiherr von Lerchenfeld, *Aus den Papieren des k.[öniglichen] b.[ayerischen] Staatsministers Maximilian Freiherrn von Lerchenfeld*, ed. Maximilian Baron von Lerchenfeld (Nördlingen, 1887), 176. That the Austrians prepared plans for their defense against Russia and Prussia is mentioned in Treitschke, *Deutsche Geschichte*, 3: 739. There are also indications of Austrian hopes that Electoral Hesse, Saxony, Hanover, Braunschweig, Mecklenburg, and the Free Cities could be united in a military alliance to protect their independence and preserve the German Confederation as it then existed. See Lindenau to Einseidel, 22 April 1828, in Hermann Oncken and F. E. M. Saemish, eds., *Vorgeschichte und Begründung des deutschen Zollvereins 1815–1834: Akten der Staaten des Deutschen Bundes und der europäischen Mächte*, 3 vols. (Veröffentlichungen der Friedrich List Gesellschaft E. V., vols. 8–10; Berlin, 1934), 2: 411–19.

7. Metternich sent General Ficquelmont to reassure Tsar Nicholas of Austrian good will in January 1829. He also had London, Paris, and Berlin inform the tsar that he had proposed no four-power intervention against Russia. See Stern, *Geschichte Europas*, 3: 168–69. Metternich's instructions to Ficquelmont on 17 January 1829 can be seen in NP, 4: 558–78.

8. Metternich's assessment of Prussia's politics in the Eastern Question can be found in his dispatch to the Austrian ambassador in London, Prince Paul Esterhazy, of 12 December 1828, NP, 4: 519–23. For confirmation of some of Metternich's fears, but also the peace keeping interests of the Prussian foreign minister, see Baack, *Bernstorff*, 160–62.

9. Hammer, *Französische Diplomatie*, 195.

10. Ibid., 229.

11. For one recent evaluation of Ludwig I, see Wolf D. Gruner, "Die Deutsche Politik Ludwig I.," *Zeitschrift für bayerische Landesgeschichte*, 49 (Heft 2, 1986): 449–507. See also the very readable and insightful work by Heinz Gollwitzer, *Ludwig I. von Bayern. Königtum im Vormärz: Eine politische Biographie* (Munich, 1986).

12. Nevertheless, some scholars remind us that in the event economic unification was not decisive to political unification, nor did it make that unification inevitable. See Hans-Werner Hahn, *Wirtschaftliche Integration im 19. Jahrhundert: Die hessischen Staaten und der Deutsche Zollverein* (Kritische Studien zur Geschichtswissenschaft, vol. 52; Göttingen, 1982), 313. See also Thomas Nipperdey, *Deutsche Geschichte 1800–1866: Bürgerwelt und starker Staat* (Munich, 1983), 361; and Gollwitzer, *Ludwig I*, 644–45.

13. See Adolf Beer, *Die Österreichische Handelspolitik im neunzehnten Jahrhundert* (Vienna, 1891), 54–55, 60–61; Albert Branchert, "Österreich und die Anfänge der preussisch-deutschen Zollvereins" (Ph.D. diss., University of Marburg, 1930), 42.

14. Huber, *Deutsche Verfassungsgeschichte*, 1: 798, 803–4; Beer, *Österreichische Handelspolitik*, 55–56; Oncken, *Zollverein*, 1: xxxiv.

15. For the Bavarian political position, see M. Doeberl, "Bayern und die wirtschaftliche Einigung Deutschlands," *Abhandlungen der Königlich Bayerischen Akademie der Wissenschaften. Philosophisch-phililogische und historische Klasse*, vol. 29, part 2 (Munich, 1915), 19–22; and Arnold H. Price, *The Evolution of the Zollverein: A Study of the Ideas and Institutions Leading to German Economic Unification between 1815 and 1833* (University of Michigan Publications, History and Political Science, vol. 17: Ann Arbor: 1949), 78–83. For Württemberg, see Albrecht, *Triaspolitik*, 103–35. Prussian and Austrian suspicions are noted in Stern, *Geschichte Europas*, 2: 392.

16. On Motz and the Zollverein, see Huber, *Deutsche Verfassungsgeschichte*, 1: 812–13; Baack, *Bernstorff*, 127; and Hahn, *Wirtschaftliche Integration*, 78. Ludwig's early ideas of a tariff union with Prussia and the exclusion of Austria are noted in Erwin Hölzle, "Der Deutsche Zollverein: Nationalpolitisches aus seiner Vorgeschichte," *Württembergische Jahrbücher für Statistik und Landeskunde, 1932–1933*, ed. Statistisches Landesamt (Stuttgart, 1935), 133.

17. Hanns Helmut Böck, *Karl Philipp Fürst von Wrede als politischer Berater König Ludwig I. von Bayern (1825–1838): Ein Beitrag zur Geschichte der Regierung König Ludwig I.* (Miscellanea Bavarica Monacensia, no. 8; Munich, 1968), 19; Gollwitzer, *Ludwig I*, 266.

18. Price, *Evolution of the Zollverein*, 193.

19. Trauttmansdorff to Metternich, 7 December 1825, BOG, 2: 48.

20. Hölzle, "Der Deutsche Zollverein," 133; Oncken, ed., *Zollverein*, 1: lxxi.

21. The economic motives of the King of Württemberg are stressed by Doeberl, "Bayern und die wirtschaftliche Einigung Deutschlands," 25–27; Price, *The Evolution of the Zollverein*, 192; and W. O. Henderson, *The Zollverein* (Cambridge, 1939), 62. Treitschke, *Deutsche Geschichte*, 3: 629, notes the attraction of the "pure Germany" idea. Hölzle, "Der Deutsche Zollverein," 133, stressed the motive of gaining strength for favorable negotiations with the Prussian Zollverein.

22. Baack, *Bernstorff*, 124–25; Hahn, *Wirtschaftliche Integration*, 78.

23. Treitschke, *Deutsche Geschichte*, 3: 630; Price, *Evolution of the Zollverein*, 203–6; and Oncken, ed., *Zollverein*, 1: xlvi–xlviii.

24. Oncken, ed., *Zollverein*, 1: xlix–liv; Price, *Evolution of the Zollverein*, 208, 210–11, 225; Henderson, *The Zollverein*, 51; Hahn, *Wirtschaftliche Integration*, 78.

25. Spiegel to Metternich, 27 February 1828, BOG, 2: 181.

26. Stern, *Geschichte Europas*, 3: 266.

27. Metternich to Trauttmansdorff, 18 March 1828, quoted and translated in Baack, *Bernstorff*, 126.

28. Ibid.

29. Baack, *Bernstorff*, 128–30, notes Prussian suspicions of Austrian influence here to encourage this union of Saxony, Hanover, Electoral Hesse, Weimar, Nassau, and several other small states.

30. Branchert, "Österreich und die Anfänge der preussisch-deutschen Zollverein," 9, 58–59. See also Stern, *Geschichte Europas*, 3: 267; and Oncken, ed., *Zollverein*, 1: lx.

31. Treitschke, *Deutsche Geschichte*, 3: 640.

32. Foreign diplomats noted rising Austro-Prussian tensions. See Baack, *Bernstorff*, 127.

33. Hölzle, "Der Deutsche Zollverein," 134; Doeberl, "Bayern und die wirtschaftliche Einigung Deutschlands," 32; and Oncken, ed., *Zollverein*, 1: liii. Regarding Ludwig's complaints to France, see Gollwitzer, *Ludwig I*, 312.

34. This and the following material on the Württemberg proposal and the Bavarian rejection can be found in Hölzle, "Der Deutsche Zollverein," 134–35, and documents 139–40. This source is also the basis for the data in Price, *Evolution of the Zollverein*, 230–31.

35. For further mention of the importance of the Sponheim dispute to Ludwig I, see Gruner, "Die Deutsche Politik Ludwig I," 470–74; and Gollwitzer, *Ludwig I*, 287–98. For details of the dispute, see Liselotte von Hörmann, *Der bayerisch-badische Gebeitstreit (1825–1832)* (Historische Studien, no. 336; Berlin, 1938).

36. This information on the Cotta mission is mainly from Hölzle, "Der Deutsche Zollverein," 135–36, 141–44. See also Baack, *Bernstorff*, 133–35.

37. Hölzle, "Der Deutsche Zollverein," 135–36, 141–44.

38. See n. 1 in BOG, 2: 225–26.

39. Metternich to Spiegel, 14 April 1829, BOG, 2: 225.

40. The French ambassador in Munich reported Austrian attempts to gain entrance to a Prussian-South German treaty. See Rumigny to Portalis, 26 May 1829, and n. 2 in BFG, 2: 182. Beer, *Österreichische Handelspolitik*, 58–66, mentions the Prussian offer, Metternich's attempts to convince the Austrian authorities of the need to participate in German free trade arrangements, and Austrian efforts to improve commercial relations with Bavaria.

41. See Baack, *Bernstorff*, 133–40, for an evaluation.

42. Doeberl, "Bayern und die wirtschaftliche Einigung Deutschlands," 36–49, traces the torturous negotiations and their importance. Price, *Evolution of the Zollverein*, 232–35, notes the highlights of the same material. See also Henderson, *The Zollverein*, 90–91.

43. Baack, *Bernstorff*, 136–40, rightly suggests the still imprecise interest that Prussian officials had in uniting Germany under the aegis of Prussia. Motz was more definite than Bernstorff in his anti-Austrian interests.

44. The text is in Oncken, ed., *Zollverein*, 3: 525–41, and mentioned in Treitschke, *Deutsche Geschichte*, 3: 669–70.

45. Metterneich to Emperor Francis (Vortrag), 9 October 1829, NP 4: 598–605.

Chapter 3. Search for Security, 1830

1. This twofold danger is well stated by Franz Richter, *Das europäische Problem der preussischen Staatspolitik und die revolutionäre Krisis von 1830 bis 1832* (Forschungen zur neueren und neuesten Geschichte, no. 2; Leipzig, 1933), 4.

2. Eugène de Guichen, *La révolution de Juillet 1830 et l'Europe* (Paris, 1913), 5, 30, 95.

3. Ibid., 11, 30, 86; Baack, *Bernstorff*, 163.

4. Theodor Schiemann, *Geschichte Russlands unter Kaiser Niklaus I.*, 4 vols. (Berlin, 1904–1919), 3: 20; Treitschke, *Deutsche Geschichte*, 4: 36, 41. Metternich reported his talks with Nesselrode to the emperor on 31 July 1830. This report is in NP, 5: 9–12. The King of Prussia was returning from Teplitz when he received first word of the July Revolution. See Baack, *Bernstorff*, 166.

5. Stern, *Geschichte Europas*, 4: 49–50; Karl Hillebrand, *Geschichte Frankreichs von der Thronbesteigung Louis Philipp's bis zum Falle Napoleon's III*, 3 vols. (Gotha, 1877–1898), 1: 22–24; Alan J. Reinerman, *Austria and the Papacy in the Age of Metternich*, 2 vols. (Washington, D.C., 1979–1989), 1: 168.

6. Schiemann, *Geschichte Russlands*, 3: 20–21. The words of the agreement are given in NP, 5: 18–19. See also Baack, *Bernstorff*, 169–70.

7. Kurt M. Hoffmann, *Preussen und die Julimonarchie 1830–1834* (Historische Studien, no. 288; Berlin, 1936), 16–17; Johann Gustav Droysen, "Zur Geschichte der preussischen Politik in den Jahren 1830–1832," *Abhandlungen zur neueren Geschichte* (Leipzig, 1876), 10; Baack, *Bernstorff*, 167.

8. Hoffmann, *Preussen und die Julimonarchie*, 21–22. Hoffmann, using

Prussian diplomatic reports from France, notes how Prussia was the first of the Eastern Powers to recognize France and the resulting gratitude on the part of France. Actually, Austria presented a letter of recognition to a French ambassador on 8 September and Prussia did so on 9 September. See Baack, *Bernstorff*, 170–73. Thus, although France rightfully gave Prussia credit—in terms of intentions and receipt of official documentation—for early recognition of Louis Philippe's government, the Austrian document of recognition was actually dated one day earlier. See also Hillebrand, *Geschichte Frankreichs*, 1: 26.

9. British recognition of Louis Philippe came on 27 August 1830. See Baack, *Bernstorff*, 169.

10. See Metternich's note regarding his third interview with General Belliard, 8 September 1830, and Metternich to Apponyi, 12 September 1830, NP, 5: 25–28, 31–34. See also Srbik, *Metternich*, 1: 651–52.

11. Baack, *Bernstorff*, 171.

12. Gasser to King Ludwig, 16 August 1830, BGSA, MA 2403; Blomberg's report, 14 August 1830, WHSA, E 70, Bü. 45.

13. Blomberg's report, 14 August 1830, WHSA, E 70, Bü. 45.

14. Bray's report, 24 August 1830, BGSA, MA 2403; Metternich's instructions to Schönburg, 25 August 1830, HHSA, Württemberg, Fasc. 41; Schönburg's report of his meeting with King Ludwig, 27 August 1830, ibid.; Schönburg's report of his talks with King William, 30 August 1830, ibid.

15. See Schönburg reports cited in n. 14.

16. Metternich's instructions to Schönburg, 25 August 1830, HHSA, Württemberg, Fasc. 41.

17. Buol's report of 21 August 1830, HHSA, Baden, Fasc. 36ª.

18. For South German interests, see Billinger, "The War Scare of 1831," 205–10; Peter Burg, "Die französische Politik gegenüber Föderationen und Föderationsplänen deutscher Klein und Mittelstaaten 1830–1833," in Raymond Poidevin and Heinz Otto Sieburg, eds., *Aspects des relations franco-allemandes 1830–1848*, (Publications du centre de recherches relations internationales de l'université de Metz, no. 9; Metz, 1978), 19–30; and Peter Burg, *Der Wiener Kongress. Der Deutsche Bund und das europäische Staatensystem* (Munich, 1984), 154–59.

19. The intent of Armansperg's proposals can be gathered from the reply of the King of Württemberg and from later comments by several foreign diplomats in Munich. See Harttmann (for King William) to Holz, 13 August 1830, WHSA, E 75, Bü. 172; Fahnenberg to Grand Duke Leopold, 18 August 1830, BGLA 48/1874; Rumigny to Molé, 23 August 1830, BFG, 2: 279–80.

20. This can be gathered from Fahnenberg's report to Grand Duke Leopold, 18 August 1830, BLGA, 48/1874.

21. Harttmann (for King William) to Holz, 13 August 1830, WHSA, E 75, Bü. 172.

22. Beroldingen to Holz, 31 August 1830, ibid.

23. Fahnenberg to Grand Duke Leopold, 1 September 1830, BGLA, 48/1874.

24. Rumigny to Polignac, 8 September 1830, BFG, 2: 281.

25. Rumigny to Molé, 29 September, 2, 7 October 1830, BFG, 2: 289, 291, 295; Beroldingen to Schmitz-Grollenburg, 2 October 1830, WHSA, E 75, Bü. 172.

26. Accounts of these north German revolts can be found in Treitschke, *Deutsche Geschichte*, 4: 98–153; and Stern, *Geschichte Europas*, 4: 267–85. A particularly interesting examination of these revolutions is found in Margaret

Kruse Wallenberger, "The Revolutions of the 1830's and the Rise of German Nationalism" (Ph.D. diss., Radcliffe College, 1962).

27. Droysen, "Preussischen Politik," 44, 47–48.

28. Münch to Metternich, 24 September 1830, HHSA, Deutsche Akten, Fasc. 58. Münch's action before his home government had consulted fully with Berlin is commented on by Droysen, "Preussischen Politik," 47–48. The innovative aspects of Münch's proposals for the general delegation of the federal power of intervention and the resulting measures of 21 October 1830 are discussed by Huber, *Deutsche Verfassungsgeschichte*, 1: 151–52. The specific measures themselves can be found in PDB, 1830, 34. Sitzung (21 October 1830) § 248, 1051. See also Gruner, "Ludwig," 478, for Bavarian reports on this Austrian proposal.

29. Metternich to Münch, 30 September 1830, HHSA, Deutsche Akten, Fasc. 58; Metternich to Trauttmansdorff, 28 September 1830, cited by Droysen, "Preussischen Politik," 45–46; Blomberg to King William, 3 October 1830, WHSA, E 70, Bü. 45.

30. That this delay was caused in part by the long absence of instructions for the delegates from Bavaria and Württemberg is noted by Droysen, "Preussischen Politik," 52.

31. Baack, *Bernstorff*, 232–33.

32. See n. 44 of Chapter 2.

33. Ludwig Dehio, "Wittgenstein und das letzte Jahrzehnt Friedrich Wilhelms III.," *Forschungen zur brandenburgischen und preussischen Geschichte*, 35 (1923): 215–19; C. Spielmann, "Regierungspräsident Karl von Ibell über die preussische Politik in den Jahren 1830 und 1831," *Annalen des Vereins für Nassauische Altertumskunde und Geschichtsforschung*, 28 (1896): 66–76; Treitschke, *Deutsche Geschichte*, 4: 188.

34. Memorandum enclosed with Bernstorff to Maltzahn, 30 September 1830, ZStM, Preussische Gesandtschaften, Rep. 81, Wien I, Nr. 142. See also Baack, *Bernstorff*, 173–77.

35. Leopold Fr.[iedrich] Ilse, *Die Politik der beiden Grossmächte und der Bundesversammlung in der kurhessischen Verfassungsfrage vom Jahre 1830 bis 1860* (Berlin, 1861), 7.

36. Some of the chief Prussian and South German reservations are highlighted in Viktor Bibl, *Metternich in neuer Beleuchtung* (Vienna, 1928), 105–9.

37. Bernstorff's instructions to Nagler in this regard are discussed in Baack, *Bernstorff*, 232–33.

38. Metternich to Münch, 13 October 1830, HHSA, Deutsche Akten, Fasc. 58.

39. The Bavarian minister in Berlin reported that this was the view of the Prussian ministry. See Luxburg's report, 3 October 1830, BGSA, MA 2608.

40. Metternich to Münch, 3 October 1830, HHSA, Deutsche Akten, Fasc. 58.

41. Münch to Metternich, 29 October 1830, ibid. This report is discussed in Bibl, *Metternich in neuer Beleuchtung*, 109–10. The new federal laws enacted on 21 October 1830 (PDB, 1830, 34. Sitzung, § 258, 1124–25) can be found in Huber, ed., *Dokumente*, 1: 117–19.

42. Münch to Metternich, 29 October 1830, HHSA, Deutsche Akten, Fasc. 58.

43. PDB, 1830, 32. Sitzung (14 October 1830) § 248, 1053, 1056; and 34. Sitzung (21 October 1830) § 258, 1123. See also Baack, *Bernstorff*, 233.

44. Stern, *Geschichte Europas*, 4: 308; Baack; *Bernstorff*, 233.

45. Spiegel to Metternich, 15 October 1830, BOG, 2: 280–81. Also noted by Baack, *Bernstorff*, 234.

46. Gruner, "Ludwig," 506. See also Gollwitzer, *Ludwig I*, 303, which notes

the continuity of King Ludwig's feelings since his days as a crown prince during the Carlsbad Conferences of 1819.

47. Werner, *Bavaria in the German Confederation*, 102.

48. Huber, *Deutsche Verfassungsgeschichte*, 2: 65; Werner, *Bavaria in the German Confederation*, 94.

49. Münch to Metternich, 17 October 1830, HHSA, Deutsche Akten, Fasc. 58.

50. Münch to Metternich, 30 September 1830, *ibid.*; PDB, 1830, 29. Sitzung (30 September 1830), § 227, 991–99.

51. PDB, 1830, 30. Sitzung (1 October 1830), § 233, 1013–14; Droysen, "Preussischen Politik," 42–43. See also Werner, *Bavaria and the German Confederation*, 95.

52. Declarations by the delegates from Nassau and Baden on 7 October 1830, PDB, 1830, 31. Sitzung, § 238, 1022–23; Beroldingen to Schmitz-Grollenburg, 5 October 1830, WHSA, E 75, Bü. 172; Trauttmansdorff to Metternich, 7 October 1830, HHSA, Deutsche Akten, Fasc. 58. See Werner, *Bavaria in the German Confederation*, 95–97, for background on the Bavarian position.

53. Report of the Baden minister in Munich, 5 October 1830, excerpted in Berstett to Blittersdorff, 8 October 1830, BGLA 49/488; and Spiegel to Metternich, 7 October 1830, BOG, 2: 280. Regarding warnings of Bavarian isolation, see Gruner, "Ludwig," 482.

54. Copies of the instructions of the Bavarian Ministry of State to the Bavarian ministers, and specifically to Lerchenfeld at Frankfurt, 6 October 1830, WHSA, E 75, Bü. 172; report of the minister of Baden in Munich, excerpted in Berstett to Blittersdorff, 8 October 1830, BGLA 49/488; Spiegel to Metternich, 25 October 1830, 2: 287. See also Gruner, "Ludwig," 480–81.

55. PDB, 1830, 31. Sitzung (7 October 1830), § 238, 1028–31.

56. Ibid., 32. Sitzung (13 October 1830), § 249, 1066–67.

57. Ibid., 34. Sitzung (21 October 1830), § 259, 1025–26.

58. Metternich to Münch, 13 October 1830, HHSA, Deutsche Akten, Fasc. 58. See also Bibl, *Metternich in neuer Beleuchtung*, 110.

59. Metternich to Emperor Francis (Vortrag), 21 September 1830, HHSA, Staatskanzlei, Acta Secreta, Fasc. 3. A note by Armansperg on Bray's report of 26 September 1830 indicated his anger with the similarity of the views held by Bray and Metternich. Armansperg felt that they both were seeing ghosts and were trying to frighten others, too. See Bray's report, 26 September 1830, BGSA, MA 2403.

60. The foreign minister of Baden learned that Bray said the Austrian government was worried by a remark made by Baden's federal representative, Friedrich von Blittersdorff, that the South German kingdoms intended to pursue their own course and maintain their neutrality. Blittersdorff denied saying any such thing, and Berstett promptly communicated this to Berlin and Munich. See Berstett to Blittersdorff, 26 October 1830; Blittersdorff to Berstett, 27 October 1830; Berstett to Blittersdorff, 29 October 1830, BGLA 49/488.

61. Metternich's explanation to Spiegel, 9 November 1830, BOG, 2: 289.

62. Bray's report, 26 September 1830, and the Austrian memorandum, "Points pour Mr. le Comte de Bray," n.d., BGSA, MA 2403.

63. The Austrian memorandum, "Points pour Mr. le Comte de Bray," n.d., ibid.

64. Copy of a report to the King of Württemberg from Schmitz-Grollenburg, 26 October 1830, WHSA, E 75, Bü. 172; Bibl, *Metternich in neuer Beleuchtung*, 112.

65. Armansperg to King Ludwig (Vortrag), 13 October 1830, BGSA, MA 2403.

66. Bray to Metternich, 22 October 1830, BOG, 2: 282–83.

67. Instructions for Bray in Vienna, 24 October 1830, and a copy of King Ludwig's note to Emperor Francis, 24 October 1830, BGSA, MA 2403.

68. Schmitz-Grollenburg to King William, 26 October 1830, WHSA, E 75, Bü. 172; and a copy of a letter, Armansperg to Luxburg in Berlin, 29 October 1830, BGSA, MA 2403.

69. Note exchange between Armansperg and King Ludwig, 24 and 25 October 1830, BGSA, MA 2403.

70. This is what the French minister in Munich learned as a result of his conversations with Armansperg. See Rumigny to Molé, 23 August, 2, 16 October, and 4 November 1830, BFG, 2: 279–280, 299, 306.

71. Luxburg's report, 22 October 1830, BGSA, MA 2608.

72. Huber, *Deutsche Verfassungsgeschichte*, 1: 117–18. The Prussian position is discussed in Hoffman, *Preussen und die Julimonarchie*, 28–30. As early as 28 August the King of the Netherlands had asked for Prussian military support. See Baack, *Bernstorff*, 177–94.

73. Rumigny to Molé, 4 November 1830; Rumigny to Sebastiani, 24 November 1830, BFG, 2: 306, 312.

74. Burg, "Französische Politik," 26–27. See also Gollwitzer, *Ludwig I*, 436.

75. Böck, *Wrede*, 146–47. See also Baack, *Bernstorff*, 265–66.

76. Droysen, "Preussischen Politik," 51–52. For a review of Prussian military interests at this time, see Baack, *Bernstorff*, chap. 9: "Prussia and the Federal Military System."

77. Schönburg to Metternich, 1 November 1830; and Metternich to Schönburg, 9 November 1830, HHSA, Württemberg, Fasc. 41.

78. The Russian questioning in Munich was reported by Rumigny to Sebastiani, 30 November 1830, BFG, 2: 314–16. A similar occurrence in Stuttgart was reported by Fahnenberg to Grand Duke Leopold, 29 November 1830, BGLA 48/1874.

79. Rumigny to Sebastiani, 30 November, BFG, 2: 314–16.

80. Rumigny to Molé, 4 November 1830, ibid., 306.

81. Instructions to Schmitz-Grollenburg, 30 November 1830, WHSA, E 9, Bü. 25, No. 8. In this dispatch Schmitz was informed that he and Armansperg would be told the contents of the communication later. Rumors of supposed armed neutrality plans of the South German states were denied. It was not until 6 December that Schmitz was sent a copy of the king's memorandum. Finally on 19 December he was allowed to show this secret material to Armansperg. This later correspondence can also be found in WHSA, E 9, Bü. 25, No. 8. By 3 December 1830, the French already knew of the King of Württemberg's initiative. See Burg, "Französische Politik," 20.

82. Fahnenberg to Grand Duke Leopold, 29 November 1830, BGLA 48/1874. Fahnenberg later told Leopold that Armansperg had told him all of this. See Fahnenberg to Leopold, 10 December 1830, ibid.

83. The material in this and the next paragraph is from King William's memorandum, "Betrachtungen über die politisch-militärische Stellung von Süddeutschland," November 1830, WHSA, E 9, Bü. 25, No. 8.

84. Fahnenberg to Grand Duke Leopold, 8 December 1830, BGLA, 48/1874. As was noted in n. 82, Fahnenberg got his information from Armansperg. Armansperg, as has been said before, was in on King William's proposals and knew the contents of the correspondance between the two South German kings despite his own king's secrecy. Regarding Ludwig's persistent interest in a

territorial settlement with Baden concerning the Sponheim Question, even as a precondition to a South German military agreement, see Gollwitzer, *Ludwig I*, 436.

85. Fahnenberg to Grand Duke Leopold, 29 November and 5, 8, 10 December 1830, ibid. On 10 December Fahnenberg reported to Leopold that the reason why he had written directly to him, rather than corresponding through his foreign minister, Berstett, was that he had given his word to Armansperg that he would not report to Berstett regarding the plans for the erection of a South German military union. When King William was informed by Schmitz that Armansperg talked to Fahnenberg about the alliance proposals, the king feared that Berstett and, then through him, Metternich would learn of these proposals. William insisted that Württemberg and Bavaria first work out an agreement on a system before including Baden. See Schmitz to King William, 23 December 1830, WHSA, E 9, Bü. 25, No. 8.

86. Fahnenberg reported this Bavarian view to Leopold in his dispatch of 8 December 1830, BGLA 48/1874.

87. Grand Duke Leopold to Fahnenberg, 15 December 1830, ibid.

88. Fahnenberg to Grand Duke Leopold, 23 December 1830, ibid. The French minister in Munich reported that Armansperg elaborated a similar plan to him. See Rumigny to Sebastiani, 22 December 1830, BFG, 2: 334.

89. Schmitz-Grollenburg to King William, 23 December 1830, WHSA, E 9, Bü. 25, No. 8.

90. Instructions for Schmitz-Grollenburg, 13 December 1830, ibid.

91. Cotta to Schmitz-Grollenburg, 29 January 1831, WHSA, E 75, Bü. 173.

Chapter 4. South German, Prussian, and Austrian Options, 1831

1. Notation for December 1830 in Carl Friedrich Freiherr Kübeck von Kübau, *Tagebücher des Carl Friedrich Freiherrn Kübeck von Kübau*, ed. Max Freiherr von Kübeck, 2 vols. (Vienna, 1909), 1, Pt. 2, 302.

2. Metternich to Esterhazy, 21 October 1830, NP, 5: 47–48; notation on 28 November 1830 in Friedrich von Gentz, *Tagebücher von Friedrich von Gentz (1829–1831)*, ed. August Fournier and Arnold Winkler (Vienna, 1920), 236, 386; Srbik, *Metternich*, 1: 658.

3. Baack, *Bernstorff*, 191–92.

4. Droysen, "Preussischen Politik," 50–52, 57–58; Franz Richter, *Das europäische Politik und der revolutionäre Krisis von 1830 bis 1832* (Forschungen zur neueren und neuesten Geschichte, no. 2; Leipzig, 1933), 167; Trauttmansdorff to Metternich, 6 January 6 1831, HHSA, Preussen, Fasc. 139ᵃ.

5. Droysen, "Preussichen Politik," 58; Baack, *Bernstorff*, 266.

6. Droysen, "Preussichen Politik," 58–60. See also Baack, *Bernstorff*, 266–67.

7. Droysen, "Preussischen Politik," 61.

8. Ibid., 68. Baack, *Bernstorff*, 268, suggests that the evidence is not really clear whether Metternich meant to secure Prussian support or merely to say that because of Austrian problems in Italy she would not be able to assist Prussia in Belgium. Röder, however, suggested that the implication was that of a quid pro quo: "As inexact and as general as the insinuations were expressed,

nevertheless, they may have had the intention of suggesting that Austria would handle Belgian affairs in a way similar to what Prussia might do in Italian affairs. See Röder to King Frederick William, 11 February 1831, ZStA, 2.4.1., Abt. 1, Nr. 10067. (Note that this is the same source used by Baack. The *Signaturs* of the documents have just been changed by the archivists from AAI, Rep. 5, Nr. 592 to 2.4.1., Abt. 1. Nr. 10067 in the archives in Merseburg.)

9. Guichen, *La révolution de Juillet*, 249; Hillebrand, *Geschichte Frankreichs*, 1: 194.

10. Metternich to Apponyi, 15 February 1831, NP, 5: 149–54; Hillebrand, *Geschichte Frankreichs*, 1: 204; Guichen, *La révolution de Juillet*, 326; Droysen, "Preussischen Politik," 69. It should be remembered that Francis Charles, the son of Napoleon and Maria Louise, resided at Schönbrunn until his death in July 1832. See Guillaume Bertier de Sauvigny, *Metternich* (Paris, 1986), 428–29.

11. Princes Melanie Metternich's diary, 2 March 1831, NP, 5: 92.

12. Beroldingen informed his representative in Munich, Schmitz-Grollenburg, of his view and actions. See Beroldingen to Schmitz, 26 February 1831, WHSA, E 75, Bü. 173.

13. Spiegel to Metternich, 4 March 1831, BOG, 2: 307–8; Bibl, *Metternich in neuer Beleuchtung*, 121.

14. Eduard Wertheimer, "Erzherzog Karl und das Juli-Königtum," *Beilage zur Allgemeinen Zeitung* (Munich), nr. 126 (4 June 1902), 418.

15. Ibid., 418–19.

16. Trauttmansdorff to Metternich, 14 March 1831, HHSA, Preussen, Fasc. 139a. Regarding the rather "liberal" inclinations of General Rühle, see Baack, *Bernstorff*, 270.

17. Droysen, "Preussischen Politik," 71.

18. Ibid.

19. Ibid., 71–72. See also Baack, *Bernstorff*, 269, which uses Röder's reports.

20. Röder to King Frederick William, 24 April 1831, ZStA, 2.4.1., Abt. 1, Nr. 10067.

21. Droysen, "Preussischen Politik," 73–75.

22. Ibid., 74–75.

23. See Metternich to Werner, 29 August 1830, HHSA, Preussen, Fasc. 142.

24. See chapter 3, n. 89. Cotta also continued to work on King Ludwig with the idea of a Prussian-South German neutrality alliance. See Cotta to King Ludwig, 17 February 1831, printed in Peter Burg, *Der Wiener Kongress: Der Deutsche Bund im europäischen Staatensystem* (Munich, 1984), 154–59.

25. See chapter 3, n. 91.

26. Luxburg to Armansperg, 29 February 1831, BGSA, MA 24076.

27. Ancillon to Salviatti, 25 February 1831 (shared with the Württemberg ministry), WHSA, E 65–68, Verz. 57, Fasc. 162.

28. Rühle and Küster to King Frederick William III, 7 March 1831, BPG, 2: 193–96.

29. Fahnenberg to Jolly, 5, 7 March 1831, BGLA 48/1629.

30. Rumigny to Sebastiani, 10 March 1831, BFG, 2: 364; Fahnenberg to Jolly, 16 March 1831, BGLA 48/1629.

31. Rühle's memorandum of 13 March 1831, as shared by the Bavarian ministry with the Württemberg embassy in Munich, WHSA, E 65–68, Verz. 57, Fasc. 162.

32. Rumigny to Sebastiani, 15 March 1831, BFG, 2: 368.

33. Fahnenberg to Jolly, 23 March 1831, BGLA 48/1629; Rumigny to Sebastiani, 24 March 1831, BFG, 2: 377–78.

34. Armansperg explained this to his minister in Berlin, Luxburg, 28 March 1831, BGSA, MA 24076.

35. Armansperg to King Ludwig and Ludwig's reply, 27 and 28 March 1831, ibid.

36. Armansperg to Ling Ludwig, 27 March 1831, ibid. See also Baack, *Bernstorff*, 272, for Rühle's report of 28 March 1830 to King Frederick William.

37. Rühle to King Frederick William, 5 April 1831, cited by Baack, *Bernstorff*, 273.

38. Beroldingen to Schmitz, 30 March 1831, WHSA, E 75, Bü. 173; Blomberg to King William, 24 March 1831, WHSA, E 70, Bü. 46.

39. Blomberg to King William, 29 March 1831, WHSA, E 65–68, Verz. 57, Fasc. 162.

40. Rühle's memorandum for the foreign ministry of Württemberg, 4 April 1831, ibid.

41. Friedrich's report from Stuttgart, April 1831, BGLA 48/1629.

42. Proposed response to Rühle's memorandum of 4 April and King William's approval for this response, 7 April 1831, WHSA, E 65–68, Verz. 57, Fasc. 162.

43. See Rühle to King Frederick William, 17 and 18 April 1831, cited by Baack, *Bernstorff*, 273.

44. Fahnenberg's reports from Munich and Friedrich's reports from Stuttgart can be found in BGLA 48/1629.

45. Fahnenberg to Grand Duke Leopold, 29 March 1831, and Jolly to Fahnenberg, 2 April 1831, ibid.

46. That is the way the foreign minister of Württemberg evaluated it. See Beroldingen to Schmitz, 21 April 1831, WHSA, E 75, Bü. 173.

47. Baden's reply to Rühle, 16 April 1831, BGLA 48/1629; copy of Baden's reply to Rühle of 16 April 1831, WHSA, E 65–68, Verz. 57, Fasc. 162. Instructions to Fahnenberg in Munich, 20 April 1831, explained the high points of the memorandum. See BGLA 48/1629.

48. Baack, *Bernstorff*, 273.

49. Rühle's final report of 14 May 1831, as reported in Droysen, "Preussischen Politik," 80–81. See also Baack, *Bernstorff*, 274.

50. Baack, *Bernstorff*, 274–75, insightfully points out that this alternative, if it had been successful, would probably have represented more a change in traditional alliance politics than a direct route to a Prussian-ruled *Kleindeutschland*.

51. Richter, *Das europäische Problem*, 169.

52. Kurt M. Hoffmann, *Preussen und die Julimonarchie 1830–1834* (Historische Studien, no. 288; Berlin, 1936), 57–64.

53. Heinrich Ritter von Srbik, *Deutsche Einheit*, 4 vols. (Vienna, 1935), 1: 274.

54. Metternich made overtures to Prussia for the formation of a continental entente in January, March, and August 1831. See Droysen, "Preussischen Politik," 91–92, 105–6.

55. Metternich to Emperor Francis (Vortrag), 22 March 1831, HHSA, Acta Secreta, Fasc. 4.

56. See nn. 13 and 16.

57. Bernstorff's declining health at this time is noted by Baack, *Bernstorff*, 277.

58. Trauttmansdorff mentioned Metternich's instructions of 2 April in his report of 13 April 1831, HHSA, Preussen, Fasc. 139a.

59. Trauttmansdorff to Metternich, 13 April 1831, ibid.
60. Blomberg to King William, 6, 8, and 11 April 1831, WHSA, E 70, Bü. 46.
61. Buol to Metternich, 25 March 1831, HHSA, Baden, Fasc. 37.
62. Metternich to Münch, 5 May 1831, HHSA, Deutsche Akten, Fasc. 59.
63. Metternich to Schönburg, 21 April 1831, HHSA, Württemberg, Fasc. 42.
64. Metternich's personal offensive against Armansperg in 1831 and against Bernstorff in 1832 will be detailed further subsequently.
65. Metternich to Schönburg, 21 April 1831, HHSA, Württemberg, Fasc. 42.
66. Memorandum of 20 April 1831, enclosed with Metternich's instructions for Schönburg, ibid.
67. Military memorandum, n.d., enclosed with Metternich's instructions for Schönburg, ibid.
68. Spiegel to Metternich, 30 April 1831, BOG, 2: 319.
69. King Ludwig to Wrede, 30 April 1831, BGSA, MA 24076.
70. Droysen, "Preussischen Politik," 80.
71. Bangold to Wrede, 11 June 1831, BGSA, MA 24076; Wrede's letter of thanks to King William, 13 June 1831, WHSA, E 9, Kabinettsakten III, Bü. 25, Nr. 9; Böck, Wrede, 148.
72. Rühle finally assured Wrede that Prussia would agree to the South German proposals. See Rühle to Wrede, 26 July 1831, BGSA, MA 24076. Wrede wrote several times before this happened. See Rühle to Wrede, 12 June 1831, and Bangold to Wrede, 25 June 1831, ibid.; Fahnenberg to Jolly, 22 June, 2, 8, July, and 5 August 1831, BGLA 48/1629.
73. Two communications from Trauttmansdorff to Metternich, 5 May 1831, HHSA, Preussen, Fasc. 139ᵃ.
74. Schönburg to Metternich, 9 May 1831, HHSA, Deutsche Akten, Fasc. 59.
75. Buol to Metternich, 25 March 1831, HHSA, Baden, Fasc. 37; Spiegel to Metternich, 19 May 1831, BOG, 2: 323–27.
76. Treitschke, Deutsche Geschichte, 4: 149.
77. Ibid., 137.
78. Ibid., 120–21.
79. Notations on 20, 26 and 31 May 1831, in Gentz, Tagebücher, 289–92; Blomberg to King William, 10, 11, 12, 16, and 22 May 1831, WHSA, E 70, Bü. 46; Gasser to King Ludwig, 14 May 1831, BGSA, MA 2404.
80. Blomberg to King William, 31 May 1831, WHSA, E 7, Bü. 46.
81. Regarding Eichhorn's promotion, on 16 May 1831, as director of the Second Division (German affairs) of the Prussian foreign ministry, see Baack, Bernstorff, 278.
82. Münch to Metternich, 2 July 1831, HHSA, Frankfurt, Fasc. 56.
83. Maltzahn's report of 7 July 1831, cited by Droysen, "Preussischen Politik," 94.
84. Metternich to Wittgenstein, 5 August 1831, HHSA, Preussen, Fasc. 142. It is also cited in Bibl, Metternich in neuer Beleuchtung, 134.
85. Metternich explained his views and strategy to Münch in a dispatch of 25 August 1831, HHSA, Frankfurt, Fasc. 56.
86. Ibid.
87. Metternich to Werner, 31 July 1831, HHSA, Preussen, Fasc. 142. The Werner mission is discussed and several of Metternich's memoranda cited by Bibl, Metternich in neuer Beleuchtung, 130–34. See also Baack, Bernstorff, 280–81.
88. Metternich to Werner, 31 July and 5 August 1831, HHSA, Preussen, Fasc. 142.

89. Werner to Metternich, 12 August 1831, ibid. Baack, *Bernstorff*, 282, quotes a letter from Wittgenstein to Metternich of 12 August 1831, which said that now "all ministerial intrigue shall be prevented, at least at the moment when your dispatches arrive."

Chapter 5. Undermining the Opposition, 1831–1832

1. Droysen, "Preussischen Politik," 100–101; Baack, *Bernstorff*, 282–83.

2. Bernstorff to Küster, the political circular, 15 August 1831, BGSA, MA 24076.

3. Bernstorff to Küster, the military circular, 15 August 1831, ibid. Baack, *Bernstorff*, 283, only mentions this military note.

4. The minister of Baden in Munich reported the cautious attitude of the Bavarian foreign minister. See Fahnenberg to Türckheim, 26 August and 9 September 1831, BGLA 48/1629. Wrede's proposals for a Bavarian reply, 31 August 1831, and Ludwig's approval, 3 September 1831, BGSA, MA 24076; notes on a Württemberg reply to the Prussian circular and Beroldingen to Linden, 16 September 1831, WHSA, E 65–68, Verz. 57, Fasc. 162; Baden's reply: Türckheim to Otterstedt, 7 September 1831, BGLA 48/1629.

5. Bernstorff to Maltzahn, 21 August 1831, HHSA, Deutsche Akten, Fasc. 59; Metternich to Werner, 29 August 1831, HHSA, Preussen, Fasc. 142. It should be noted that Metternich had already been angered by Eichhorn's influence on Bernstorff and thus the Rühle mission. He wrote to Wittgenstein complaining that Eichhorn was blinded by liberal and doctrinaire views. See Metternich to Wittgenstein, 5 August 1831, quoted in Hans Branig, *Fürst Wittgenstein: Ein preussischer Staatsmann der Restaurationszeit* (Veröffentlichungen aus den Archiven Preussischer Kulturbesitz, Band 17; Cologne, 1981), 160.

6. Tettenborn to Türckheim, 16 September 1831, BGLA 48/1629.

7. Metternich to Trauttmansdorff, 5 September 1831, HHSA, Deutsche Akten, Fasc. 59.

8. Metternich to Clam, 11 September 1831, HHSA, Preussen, Fasc. 142.

9. Droysen, "Preussischen Politik," 105–6. Bernstorff explained that his 26 September dispatch to Maltzahn was in response to the Austrian overture of 5 September. See Bernstorff to Maltzahn, 26 September 1831, copy enclosed with Bernstorff to Nagler, 27 April 1832, ZStA, Gesandtschaft am deutschen Bundestag, Rep. 75A, Nr. 457.

10. See Bernstorff to Maltzahn, 26 September 1831, ibid. Mentioned and explained in Baack, *Bernstorff*, 244.

11. See Baack, *Bernstorff*, 245.

12. Metternich to Schönburg, 8 September 1831, HHSA, Württemberg, Fasc. 42.

13. Ibid.

14. Metternich to Wrede, 8 September 1831, in Bibl, *Metternich in neuer Beleuchtung*, 242–43.

15. Schönburg to Metternich, 18 September 1831, and an enclosed letter and memorandum from King William, HHSA, Württemberg, Fasc. 42.

16. Wrede to Metternich, 23 September 1831, in Bibl, *Metternich in neuer Beleuchtung*, 245–46.

17. Blomberg's report, 23 September 1831, WHSA, E 70, Bü. 46.

18. Metternich to Wrede, 10 October 1831, in Bibl, *Metternich in neuer Beleuchtung*, 248–50.

19. Werner to Metternich, 25 September 1831, and the enclosures: Duke Carl of Mecklenburg to Wittgenstein, n.d., and Frederick William to Wittgenstein, 2 September 1831, HHSA, Preussen, Fasc. 142; Droysen, "Preussischen Politik," 108. See also Baack, *Bernstorff*, 288–89.

20. Frankenberg to Türckheim, 22 September 1831, and Fahnenberg to Türckheim, 27 September 1831, BGLA 48/1629. Frankenberg, the chargé d'affaires of Baden in Berlin, was reporting his own views. Fahnenberg, the envoy of Baden in Munich, reported the views of the Bavarian envoy in Berlin.

21. Metternich to Clam, 9 October 1831 (reserved dispatch), and enclosures, HHSA, Preussen, Fasc. 142; Droysen, "Preussischen Politik," 110.

22. Metternich to Clam, 9 October 1831 (reserved dispatch), HHSA, Preussen, Fasc. 142. See also Baack, *Bernstorff*, 290. Jena, where Napoleon defeated the Prussians in 1806, lies in the valley of the Saale River.

23. Diary notation of 30 October 1831, in Anton Franz Graf Prokesch von Osten, *Aus den Tagebücher des Grafen Prokesch von Osten, 1830–1834*, ed. Anton Graf Prokesch von Osten (Vienna, 1909), 107.

24. Private letter of Metternich to Schönburg, 24 October 1831, HHSA, Württemberg, Fasc. 42.

25. Metternich to Schönburg, 24 October 1831, ibid.

26. Ibid.

27. This material is from the memorandum enclosed with Metternich's dispatch to Schönburg of 24 October 1831, ibid.

28. See n. 27.

29. Information in this and the next paragraph is from Metternich to Wrede, 24 October 1831, in Bibl, *Metternich in neuer Beleuchtung*, 253–56. Refer also to Wrede to Metternich, 13 October 1831, ibid., 250–52.

30. Metternich's secret dispatch to Wrede, 24 October 1831, ibid., 256–58.

31. See n. 30.

32. Bibl, *Metternich in neuer Beleuchtung*, 143. See also Baack, *Bernstorff*, 245–46.

33. Diary notation of 29 October 1831, in Prokesch, *Tagebücher*, 106; editorial note regarding Gentz's diary entry of 29 October 1831, in Gentz, *Tagebücher*, 328, 404.

34. Metternich's private letter to Schönburg, 2 November 1831, HHSA, Württemberg, Fasc. 42.

35. Diary notation of 13 November 1831, in Gentz, *Tagebücher*, 331.

36. Instructions for Maltzahn in Vienna, 6 November 1831, copy with Bernstorff to Nagler, 27 April 1831, ZStA, Gesandtschaft am deutschen Bundestag, Rep. 75A, Nr. 457.

37. Bernstorff memorandum, 6 November 1831, ibid. Explained in Baack, *Bernstorff*, 246.

38. See n. 37.

39. Regarding the earlier suppression of the published Federal Diet protocols, see chapter 1, n. 63.

40. Bernstorff memorandum, 6 November 1831, ZStA, Rep. 75A, Nr. 457; Baack, *Bernstorff*, 247–48.

41. Trauttmansdorff to Metternich, 8 November 1831, HHSA, Deutsche Akten, Fasc. 61.

42. A second dispatch from Trauttmansdorff to Metternich, 8 November 1831, ibid.

43. Metternich explained his strategy to his envoys in Frankfurt and Stuttgart. See Metternich to Münch, 15 November 1831, HHSA, Frankfurt, Fasc. 56; Metternich to Schönburg, 15 November 1831, HHSA, Württemberg, Fasc. 42.

44. Wrede and Schönburg informed Metternich that the envoys from Bavaria and Württemberg were empowered to participate in the secret talks. See Wrede to Metternich, 2 November 1831, in Bibl, *Metternich in neuer Beleuchtung*, 262–63; Schönburg to Metternich, 4 November 1831, HHSA, Württemberg, Fasc. 42.

45. Metternich to Schönburg, 15 November 1831, and Schönburg to Metternich, 25 November 1831, HHSA, Württemberg, Fasc. 42; Metternich to Wrede, 15 November 1831, and editor's citation of Metternich to Spiegel, 15 November 1831, in Bibl, *Metternich in neuer Beleuchtung*, 268–270, 155; Metternich to Spiegel, 15 November 1831, BOG, 2: 372–73.

46. Memorandum enclosed with Metternich's dispatch to Schönburg, 15 November 1831, HHSA, Württemberg, Fasc. 42.

47. Ibid.

48. Metternich to Schönburg, 30 October 1831, and Schönburg to Metternich, 4–11 and 24 November 1831, ibid.; Wrede to Metternich, 18 November 1831, and the editor's citations from Metternich to Spiegel, 9 and 30 November 1831, in Bibl, *Metternich in neuer Beleuchtung*, 270–73, 267, 277–78; Metternich to Spiegel, 15 November 1831, BOG, 2: 372–73.

49. Clam to Metternich, 20 November 1831, HHSA, Preussen, Fasc. 142. See also Baack, *Bernstorff*, 289–92.

50. Diary notation of 20 November 1831, in Prokesch, *Tagebücher*, 114.

51. Metternich to Clam, 21 November 1831, HHSA, Preussen, Fasc. 142.

52. Ibid. This is basically the thesis sentence from Billinger, "The War Scare of 1831."

53. Droysen, "Preussischen Politik," 113–18. See also Baack, *Bernstorff*, 292.

54. Droysen, "Preussischen Politik," 110; Bibl, *Metternich in neuer Beleuchtung*, 150–51; Baack, *Bernstorff*, 290–91.

55. Hoffmann, *Preussen und die Julimonarchie*, 85–91.

56. Droysen, "Preussischen Politik," 116.

57. Richter, *Das europäische Problem*, 181; Baack, *Bernstorff*, 292–93.

58. Spiegel to Metternich, 21 November 1831, BOG, 2: 376–77.

59. Wrede to Metternich, 24 November 1831, in Bibl, *Metternich in neuer Beleuchtung*, 276.

60. Schönburg to Metternich, 25 and 30 November 1831, HHSA, Württemberg, Fasc. 42.

61. Metternich to Wrede, 1 December 1831, in Bibl, *Metternich in neuer Beleuchtung*, 281–82. Prokesch's diary notation of 25 December 1831, states that a courier from Berlin brought Prussian agreement to negotiations with Munich and Stuttgart regarding German affairs. See Prokesch, *Tagebücher*, 122. Bibl, *Metternich in neuer Beleuchtung*, 158, says the courier arrived on 26 December.

62. Regarding editing, see Prokesch's diary notation of 30 December 1831, Prokesch, *Tagebücher*, 124. Explained by Baack, *Bernstorff*, 248.

63. Bibl, *Metternich in neuer Beleuchtung*, 157, cites Trauttmansdorff's report of 15 December 1831.

64. See Baack, *Bernstorff*, 248.

Chapter 6. Fear, Finesse, and Federal Duties, 1832

1. Srbik, *Metternich*, 1: 676. For more on Metternich and Ancona, see Reinerman, *Austria and the Papacy*, 2: 109–128.

2. Spiegel to Metternich, 2 January 1832, BOG, 2: 387. Metternich had been trying indirectly to influence Ludwig to get rid of Armansperg since the spring of 1831. See Metternich to Wrede, 16 April 1831, and 24 October 1831, Bibl, *Metternich in neuer Beleuchtung*, 221–23, 253–56; Böck, *Wrede*, 168–69. Wrede told Metternich of Ludwig's plans for a change of ministry as early as 2 November. See Wrede to Metternich, 2 November 1831, in Bibl, *Metternich in neuer Beleuchtung*, 262. Regarding Ludwig's increasing alienation from Armansperg since 1830, see Gollwitzer, *Ludwig I*, 454, 456.

3. Schönburg to Metternich, 11 January 1832, HHSA, Württemberg, Fasc. 43; Treitschke, *Deutsche Geschichte*, 4: 271.

4. Metternich to Spiegel, 21 February 1832, BOG, 2: 395–98; Metternich to Wrede, 21 February in Bibl, *Metternich in neuer Beleuchtung*, 287–88.

5. Stern, *Geschichte Europas*, 4: 309–10; Treitschke, *Deutsche Geschichte*, 4: 269. According to Treitschke, the Eichhorn censorship plan was sent to the South German courts. It called for censorship to be exercised only on political newspapers. Even this was to be done by an independent board made up of academicians and state officials. See also Baack, *Bernstorff*, 316–20. For Bernstorff's earlier overture to Metternich, see chapter 5, n. 40.

6. Metternich to Clam, 27 February 1832, HHSA, Preussen, Fasc. 146ª; Trauttmansdorff to Metternich, 5 March 1832, HHSA, Preussen, Fasc. 143ª; Bibl, *Metternich in neuer Beleuchtung*, 164.

7. Wilhelm Gauer, "Badische Staatsräson und Frühliberalismus um die Juliwende," *Zeitschrift für Geschichte des Oberrheins*, 84 (1932): 361–63; Hippel, *Blittersdorff*, 68–69.

8. Hippel, *Blittersdorff*, 70; PDB, 1832, 6. Sitzung (9 February 1832), § 38, 179–80.

9. PDB, 1832, 7. Sitzung (20 February 1832), § 55, 228–44.

10. The Prussian federal delegate noted that these papers outdid all others in preaching insurrection. He proposed, therefore, that the Diet consider what should be done to stop this. See ibid., § 48, 219–20. Samples from the articles of these papers are given in the PDB, too. See ibid., 9. Sitzung (2 March 1832), § 67, 309–83.

11. Werner, *Bavaria and the German Confederation*, 113–15.

12. Handel to Metternich, 22 February 1832, HHSA, Frankfurt, Fasc. 58; Buol to Metternich, 2 March 1832, HHSA, Baden, Fasc. 38ᵇ.

13. Regarding the question of the relationship between federal and state legislation, see Huber, *Deutsche Verfassungsgeschichte*, 1: 601–2.

14. Metternich to Schönburg, 25 February 1832, HHSA, Württemberg, Fasc. 43. See also Gruner, "Ludwig," 495.

15. PDB, 1832, 9. Sitzung (2 March 1832), § 67, 385–88.

16. Ibid., 10. Sitzung (8 March 1832), § 80, 415.

17. See Werner, *Bavaria and the German Confederation*, 114, and Gruner, "Ludwig," 496.

18. Schönburg to Metternich, 8, 13, and 14 March 1832, BOG, 2: 404, 408–11, 420–21. See also Werner, *Bavaria and the German Confederation*, 116–18, for the Schönburg visit.

19. Schönburg to Metternich, 18 March 1832, BOG, 2: 429–33.
20. Metternich to Wrede, 26 March 1832, in Bibl, *Metternich in neuer Beleuchtung*, 295–97.
21. Metternich to Schönburg, 26 March 1832, HHSA, Württemberg, Fasc. 43.
22. Böck, *Wrede*, 139–40; Werner, *Bavaria and the German Confederation*, 120. For background, see Gruner, "Ludwig," 497–500.
23. PDB, 1832, 12. Sitzung (12 April 1832), § 106, 481. Wrede explained the Bavarian declaration to Metternich before it was given at Frankfurt. See Wrede to Metternich, 1 April 1832, in Bibl, *Metternich in neuer Beleuchtung*, 299.
24. Hippel, *Blittersdorff*, 71–72.
25. PDB, 1832, 14. Sitzung (26 April 1832), § 118 and § 119, 528–38. Werner, *Bavaria and the German Confederation*, 122, explains the seemingly contradictory Bavarian position by noting that Baden had unconditionally accepted the earlier Carlsbad Decrees while Bavaria had accepted them with reservations designed to protect her sovereignty.
26. The protocols and agreements of each state of the talks can be found in HHSA, Deutsche Akten, Fasc. 61.
27. For example, see Metternich's complaint to Wrede of 21 February 1832, in Bibl, *Metternich in neuer Beleuchtung*, 288, and Gise's call for clarification of 16 March 1832, copy in HHSA, Deutsche Akten, Fasc. 62.
28. See Metternich to Clam, 27 February 1832, HHSA, Preussen, Fasc. 146[a]; Werner to Metternich, 4 February 1832, and Trauttmansdorff to Metternich, 5 and 15 March 1832, HHSA, Preussen, Fasc. 143[a].
29. Protocol of 4 April 1832 and memorandum of 12 April 1832, HHSA, Deutsche Akten, Fasc. 61. Regarding the Bavarian desire to limit the federal commission to six years, see Metternich to Spiegel, 26 March 1832, HHSA, Deutsche Akten, Fasc. 62. This business is also noted in Bibl, *Metternich in neuer Beleuchtung*, 291.
30. Copy of the 12 April 1832 memorandum, HHSA, Deutsche Akten, Fasc. 62. Its text is printed in NP, 5: 347–57.
31. Metternich to Buol, 21 February 1832, HHSA, Deutsche Akten, Fasc. 62; Fahnenberg's reports of 2 January and 18 February 1832: the first is copied in its entirety, the second summarized, in Türckheim's 24 February digest of recent diplomatic correspondence for Grand Duke Leopold., BGLA 48/1854.
32. See Metternich to Buol, 21 February 1832, HHSA, Deutsche Akten, Fasc. 62; Buol to Metternich, 2 March 1832, HHSA, Baden, Fasc. 38[b].
33. Schönburg to Metternich, 18 April 1832, HHSA, Württemberg, Fasc. 43.
34. Buol to Metternich, 27 April 1832, HHSA, Baden, Fasc. 38[b].
35. Spiegel to Metternich, 3 May 1832, HHSA, Deutsche Akten, Fasc. 61; Bibl, *Metternich in neuer Beleuchtung*, 169. King William informed the Austrian mininster in Stuttgart that Bavaria had contacted his government in the hope that it would support her stand. See Schönburg to Metternich, 10 May 1832, HHSA, Württemberg, Fasc. 43.
36. Metternich to Wrede, 25 March 1832, and Wrede to Metternich, 1 April 1832, in Bibl, *Metternich in neuer Beleuchtung*, 293, 301.
37. Bray to King Ludwig, 24 April 1832, BGSA, Ma 2404; Böck, *Wrede*, 141–43.
38. Bibl, *Metternich in neuer Beleuchtung*, 161.
39. Metternich to Wrede, 16 May 1832, ibid., 310.
40. Buol to Metternich, 2 March 1832, HHSA, Baden, Fasc. 38[b]. Early correspondence between the Baden ministry and Falkenstein regarding this project can be found in BGLA 48/2546.

41. Buol to Metternich, 26 April 1832, HHSA, Baden, Fasc. 38[b]. The Baden ministry explained to its chargé in Berlin the original reason and the later necessity for sending Falkenstein to Vienna. See instructions to Frankenberg, 30 April 1832, BGLA 48/2546.

42. Falkenstein's reports of 7 and 11 May 1832, BGLA 48/2546.

43. These reports can be found in HHSA, Deutsche Akten, Fasc. 62.

44. Buol to Metternich, 22 May 1832, HHSA, Baden, Fasc. 38[b].

45. Treitschke pointed this out, but many historians still cling to the mistaken view expressed by contemporary organs of public opinion. See Treitschke, *Deutsche Geschichte*, 4: 273.

46. Metternich to Wrede, 8 June 1832, HHSA, Deutsche Akten, Fasc. 62.

47. Veit Valentin, *Das Hambacher Nationalfest* (Berlin, 1932), 31, 60–62. For more on the Hambach and related festivals, see Burg, *Der Wiener Kongress*, 33–50. For further bibliography, see also Max Spindler, "Die Regierungszeit Ludwig I (1825–1848), *Bayerische Geschichte im 19. und 20. Jahrhundert, 1800–1970*, 2 part vol., (Munich, 1978) (Special ed. and unchanged repro. of Max Spindler, ed., *Handbuch der bayerischen Geschichte*, vol. 4: *Das neue Bayern. 1800–1970*, 2 part vol., Munich, 1974/75]), pt. 1, 182–86.

48. Buol to Metternich, 1, 6, and 7 June 1832, HHSA, Baden, Fasc. 38[b].

49. PDB, 1832, 19. Sitzung, III. Separat Protokoll (30 May 1832), § 1 and § 2, 779–780.

50. Handel to Metternich, 8 June 1832, HHSA, Deutsche Akten, Fasc. 62; PDB, 1832, 20. Sitzung, III. Separat Protokoll (7 June 1832), § 1, 795–98.

51. Metternich to Emperor Francis, 12 June 1832 (Vortrag), HHSA, Deutsche Akten, Fasc. 62.

52. This was done. On 24 June, Field Marshal Wrede with a command of more than 8,000 men moved into the Rheinkreis. See Spindler, ed., *Bayerische Geschichte*, 1: 184. For Wrede's role, see Helmut Renner, "Fürst Karl Philipp von Wrede," in Kurt Baumann, ed., *Das Hambacher Fest, 27. Mai 1832: Männer und Ideen* (Speyer, 1982 [1957], 318–22.

53. Metternich to Wrede, 8 June 1832, and Metternich to Gise, 8 June 1832, HHSA, Deutsche Akten, Fasc. 62; Metternich to Wrede, 8 and 16 June 1832, in Bibl, *Metternich in neuer Beleuchtung*, 326–30.

54. Metternich to Trauttmansdorff, 10 June 1832, in Valentin, *Hambacher Nationalfest*, 141.

55. See Metternich to Trauttmansdorff, 10 June 1832, and Metternich to Emperor Francis, 12 June 1832 (Vortrag), HHSA, Deutsche Akten, Fasc. 62.

56. Metternich to Münch, 17 June 1832, HHSA, Frankfurt, Fasc. 58.

57. Ibid.

58. Münch to Metternich, 22 June 1832, BOG, 2: 462–64; Münch to Metternich, 26 June 1832, HHSA, Deutsche Akten, Fasc. 62; Schönburg to Metternich, 27 June 1832, HHSA, Deutsche Akten, Fasc. 59. The military affairs mentioned here will be the subject of the next chapter.

59. Münch to Metternich, 29 June 1832, HHSA, Deutsche Akten, Fasc. 62.

60. Münch to Metternich, 29 June and 8 July 1832, ibid.; PDB, 1832, 22. Sitzung (28 June 1832), Öffentliches Protokoll, 852–64. The Six Articles are printed in Huber, ed., *Dokumente*, 1: 119.

61. A *Bogen* was sixteen pages. Twenty *Bogen* was thus 320 pages. See Huber, *Deutsche Verfassungsgeschichte*, 1: 743.

62. PDB, 1832, 24. Sitzung (5 July 1832), § 231, 942–53. The Ten Acts are also printed in Huber, ed., *Dokumente*, 1: 120.

63. Münch to Metternich, 6 July 1832, HHSA, Deutsche Akten, Fasc. 62. Metternich had already been informed in regard to these Bavarian efforts. See Handel to Metternich, 13 and 15 June 1832, HHSA, Frankfurt, Fasc. 58; Buol to Metternich, 21 June 1832, HHSA, Baden, Fasc. 38b.

64. Gauer, "Badische Staatsräson und Frühliberalismus," 366; Mortier to Perier, 7 March 1832, BFG, 3: 29–30; PDB, 1832, 24. Sitzung (5 July 1832), § 230, 940–41, and 25. Sitzung (12 July 1832), § 238, 959–61.

65. Gauer, "Badische Staatsräson and Frühliberalismus," 367; Hippel, *Blittersdorff*, 72–73; PDB, 1832, 28. Sitzung (31 July 1832), § 282, 1057–59.

66. Treitschke, *Deutsche Geschichte*, 4: 272–73; Kress to Metternich, 24 July 1832, BOG, 2: 474; Bibl, *Metternich in neuer Beleuchtung*, 175–77.

67. Weissenburg to Metternich, 21 July 1832, HHSA, Deutsche Akten, Fasc. 62; Bibl, *Metternich in neuer Beleuchtung*, 177. See Werner, *Bavaria and the German Confederation*, 129–30, for a discussion of federal versus state legislation issues.

68. Münch to Metternich, 21, 28 July and 4 August 1832, HHSA, Deutsche Akten, Fasc. 62; Buol to Metternich, 21 July and 20 August 1832, HHSA, Baden, Fasc. 38b; Huber, *Deutsche Verfassungsgeschichte* 2: 160–62; Bibl, *Metternich in neuer Beleuchtung*, 178. For more on the British position, see Gruner, "Ludwig," 503–5; Gruner, "Europäischer Friede als Nationales Interesse. Die Rolle des Deutschen Bundes in der Britischen Politik 1814–1832," *Jahrbuch des Collegium Carolinum*, vol. 18 (Munich, 1977), 119–22; Charles Webster, *The Foreign Policy of Palmerston, 1830–1841; Britain, the Liberal Movement and the Eastern Question*, 2 vols. (New York, 1969), 1: 226–36. For both French and British official and press attitudes and their rejection even by the constitutional German governments, see Peter Burg, "Der Bund des konstitutionellen Deutschland in der europäischen Mächtkonstellation nach den Plänen aus der Zeit der Revolutionen von 1830 und ihrer Folgewirkungen" (Paper presented to the Working Group on the Revolutions of 1830 at the International Historical Congress in Bucharest, 1980), 16–19.

69. Metternich to Apponyi, 4 August 1832, in NP, 5: 271–81.

70. PDB, 1832, 26, 29, 31. Sitzung (19 July, 9 August, and 23 August 1832), § 246, § 288, § 333, 974–75, 1066–67, 1138–40.

71. Bentzel to Metternich, 30 July 1832, HHSA, Deutsche Akten, Fasc. 62; Bibl, *Metternich in neuer Beleuchtung*, 180.

72. Münch to Metternich, 25 August 1832, and Metternich to Münch, 31 August 1832, HHSA, Deutsche Akten, Fasc. 62; BIbl, *Metternich in neuer Beleuchtung*, 180.

73. Treitschke, *Deutsche Geschichte*, 4: 278. See also Werner, *Bavaria and the German Confederation*, 133, which cites PDB of 8 November 1832.

74. Schönburg to Metternich, 20 October 1832, HHSA, Württemberg, Fasc. 43.

75. Schönburg to Metternich, 29 October 1832, ibid.

76. Buol to Metternich, 25 September 1832, HHSA, Baden, Fasc. 38b. For background on Reitzenstein, see Loyd Lee, *The Politics of Harmony: Civil Service, Liberalism, and Social Reform in Baden, 1800–1850* (Newark, DE: 1980), 158.

77. Metternich to Schönburg, 19 December 1832, HHSA, Württemberg, Fasc. 43.

Chapter 7. Politics by Other Means: The Berlin Conference, 1832

1. See chapter 5, nn. 49–53.

2. Bibl, *Metternich in neuer Beleuchtung*, 163–64. See also Baack, *Bernstorff*, 293.

3. Metternich's memorandum for King Frederick William III enclosed in Metternich's dispatch to Clam, 27 February 1832, HHSA, Preussen, Fasc. 146ª; Droysen, "Preussischen Politik," 122–23.

4. Metternich to Clam, 27 February 1832, HHSA, Preussen, Fasc. 146ª.

5. Clam to Metternich, 5 March 1832, ibid.; Droysen, "Preussischen Politik," 123; Baack, *Bernstorff*, 293.

6. Bernstorff to King Frederick William III, 4 March 1832, ZStA, Geheimes Civil Cabinet, Rep. 2.2.1., Nr. 13072; Droysen, "Preussischen Politik," 124. Trauttmansdorff reported to Metternich Bernstorff's indignation at Metternich's methods and his disinclination to hear further about the negotiations. See Trauttmansdorff to Metternich, 7 April 1832, HHSA, Preussen, Fasc. 143ª. See also Baack, *Bernstorff*, 293–94.

7. Clam to Metternich, 5 March 1832, HHSA, Preussen, Fasc. 146ª.

8. He was right. For South German rejection of ideas of an alliance that might benefit France, see Burg, "Die Französische Politik," 19–29; Gruner, "Ludwig," 488.

9. These were views that Metternich held at least since the fall of 1831. See Metternich to Clam, 9, 30 October and 21 November 1831, HHSA, Preussen, Fasc. 142; Metternich to Spiegel, 9 November 1831, cited in Bibl, *Metternich in neuer Beleuchtung*, 267.

10. See chapter 6, nn. 36–39.

11. Gise to Beroldingen, 20 April 1832, WHSA, E 65–68, Verz. 57, Fasc. 162; Metternich to Wrede, 10 April 1832, and editorial note in Bibl, *Metternich in neuer Beleuchtung*, 305. Note that the Seventh Corps consisted of Bavarian troops and the Eighth of troops from Württemberg, Baden, Hesse-Darmstadt, and the tiny states of Hohenzollern-Hechingen, Liechtenstein, Hohenzollern-Sigmaringen, Hesse-Homburg, and Frankfurt. See Lutz, *Zwischen Habsburg und Preussen*, 62, for troop strengths.

12. Metternich to Wrede, 15 and 21 May 1832, in Bibl, *Metternich in neuer Beleuchtung*, 309–10, 315. Regarding the Prussian memorandum and Metternich's use of it, see ibid., 165–67; C. Spielmann, "Regierungspräsident Karl von Ibell über die preussische Politik in den Jahren 1830 und 1831," *Annalen des Vereins für Nassausische Altertumskunde und Geschichtsforschung*, 28 (1896): 66–76; Werner to Metternich, 6 May 1832, and Metternich to Emperor Francis, 17 May 1832 (Vortrag), HHSA, Acta Secreta, Fasc. 4; Metternich to Wittgenstein, 22 April 1832, HHSA, Preussen, Fasc. 145ᵇ; Wittgenstein to Metternich, 6 May 1832 ibid.; Metternich to Wittgenstein, 25 May and 10 June 1832, ibid.; Duke of Nassau to Metternich, 25 May 1832, ibid. For Metternich's original letter to Wittgenstein of 22 April 1833 and the enclosed copy of the Bernstorff memorandum of 29 January 1831, see GSA PKB, Rep. 192, Wittgenstein, VI, 3, 1.2.3. Regarding Bernstorff's resignation and Metternich's role, see also Baack, *Bernstorff*, 323–26; and Branig, *Wittgenstein*, 164–65.

13. Wrede to Metternich, 20 May 1832 and editorial note in Bibl, *Metternich in neuer Beleuchtung*, 311.

14. Blomberg to King William, 26 April 1832, WHSA, E 65–68, Verz. 57, Fasc. 162.

15. Editorial notes in Bibl, *Metternich in neuer Beleuchtung*, 311–12; Gisbert Rieg, "Die württembergische Aussenpolitik und Diplomatie in der vormärzlichen Zeit" (Ph.D. diss., University of Munich, 1954), 417–18.

16. Wrede to Metternich, 20 May 1832, in Bibl, *Metternich in neuer Beleuchtung*, 311–12; Wrede to Knesebeck, 18 May 1832, in Rieg, "Württembergische Aussenpolitik," 419–21.

17. Metternich to Wrede, 27 May 1832, in Bibl, *Metternich in neuer Beleuchtung*, 317–20; Wrede to Beroldingen, 31 May 1832, WHSA, E 65–68, Verz. 57, Fasc. 162.

18. This is what the minister of Baden in Munich learned about General Hertling's report. See Fahnenberg to Türckheim, 6 June 1832, BGLA 48/1629.

19. General Bangold to Grand Duke Leopold, 6 June 1832, ibid.; Hertling's report of 8 June 1832, cited in Bibl, *Metternich in neuer Beleuchtung*, 185.

20. Bangold to Leopold, 13 June 1832, BGLA 48/1629.

21. Private letter of Metternich to Clam, 10 June 1832, HHSA, Preussen, Fasc. 146a.

22. Ibid. For the list of states represented in the Ninth and Tenth Federal Corps, see Lutz, *Zwischen Habsburg und Preussen*, 62. In the Ninth Corps, Saxony and Electoral Hesse had the largest units; Reuss had the smallest. In the Tenth Corps, Hanover had the largest; Lippe-Schaumberg had the smallest.

23. Copies of Wrede to Metternich, 16 and 23 June 1832, enclosed in Wrede's letters to Beroldingen of 16 and 24 June 1832, WHSA, E 65–68, Verz. 57, Fasc. 162. Copies of these letters from Wrede to Metternich are printed in Bibl, *Metternich in neuer Beleuchtung*, 330–32, 333–34.

24. Bangold to Grand Duke Leopold, 25 June 1832, BGLA 48/1629.

25. Clam to Metternich, 25 June 1832, cited in Bibl, *Metternich in neuer Beleuchtung*, 185.

26. Blomberg to King William, 3 and 6 July 1832, WHSA, E 70, Bü. 47; Gasser to King Ludwig, 9 July 1832, BGSA, MA 2404.

27. Metternich to Münch, 21 July 1832, HHSA, Deutsche Akten, Fasc. 59.

28. Metternich to Wrede, 10 August 1832, in Bibl, *Metternich in neuer Beleuchtung*, 342. Droysen, "Preussischen Politik," 126, notes that the north German delegates joined the conference on 19 August.

29. Regarding the mobilization system see Droysen, "Preussischen Politik," 128. See also Baack, *Bernstorff*, 295.

30. Metternich to Wrede, 10 September 1832, in Bibl, *Metternich in neuer Beleuchtung*, 344. This communication was prompted by the report that Wrede saw in the new mobilization system a concession to Prussian primacy in Germany. See Kress to Metternich, 23 August 1832, BOG, 2: 478. See also Baack, *Bernstorff*, 295–96.

31. Wrede to Metternich, 17 October 1832, in Bibl, *Metternich in neuer Beleuchtung*, 346–47; Böck, *Wrede*, 153–54.

32. Metternich to Clam, 6 November 1832, HHSA, Preussen, Fasc. 146c.

33. Metternich to Wrede, 5 November 1832, in Bibl, *Metternich in neuer Beleuchtung*, 351–53.

34. Schönburg to Metternich, 12 November 1832, HHSA, Württemberg, Fasc. 43.

35. Metternich to Schönburg, 24 November 1832, ibid.

36. Gise to Beroldingen, 7 November 1832, and an enclosed copy of the

instructions for General Hertling of 5 November 1832, WHSA, E 65–68, Verz. 57, Fasc. 162.

37. Hertling's report, "Vortrag über die Verhandlungen der Berlin Militär-Conferenz," 7 January 1833, BGSA, MA 24080; Luxburg to King Ludwig, 7 December 1832, BGSA, MA 2610.

38. Droysen, "Preussischen Politik," 128–29. Baack, *Bernstorff*, 295, citing Droysen, gives the same information.

39. Metternich to Emperor Francis, 6 January 1832 (Vortrag), HHSA, Deutsche Akten, Fasc. 60.

40. Ibid.

41. Emperor Francis' note of approval and thanks, 13 January 1833, appended to Metternich's report of 6 January 1833, ibid.; Bibl, *Metternich in neuer Beleuchtung*, 187–88.

42. Proposed Bavarian ratification formula accepted by King Ludwig, 11 February 1833, BGSA, MA 24080. Württemberg agreed to use the same formula and persuaded the other major states of the Eighth Corps, Baden and Darmstadt, to agree to this, too. See Beroldingen to Gise, 1 February and 3 March 1833, ibid.

43. Beroldingen to Gise, 3 March 1833, BGSA, MA 24080; Gise's report to King Ludwig, 8 March 1833, and Ludwig's response that he would stand by his decision, 9 March 1833, ibid.; Türckheim to Beroldingen, 18 March 1833, BGLA 48/1629.

44. Metternich's report to Emperor Francis, 6 May 1833, with a copy of his instructions to the Austrian embassies in Munich and Stuttgart of 1 May 1833, HHSA, Deutsche Akten, Fasc. 60; Schönburg to Metternich, 10 May 1833, ibid.; Spiegel to Gise, 6 May 1833, BGSA, MA 24080; Gise's report to King Ludwig, 9 May 1833, with Ludwig's decision to stand by his position, 10 May 1833, ibid.; Beroldingen to Gise, 3 June 1833, informing him that the states of the Eighth Corps would stand by Bavaria, ibid.; Beroldingen to King William, 29 May 1833, and King William to Beroldingen, 1 June 1833, WHSA, E 65–68, Verz. 56, Fasc. 162; Beroldingen to Türckheim, 3 June 1833, BGLA 48/1629; Türckheim to Grand Duke Leopold, 12 June 1833, with a notation of Leopold's decision to stand by Bavaria and Württemberg, ibid.

45. Schönburg to Metternich, 22 June 1833, HHSA, Deutsche Akten, Fasc. 60; Beroldingen to Gise, 5 July and 11 September 1833, BGSA, MA 24080; King William to Beroldingen, 18 August 1833, WHSA, E 65–68, Verz. 57, Fasc. 162; Beroldingen to Türckheim, 22 August 1833, ibid.; Türckheim to Beroldingen, 7 September 1833; Beroldingen to Gise, 11 September 1833, ibid.; Türckheim to Beroldingen, 27 June and 7 September 1833, BGLA 48/1629.

46. Irmline Veit-Brause, "Die deutsch-französische Krise von 1840: Studien zur deutschen Einheitsbewegung" (Ph.D. diss., Cologne, 1967); Robert D. Billinger, Jr., "They Sing the Best Songs Badly: Metternich, Frederick William IV and the German Confederation during the War Scare of 1840–41," *Wiener Beiträge zur Geschichte der Neuzeit*, vol. 16/17 (Vienna, 1990).

47. For the conflicting interests and differences within the Prussian government and the final undermining of Bernstorff, see Baack, *Bernstorff*, 295–98.

Chapter 8. More Dangerous than Street Revolts, 1833

1. Metternich to Schönberg, 19 December 1832, HHSA, Württemberg, Fasc. 43; Hippel, *Blittersdorff*, 75.
2. Schönburg to Metternich, 31 December 1832, HHSA, Württemberg, Fasc. 43; Türckheim to Tettenborn, 20 January 1833, BGLA 49/1675.
3. Schönburg to Metternich, 2 and 28 February 1833, HHSA, Württemberg, Fasc. 44; Wilhelm Lang, "Paul Pfizer," *Von und aus Schwaben* 3 vols. (Stuttgart, 1885–86), 1: 26–27; Treitschke, *Deutsche Geschichte*, 4: 291–92.
4. Buol to Metternich, 22 February 1833, HHSA, Baden, Fasc. 39ᵃ.
5. Wrede to Metternich, 16 February 1833, in Bibl, *Metternich in neuer Beleuchtung*, 361.
6. Metternich to Münch, 5 January 1833, HHSA, Frankfurt, Fasc. 60; Bibl, *Metternich in neuer Beleuchtung*, 190–91; Fritz Reinöhl, "Die österreichischen Informationsbüros des Vormärz, ihre Akten und Protokolle," *Archivalische Zeitschrift* 38 (1929): 261.
7. Wittgenstein to Metternich, 24 February 1833, HHSA, Deutsche Akten, Fasc. 194; Metternich to Wrede, 26 February 1833, ibid.; Metternich to Schönburg, 26 February 1833, ibid. See also Metternich to Wrede, 26 February 1833, and editor's text in Bibl, *Metternich in neuer Beleuchtung*, 191, 363–66; Reinöhl, "Österreichischen Informationsbüros," 262.
8. "Österreichischen Informationsbüros," 262.
9. Wittgenstein to Metternich, 3 March 1833, and Metternich to Wittgenstein, 20 March 1833, HHSA, Deutsche Akten, Fasc. 194; Reinöhl, "Österreichischen Informationsbüros," 262–63.
10. Initial report of the Saxon delegate, Freiherr von Manteuffel, to the Federal Diet regarding the putsch attempt, PDB, 1833, 13. Sitzung (4 April 1833), § 130, 381–82; Treitschke, *Deutsche Geschichte*, 4: 297–302; Huber, *Deutsche Verfassungsgeschichte*, 2: 165–67; Paul Sauer, *Das württembergische Heer in der Zeit des Deutschen und des Norddeutschen Bund* (Veröffentlichungen der Kommission für Geschichtliche Landeskunde in Baden-Württemberg, Reihe B: Forschungen, vol. 5; Stuttgart, 1958), 69–71. For further details on the Frankfurt Putsch, see Georg Heer, *Geschichte der Deutschen Burschenschaft*, vol. 2: *Die Demagogenzeit: Von den Karlsbader Beschlüssen bis zum Frankfurter Wachensturm (1820–1833)* (Quellen und Darstellungen zur Geschichte der Burschenschaft und der deutschen Einheitsbewegung, vol. 10; Heidelberg, 1927), 299–300. See also "Aktenmässige Darstellung des Ergebnisse der gerichtlichen Untersuchungen gegen die Teilnehmer an dem hochverrätischen Komplotte, welches am 3. April 1833 in Frankfurt a. M. zum Ausbruche gekommen ist; nach den der Bundes-Zentral-Behörde bis Ende März 1834 zugekommenen Akten," in Reinhard Görisch and Thomas Michael Mayer ed., *Untersuchungsberichte zur republikanischen Bewegung in Hessen 1831–1834* (Frankfurt, 1982), 39–138.
11. Handel to Metternich, 4 April 1833, HHSA, Deutsche Akten, Fasc. 194; Metternich to Emperor Francis, 8 April 1833 (Vortrag), ibid. For details regarding the warning the authorities had of a forthcoming putsch, see Harry Gerber, "Der Frankfurter Wachensturm von 3. April 1833. Neue Beiträge zu seinem Verlauf und seiner behördlichen Untersuchung," *Quellen und Darstellungen zur Geschichte der Burschenschaft und der deutschen Einheitsbewegung*, 14

(1934): 172–76, and Franz Leininger and Herman Haupt, "Zur Geschichte des Frankfurter Attentats," ibid., 5 (1920): 133–48.

12. Metternich to Schönburg, 1 May 1833, HHSA, Württemberg, Fasc. 44.

13. Metternich to Wittgenstein, 24 April 1833, HHSA, Deutsche Akten, Fasc. 194; Metternich to Schönburg, 1 May 1833, and an enclosed copy of a letter: Metternich to Wrede, 29 April 1833, HHSA, Württemberg, Fasc. 44. See also Branig, Wittgenstein, 172–73.

14. Trauttmansdorff to Metternich, 22 April 1833, HHSA, Preussen, Fasc. 148ᵃ; Blomberg to King William, 21 April 1833, WHSA, E 70, Bü. 48; Blittersdorff's report of 22 April 1833, noted in Türckheim's report to Grand Duke Leopold, 26 April 1833, BGLA 48/1855. The attributes of the old Mainz Commission can be found in Huber, ed., Dokumente, 1: 93–95.

15. Trauttmansdorff to Metternich, 22 April 1833, HHSA, Preussen, Fasc. 148ᵃ; Schönburg to Metternich, 7 May 1833, HHSA, Württemberg, Fasc. 44; Bavarian ministerial note of 12 April 1833, cited in BOG, 2: 520.

16. Metternich to Wrede, 29 April 1833, in Bibl, Metternich in neuer Beleuchtung, 370–71.

17. Treitschke, Deutsche Geschichte, 4: 302; Werner, Bavaria and the German Confederation, 137. The attributes of the Mainz and Frankfurt investigating agencies can be found in Huber, ed., Dokumente, 1: 93–95, 122–23.

18. Reinöhl, "Österreichischen Informationsbüros," 264–65.

19. Markgraf Wilhelm of Baden informed Wrede of this in a letter of 16 April 1833. See Wrede to Metternich, 8 May 1833, in Bibl, Metternich in neuer Beleuchtung, 373.

20. De Longsdorff to Broglie, 28 April 1833, BFG, 3: 123.

21. Meyendorff to Nesselrode, 23 April 1833, in Peter Baron von Meyendorff, Peter von Meyendorff: Ein russischer Diplomat an den Höfen von Berlin und Wien: Politischer und privater Briefwechsel, 1826–1863, ed. Otto Hoetzsch (Berlin, 1923), 32.

22. Metternich to Emperor Francis, 25 April 1833 (Vortrag), HHSA, Deutsche Akten, Fasc. 60; Metternich to Wrede, 29 April 1833, in Bibl, Metternich in neuer Beleuchtung, 371–72; Metternich to Buol, 30 April 1833, with note that the same information was sent to Stuttgart on 30 April 1833, HHSA, Baden, Fasc. 39ᵃ.

23. Schönburg to Metternich, 8 and 10 May 1833, HHSA, Württemberg, Fasc. 44.

24. Instructions to Schönburg, 24 May 1833, consisting of three memoranda, ibid. The first and third memoranda are printed in NP, 5: 494–502. Lichnowsky's mission and the memoranda he brought are mentioned briefly in Treitschke, Deutsche Geschichte, 4: 336.

25. Metternich to Wrede, 1 June 1833, in Bibl, Metternich in neuer Beleuchtung, 376–77.

26. Instructions to Schönburg, 24 May 1833, memorandum nr. 1, HHSA, Württemberg, Fasc. 44.

27. The proposed reforms are noted in memorandum nr. 1, and the means to achieve them are presented in nr. 3. See ibid.

28. Memorandum nr. 3, ibid.

29. See Branig, Wittgenstein, 168–72.

30. Metternich asked the Bavarian minister to consider if Bavaria's economic outlets were on the Elbe or the Danube. See Bray to Gise, 12 June 1833, HHSA, Deutsche Akten, Fasc. 79ᵃ and BOG, 2: 253. Metternich also had Schönburg

encourage the King of Württemberg to enter a commercial treaty with Austria, so as to balance the Zollverein. See Metternich to Schönburg, 21 June 1833, HHSA, Deutsche Akten, Fasc. 79[b].

31. Metternich to Spiegel, 13 July 1833, noted in BOG, 2: 524–25; Metternich to Schönburg, 21 June 1833, HHSA, Deutsche Akten, Fasc. 79[b].

32. Metternich to Emperor Francis, June 1833 (Vortrag), NP, 5: 502–19; Branchert, "Österreich und die Anfänge des preussisch-deutschen Zollvereins," 68–72; Treitschke, Deutsche Geschichte, 4: 384–86.

33. Ludwig Dehio, "Wittgenstein und das letzte Jahrzehnt Friedrich Wilhelms III," Forschungen zur brandenburgischen und preussischen Geschichte, 35/1 (1923), 226–27; Branig, Wittgenstein, 171–72; Baack, Bernstorff, 327. Count Carl von Lottum was a member of the Ministry of State and generally in charge of domestic affairs. See Baack, Bernstorff, 99.

34. Metternich to Schönburg, 27 July 1833, HHSA, Württemberg, Fasc. 44.

35. Metternich to Emperor Francis, 19 August 1833 (Vortrag), HHSA, Deutsche Akten, Fasc. 37[a]; Treitschke, Deutsche Geschichte, 4: 336. Werner, Bavaria and the German Confederation, 146, basing his ideas on Weech, Correspondencen und Aktenstücke, 130–31, suggests that all this was a Prussian initiative, but Metternich's correspondence noted here and in n. 32 indicates the Austrian lead.

36. This information on the 24 August 1833 circular was derived from a copy of the circular sent by Metternich to Schönburg. See Metternich to Schönburg, 24 August 1833, WHSA, E 36–38, Verz. 58, Fasc. 5.

37. Details of the Schönburg mission and its special character are noted in Wrede to Metternich, 29 August 1833, in Bibl, Metternich in neuer Beleuchtung, 387–88, and in the text of the same book, 197–99. See also Schönburg to Metternich, 1 September 1833, BOG, 21: 555.

38. Metternich to Wrede, 25 August 1833, BGSA, MA 1104, and in Bibl, Metternich in neuer Beleuchtung, 385–87; Böck, Wrede, 185–86.

39. Schönburg to Metternich, 28 August 1833, HHSA, Deutsche Akten, Fasc. 37[a]; Schönburg to Metternich, 1 September 1833, BOG, 2: 555.

40. Schönburg to Metternich, 1 September 1833, HHSA, Württemberg, Fasc. 44.

41. Metternich to Emperor Francis, 17 September 1833 (Vortrag), HHSA, Deutsche Akten, Fasc. 37[a]. It should be remembered that Frederick William III did not participate in the Münchengrätz meetings, and to Metternich's chagrin only halfheartedly joined in the Austro-Russian proclamation of the right of intervention against revolutionary movements. See Srbik, Metternich, 1: 687–89; Treitschke, Deutsche Geschichte, 4: 329–34; Branig, Wittgenstein, 174–75; Bertier, Metternich, 434–35.

42. Metternich to Münch, 18 September 1833, ibid.

43. Metternich to Schönburg, 15 October 1833, HHSA, Württemberg, Fasc. 44. The Linz meetings are mentioned in Treitschke, Deutsche Geschichte, 4: 338, and in Böck, Wrede, 186–87. Metternich's account of how, in the course of one of his hand-waving declamations at Linz, he accidently bloodied Ludwig's nose is refreshing evidence of the mortal nature of both men. See Egon Caesar Conte Corti, Metternich und die Frauen 2 vols. (Vienna, 1948–49), 2: 353–54.

44. Tettenborn to Grand Duke Leopold, 20 October 1833, BGLA 48/1561.

45. Valeria Dcsacovszky, "Das Ministerium des Fürsten Ludwig von Öttingen-Wallerstein 1832–1837" (Ph.D. diss., University of Munich, 1932), 90–92.

46. Buol to Metternich, 27 October 1833, HHSA, Baden, Fasc. 39[a]; Buol to Metternich, 2 November 1833, HHSA, Deutsche Akten, Fasc. 37[a].

47. Gise to King Ludwig, 7 November 1833 (Vortrag), BGSA, MA 1104.

48. Ibid., and Ludwig's notation on the proposal, 9 November 1833. Information on Gise's proposals and his attempt to gain the agreement of other constitutional states to a united front at the ministerial conference can be found in Bibl, *Metternich in neuer Beleuchtung*, 201–3. See also Böck, *Wrede*, 187–88.

49. Gise to Beroldingen, 3 November 1833, BGSA, MA 1104.

50. Resumé of the secret talks held in Munich on 11 November 1833, signed by Gise, Lindenau, and Beroldingen, ibid.

51. Metternich to Münch, 18 September 1833, HHSA, Deutsche Akten, Fasc. 37[a].

52. Metternich to Schönburg, 15 October 1833, HHSA, Württemberg, Fasc. 44.

53. Metternich to Trauttmansdorff, 18 November 1833, HHSA, Deutsche Akten, Fasc. 37[a].

54. Regarding the Spanish succession question: The problem was of *Cristinos* versus *Carlistes*. When King Ferdinand VII of Spain died in 1833, his widow, Queen Christine, began to reign on behalf of their daughter, Isabella. This was because in 1832 Ferdinand had reactivated the Pragmatic Sanction of Charles IV of 1789, which replaced the Salic Law of 1713. In a return to earlier Castilian tradition, the direct female line took precedence over an indirect male line in royal succession. Ferdinand's brother, Carlos, contested the claim. At first the Eastern Powers—Austria, Prussia, and Russia—watched to see the course of developments in Spain. Then, when in 1834 Queen Christine's government proclaimed a constitution modeled on the French Charter, they opted for diplomatic support of the Carlists. The response of England and France to the conservative powers was to form a Quadruple Alliance with Spain and Portugal on 22 April 1834. This declared their support of the liberal cause in Spain and Portugal, aligning themselves with the *Cristinos* in Spain and Dom Pedro in Portugal. In Portugal, Dom Pedro represented the cause of his daughter, Maria, against the absolutism of his brother, King Miguel. See Srbik, *Metternich*, 1: 689–91; and Bertier, *Metternich*, 435.

55. The Austrian invitation is printed in NP, 5: 532–33. Trauttmansdorff informed Metternich of Ancillon's wish to hold off the conference until 1 January 1834 in the hope that the question of the Spanish succession would be settled by then. See Trauttmansdorff to Metternich, 11 November 1833, HHSA, Deutsche Akten, Fasc. 37[a]. For Metternich's response see n. 53. Because there was earlier talk of holding the conference in Prague or Linz, Metternich explained the choice of Vienna as based on his need to stay in the Habsburg capital because of Hungarian problems. See Böck, *Wrede*, 188.

56. Trauttmansdorff to Metternich, 28 November 1833, HHSA, Deutsche Akten, Fasc. 37[a].

57. Buol to Metternich, 4 December 1833, ibid.

58. Spiegel to Metternich, 11 December 1833, ibid.

59. Schönburg to Metternich, 14 December 1833, HHSA, Württemberg, Fasc. 44.

60. Ibid.

Chapter 9. The Act of Unity That Almost Failed: The Vienna Conference of 1834

1. See Metternich to Emperor Francis, 19 August 1833 (Vortrag), HHSA, DA, Fasc. 37ᵃ, mentioned already in chapter 8, n. 35.

2. Böck, *Wrede*, 187.

3. Metternich's opening speech to the conference, the subject of this and the following paragraph, is printed in NP, 5: 600–605.

4. Reitzenstein to Grand Duke Leopold, 14 January 1834, BGLA 48/1561; Weech, *Correspondenzen und Actenstücke*, 146–48; Heinrich Ulmann, ed., *Denkwürdigkeiten aus dem Dienstleben des Hessen-Darmstädtischen Staatsministers Freiherrn du Thil 1803–1848* (Deutsche Geschichtsquellen des 19. Jahrhunderts, vol. 3; Osnabrück, 1967), 449. Weech, *Correspondenzen und Actenstücke*, 140, lists the eighteen plenipotentiaries present and on pages 146–48 lists the membership of each commission. Weech, 148, also notes that unlike at the Vienna Conferences of 1820, the accredited ambassadors of the German powers in Vienna were not included because these were supposedly not formal negotiations but merely private discussions. The real reason, Weech notes, was secrecy through fewer participants.

5. Metternich to Emperor Francis, 4 February 1834 (Vortrag), with Metternich to Ancillon, 3 February 1834, as an enclosure, HHSA, Deutsche Akten, Fasc. 39ᵇ.

6. Metternich to Trauttmansdorff, 3 February 1834, enclosed with Metternich to Emperor Francis, 4 February 1834 (Vortrag), ibid.

7. Noted in chapter 8, nn. 48–50.

8. Metternich's ostensible and secret dispatches to Wrede, 20 February 1834, and Metternich to Wrede, 9 March 1834, in Bibl, *Metternich in neuer Beleuchtung*, 401–4, 409–10. See Ulmann, ed., *Du Thil*, 450, for the Bavarian search for an agreement. Du Thil, 483, also credits his own opposition within the constitutional bloc for preventing such an agreement.

9. Metternich to Wrede, 20 February and 9 March 1834, in Bibl, *Metternich in neuer Beleuchtung*, 401–4, 409–10.

10. Böck, *Wrede*, 188–89.

11. Beroldingen to King William, 27 January 1834, WHSA, E 9, Bü. 26.

12. Metternich to Wrede, 9 March 1834, in Bibl, *Metternich in neuer Beleuchtung*, 411.

13. Du Thil to the Grand Duke of Hesse-Darmstadt, 21 February 1834, in Ulmann, ed. *Du Thil*, 483.

14. Metternich to Wrede, 9 March 1834, in Bibl, *Metternich in neuer Beleuchtung*, 410.

15. Wrede to Metternich, 15 March 1834, ibid., 413–14; Böck, *Wrede*, 189. Gollwitzer, *Ludwig I*, 307–8.

16. Ludwig's resolution is noted in Bibl, *Metternich in neuer Beleuchtung*, 209.

17. Metternich to Wrede, 17 March 1834, and editor's text, ibid., 210, 415–16.

212   METTERNICH AND THE GERMAN QUESTION

18. Bibl, *Metternich in neuer Beleuchtung*, 211–12. Confounded by instructions that always put him in a negative position, Mieg turned to Wrede for help. In response Wrede worked on the ministerial council to modify Mieg's instructions. See Böck, *Wrede*, 190.

19. Trauttmansdorff to Metternich, 16 January 1834, HHSA, Deutsche Akten, Fasc. 39[b].

20. Bibl, *Metternich in neuer Beleuchtung*, 207, explains Ancillon's late arrival. The delegate from Baden reported that the early progress of the conference was slow and concluded that this was partly the result of Alvensleben's wish to hold up things until Ancillon's arrival. See Reitzenstein to Grand Duke Leopold, 27 January 1834, BGLA 48/1561. Alvensleben was a Geheim Justizrat and Kammerherr, legal counselor and chamberlain, and highly recommended to Metternich by Wittgenstein. See Branig, *Wittgenstein*, 175.

21. Weech, *Correspondenzen und Actenstücke*, 248–57, notes the Hanoverian proposal and Metternich's neutral stand. The French minister in Munich noted this and concluded that it was part of Metternich's effort to win Prussia to a close political understanding. See Vaudreuil to Broglie, 2 May 1834, BFG, 3: 182.

22. Metternich to Wrede, 7 April 1834, in Bibl, *Metternich in neuer Beleuchtung*, 418–19.

23. Metternich to Wrede, two dispatches of 21 April 1834, ibid., 419–23. When no revolt took place on 4 May and Bavarian authorities could find none of the conspirators, the French minister in Munich concluded that Metternich had been merely trying to end Bavaria's independent stand in Vienna by increasing the king's fear of revolution. See Vaudreuil to Rigny, 15 May 1834, BFG, 3: 184–85. Metternich sent the same information to the government of Württemberg as he did to Wrede. See Vollnagel to Schmitz, 18 May 1834, WHSA, E 75, Bü 174. The government of Baden wondered why Bavaria and Württemberg had been informed of the conspiracy and they had not been contacted. See Türckheim to Tettenborn, 13 May 1834, BGLA 49/1676. It is worth noting, however, that on 7 May the Vienna conferees learned that on 2 May there had been an attempt made to free the prisoners from the Frankfurt Putsch of 3 April 1833. After considering the matter, the German ministers in Vienna agreed to have their governments instruct their federal representatives to have both the political prisoners and the federal treasury moved from Frankfurt to Mainz. See Weech, *Correspondenzen und Actenstücke*, 258–59. Regarding the attempt to free the prisoners, see Stern, *Geschichte Europas*, 4: 328–29; Treitschke, *Deutsche Geschichte*, 4: 305–6.

24. Weech, *Correspondenzen und Actenstücke*, 264–66.

25. Huber, *Deutsche Verfassungsgeschichte*, 2: 180–84. The important articles of the final protocol of the conference are also discussed in Treitschke, *Deutsche Geschichte*, 4: 342–45, and Stern, *Geschichte Europas*, 4: 333–34.

26. Weech, *Correspondenzen und Actenstücke*, 266–67. The precise articles that were eventually turned into federal decrees are noted in Carl von Kaltenborn, *Geschichte der Deutschen Bundesverhältnisse und Einheitsbestrebungen von 1806 bis 1856*, 2 vols. (Berlin: 1852), 1: 459–60, and Huber, *Deutsche Verfassungsgeschichte*, 2: 178.

27. Article 3 of the Final Protocol of the Vienna Ministerial Conference of 1834. See Huber, ed., *Dokumente*, 1: 124. Regarding the general details of the arbitral court, see also Treitschke, *Deutsche Geschichte*, 4: 342.

28. Article 49, in Huber, ed, *Dokumente*, 1: 133.

29. Articles 25–27, ibid., 127–28.
30. Article 17, ibid., 126.
31. Article 21, ibid., 127.
32. Articles 33–35, ibid., 129.
33. Articles 29 and 30, ibid., 129–29.
34. Article 24, ibid., 127.
35. Weech, *Correspondenzen und Actenstücke*, 264–65.
36. This evaluation was made by the delegate from Baden. See Reitzenstein to Grand Duke Leopold, 9 June 1834, BGLA, 48/1561. Against the wishes of his ministers, who feared responsibility for wrecking the Vienna Conference, Ludwig empowered Mieg to agree to a protocol only insofar as it was consistent with the Bavarian constitution. See Böck, *Wrede*, 190.
37. Metternich to Wrede, 25 May 1834, in Bibl, *Metternich in neuer Beleuchtung*, 425–26.
38. Reitzenstein to Grand Duke Leopold, 24 May 1834, BGLA 48/1574.
39. Trauttmansdorrf to Metternich, 31 May 1834, HHSA, Deutsche Akten, Fasc. 39b.
40. Wrede to Metternich, 30 May 1834, in Bibl, *Metternich in neuer Beleuchtung*, 426–27. Regarding Wallerstein's opposition, see also Karl-Heinz Zuber, *Der "Fürst Proletarier," Ludwig von Öttingen-Wallerstein (1791–1870)* (Zeitschrift für Bayerische Landesgeschichte, Beiheft (Reihe B) nr. 10; Munich, 1978), 135; Böck, *Wrede*, 191.
41. Wrede to Metternich, 2 June 1834, Bibl, *Metternich in neuer Beleuchtung*, 427; Böck, *Wrede*, 191.
42. Weech, *Correspondenzen und Actenstücke*, 268, 273.
43. Ibid., 269. Metternich explained to his minister in Munich how Bavaria insisted that the federal court of arbitration be merely facultative and not obligatory. See Metternich to Spiegel, 14 December 1834, BOG, 2: 598, n. 1.
44. The compromise was explained in detail by the delegate from Baden in his report to Grand Duke Leopold. See Reitzenstein to Grand Duke Leopold, 9 and 13 June 1834, with the enclosed copies of the Bavarian declaration and the reply of the other delegates, BGLA 48/1561. These archival materials seem to be the basis for the explanation in Weech, *Correspondenzen und Actenstücke*, 273–74.
45. For a discussion of Bavarian assertions of both sovereignty and support for the monarchic principle within the Confederation during the Vienna Conference of 1820 see Wolfgang Quint, *Souveränitätsbegriff und Souveränitätspolitik in Bayern. Von der Mitte des 17. bis zur ersten Hälfte des 19. Jahrhunderts* (Schriften zur Verfassungsgeschichte, vol. 15) (Berlin: 1971), 503. For Articles 56 and 57 of the Vienna Final Act see Huber, ed., *Dokumente*, 1: 88.
46. Metternich's evaluation of the results of the conference was presented in his concluding speech to the delegates of the conference. It is printed in NP, 5: 606–10. Metternich presented a copy of this final speech to Emperor Francis as his evaluation of the worth of the conference. See Metternich to Emperor Francis, 17 June 1834 (Vortrag), HHSA, Vorträge, Kart. 274.
47. See Metternich's closing speech to the Vienna Conference, June 1834, NP, 5: 606–10.
48. Ibid., and Article 21 of the final protocol printed in Huber, ed., *Dokumente*, 1: 127.
49. This was what Metternich told Austrian diplomats at the German courts in a dispatch that was meant for their own private knowledge. It was, however,

also to serve as a basis for their comments if any of the results of the conference came to public attention. See Metternich to Schönburg, Spiegel, Buol, et al, 22 June 1834, HHSA, Deutsche Akten, Fasc. 38ᵃ.

50. See again Metternich to Emperor Francis, 19 August 1833 (Vortrag), HHSA, Deutsche Akten, Fasc. 37ᵃ; Metternich to Wrede, 25 May 1834, in Bibl, Metternich in neuer Beleuchtung, 425–26. See also Böck, Wrede, 191–92.

51. The Bavarian ratifiction of 1 July 1834, enclosed in a note of 9 July 1834, HHSA, Deutsche Akten, Fasc. 38ᵃ.

52. When Metternich sent the original documents of the Vienna Conference to the federal archives at Frankfurt, he included a list of the ratification instruments and their dates. See Metternich to Münch, 19 October 1834, ibid. If the dates on the list for the Württemberg and Baden ratification instruments are correct, then these instruments seem to have been antedated. Metternich thanked the foreign minister of Württemberg for sending him Württemberg's ratification in a dispatch of 17 July. See Metternich to Beroldingen, 5 August 1834, ibid. On 16 July 1834, the Austrian minister in Karlsuhe noted that Baden's Staatsrat had just decided to ratify the protocol the day before. See Buol to Metternich, 16 July 1834, ibid.

53. Frank to Metternich, 25 June 1834, HHSA, Württemberg, Fasc. 45.

54. Buol to Metternich, 8 July 1834, HHSA, Baden, Fasc. 39ᵃ; Hippel, Blittersdorff, 77.

55. Gise to King Ludwig, 25 June 1834, BGSA, MA 1110.

56. Münch to Metternich, 15 November 1834, and n. 1, BOG, 2: 595–96.

57. PDB, 1834, 37. Sitzung (30 October 1834), § 506, 938–39.

58. Meyendorff to Pozzo di Borgo, 23 November 1834, in Meyendorff, Meyendorff, 1: 50.

59. Hippel, Blittersdorff, 77–78.

60. The conservative minister of Hesse-Darmstadt, Baron Karl du Thil, reminisced that the results of the conference were words without guarantees. See Ulmann, ed., Du Thil, 455–59.

61. For an evaluation of the important "extra-constitutional," tranquilizing, although limited effect on Germany, see Werner, Bavaria and the German Confederation, 147–51.

Chapter 10. Metternich's School of Nationalism for the German Princes

1. See Austensen's discussion in "Einheit oder Einigkeit," 47–53.

2. See, for example, James J. Sheehan, "What is German History? Reflections on the Role of the Nation in German History and Historiography," Journal of Modern European History 53 (March 1981): 1–23; and Robert M. Berdahl, "New Thoughts on German Nationalism," American Historical Review 77 (February 1972); 65–80.

3. Ranke, "Über die Trennung und die Einheit von Deutschland," Sämmtliche Werke (Leipzig, 1887), vol. 49/50, 172, cited by Sheehan, "What is German History?" 1.

4. Berdahl, "New Thoughts on German Nationalism," 76.

5. See Austensen, "Einheit oder Einigkeit?"

Bibliography

Unpublished Documents

Österreichisches Staatsarchiv, Abteilung: Haus-, Hof- und Staatsarchiv, Vienna = HHSA

Staatskanzlei
ACTA SECRETA
Fasc. 3: 1827–1830

Fasc. 4: 1831–1832

Fasc. 5: 1833–1836
BADEN
Fasc. 36ª Politische Berichte, 1830

Fasc. 37 Politische Berichte, 1831

Fasc. 38ᵇ Politische Correspondenz, 1832

Fasc. 39ª Politische Correspondenz, 1833–1834
DEUTSCHE AKTEN
Fasc. 27 BundesPräsidial-Gesandtschaft, 1831–1847

Fasc. 37ª–39ᵇ Cabinetts-Conferenzen von 1834

Fasc. 58–60 Verteidigung des Bundes, 1830–1833

Fasc. 61 Leitfaden zur Besprechungen über die Deutschen Angelegenheiten mit Preussen, Bayern, und Württemberg, 1831–1832

Fasc. 62 Bundesbeschlüsse von 28. Juni und 5. Juli 1832

Fasc. 79ª, 79ᵇ Handel, Preussen Zollverein, 1832–1835

Fasc. 194 Mainzer Central Polizei, 1833ⁱ⁻ᵛ
FRANKFURT
Fasc. 56 Berichte, Weisungen, 1831

Fasc. 58 Berichte, Weisungen, 1832

Fasc. 60 Berichte, Weisungen, 1833

Fasc. 62 Berichte, Weisungen, 1834

Fasc. 64 Berichte, Weisungen, 1835
PREUSSEN
Fasc. 139ª Politische Berichte 1831ⁱ⁻ᵛⁱ

Fasc. 142 Sendung Werners nach Teplitz, Berichte, Weisungen, 1831ᵛⁱⁱ⁻ⁱˣ

Fasc. 143ª Politische Berichte, 1832ⁱ⁻ᵛⁱ

Fasc. 143ᵇ Politische Berichte, 1832ᵛⁱⁱ⁻ˣⁱⁱ

Fasc. 145ᵇ Briefwechsel Metternichs mit Wittgenstein, 1832

Fasc. 146ª Sendung Clam-Martinitz, Berichte, Weisungen, 1832[i−vi]
Fasc. 146ᶜ Sendung Clam-Martinitz, Berichte, Weisungen, 1832[x−xii]
Fasc. 148ª Politische Berichte, 1833[i−iv]
Fasc. 148ᵇ Politische Berichte, 1833[v−ix]
Fasc. 148ᶜ Politische Berichte, 1833[x−xii]
WÜRTTEMBERG
Fasc. 41−45 Berichte, Weisungen, 1830−1834
VORTRÄGE
Kart. 274 1834[v−ix]

Badisches Generallandesarchiv, Karlsruhe = BGLA

48/1561
HAUS- UND STAATSARCHIV: III. STAATSSACHEN:
Deutscher Bund, Die Wiener Conferenzen
48/1574
Deutscher Bund, Wiener Kabinettskonferenzen,
    Correspondenz des Staatsministers Freiherrn von Reitzenstein mit
    Grossherzog Leopold
48/1575
Deutscher Bund, Wiener Kabinettskonferenzen,
    Berichte, Ministerialschreiben, Denkschriften aus dem Nachlass des Min-
    isters von Reitzenstein
48/1629
Deutscher Bund, Militäria, 1831−1833
48/1853−48/1857
Diplomatische Correspondenz, Generalia,
    Referate des Ministers Freiherrn von Türckheim an Grossherzog Leopold
    über die eingegangene Gesandtschaftsberichte, 1831−1835
48/1874−48/1875
Diplomatische Correspondenz, Baiern,
    Correspondenz des Gesandten Freiherrn von Fahnenberg mit Grossherzog
    Leopold, 1830−1831
48/2546
Diplomatische Correspondenz, Österreich,
    Correspondenz des ausserordentlichen Mission an den Kaiserlichen Hof
    nach Wien entsandten Kammerherrn Freiherrn von Falkenstein mit
    Türckheim, 1832
48/2584−48/2585
Diplomatische Correspondenz, Preussen,
    Correspondenz des Ministerresidenten von Franckenberg mit Grossherzog
    Leopold, 1830−1831
49/488
HAUS- UND STAATSARCHIV: IV. GESANDTSCHAFTEN:
Deutscher Bund, Diplomatische Correspondenz,
    Korrespondenz des Ministers Frhr. v. Berstett mit dem Bundestagsge-
    sandten v. Blittersdorff, 1830
49/1671
Österreich, Diplomatische Correspondenz,

Vertrauliche Correspondenz des Staatsministers Frhr. v. Berstett mit dem badischen Gesandten Frhr. v. Tettenborn, 1818–1830
49/1673–49/1677
Österreich, Diplomatische Correspondenz,
Vertrauliche Correspondenz des Staatsministers Frhr. v. Türckheim mit dem badischen Gesandten Generalleutnant Freiherrn v. Tettenborn in Wien, 1831–1835

Bayerische Hauptstaatsarchiv, Abteilung II: Geheimes, Staatsarchiv, Munich = BGSA

MA 1104 Deutscher Bund, Konferenzen zu Wien 1834: Vorbereitenden Akten, August–December 1833

MA 1105 Generalakten, Jan.–März. 1834

MA 1110 Generalakten, Juni–Nov. 1834, Schlussprotokoll und Ratification

MA 1111 Spezialakten, Äusserung des Grafen Luxburg gegenüber dem preussischen Minister Ancillon über die Konferenzen, Okt.–Nov. 1833

MA 2403 Diplomatische Berichte, Österreich, 1830

MA 2404 Diplomatische Berichte, Österreich, 1831–1832

MA 2405 Diplomatische Berichte, Österreich, 1833–1834

MA 2608–2612 Diplomatische Berichte, Preussen, 1830–1834

MA 24076 Ministerium des K. Hauses und des Aussern, Deutscher Bund, Militärkonferenzen zu Berlin über die Defensiveaufstellung des Bundesheeres in Kriegsfalle, 1831

MA 24080 December 1832–1833

Württembergisches Hauptstaatsarchiv, Stuttgart = WHSA

E 9, Bü. 25, No. 8
Kabinettsakten III, Ministerium der Auswärtigen Angelegenheiten, Politisch-militärische Stellung Süddeutschland infloge der Revolution in Frankreich und Belgien 1830
E 9, Bü. 25, No. 9
Verhandlungen mit preuss. Generalmajor Rühle von Lilienstern. . . . Verhandlungen des württ. Generalmajors von Bangold mit dem bayer. Marschall Fürsten von Wrede in München. Sendung des Gen. Majors von Bangold nach Berlin, 1831–1833
E 9, Bü. 26–30
Ministerialkonferenz in Wien über deutsche Angelegenheiten 1833–1834
E 36–38. Verz. 13 II, Bü. 2.
Ministerium der Auswärtige Angelegenheiten. Circular Erlasse an den K. Gesandtschaften, 1821–1823.
E 36–38, Verz. 13 II, Bü. 5, Fasc. 15.
Rappel der in Stuttgart accreditierten Gesandten von Österreich, Russland u. Preussen, 1823.
E 36–38. Verz. 57, Fasc. 173.
Deutscher Bund. Verhandlungen in Wien in Jahre 1823 über Deutsche Angelegenheiten in Folge der Congress zu Verona von 1822

E 36–38, Verz. 58, Fasc. 1–5
Akten des Ministeriums der auswärtigen Angelegenheiten, Berichte über die Wiener Konferenz 1834
E 65–68, Verz. 40
Deutscher Bund, Vertrauliche Conferenzen in Wien: Bundesbeschlüsse von 28, Juni 1832
E 65–68, Verz. 57, Fasc. 162
Protokolle der Berliner Militärkonferenz, 1832
E 65–68, Verz. 57, Fasc. 173
Verhandlungen in Wien in Jahre 1823 über Deutsche Bundes-Angelegenheiten in Folge der Congresse zu Verona von 1822
E 65–68, Verz. 57, Fasc. 220
Ministerialkonferenz in Wien, 1833–1834
E 70, Bü. 45–48
Ministerium der Auswärtigen Angelegenheiten, Berichte der Gesandtschaft Wien, 1830–1833
E 70, Verz. 31, Fasc. 4
Königliche Gesandtschaft in Berlin, Schreiben des K. Gesandten an den Ministeriums von 1828–1833
E 71, Verz. 30, Carton VIII-2, 1819–1820.
Königliche Gesandtschaft in St. Petersburg, 1819–1820
E 71, Verz. 30, Carton VIII-3, 1821–1823
Relationen des K. Gesandten, General Lt. Grafen von Beroldingen, St. Petersburg
E 72, Bü. 137–141. 1820–1823
Württembergische Gesandtschaft in St. Petersburg (1808–1893), 1951 aus den Bestände E 70, E 72, E 73 augsgeliederte Akten der bis 1893 bestehenden Württembergischen Gesandtschaft in St. Petersburg
E 74 I, Bü. 2
Berlin Gesandtschaft, Allgemeine politische Ministerialschreiben, 1831–1842
E 75, Bü. 172
Württembergische Gesandtschaft München, Schriftenwechsel mit dem Aussenministerium in Stuttgart, 1830
E 75. Bü. 173
Württembergische Gesandtschaft München, Schriftenwechsel mit dem Aussenministerium, 1831
E 75, Bü. 174
1832–1834

Zentrale Staatsarchiv, Merseburg = ZStA

Auswärtiges Amt: Sektion I. Politische Abteilung, Deutscher Bund, 2.4.1., Abt. 1, Nr. 10067
(formerly AA1, Rep. 5, Nr. 592) Acta. betr. die Sendung des Generals v. Roeder nach Wien, betr. der Organisierung des deutschen Bundes Heeres
Geheimes Civil Cabinet, Rep. 2.2.1., Nr. 13072
Verhandlungen Bernstorffs mit Clam. Defensivstellung des deutschen Bundes.
Gesandtschaft am deutschen Bundestag, Rep. 75A, Nr. 457

Actebetr. die in den Jahren 1831 und 1832 zwischen den Kabinetten zu Berlin und Wien stattgefundenen Berathungen wegen Massregeln zur Herstellung und Erhaltung der Ruhe in Deutschland.
Preussischen Gesandtschaften, Rep. 81, Wien I, 142
Erlasse an Maltzahn u. Conzepte von Berichte desselber an das Ministerium des Auswärtigen. 1830.

Geheimes Staatsarchiv Preussischer Kulturbesitz, Berlin = GSA PKB

Wittgenstein, Rep. 192, VI, 3, 1.2.3.
Briefe des K. K. Oesterr. Haus-, Hof-, und Staatskanzlers Fürsten von Metternich an den Fürsten zu Wittgenstein, 1818–Juli 1832.

Primary Sources: Published Documents, Memoirs, Diaries, and Letters

Aegidi, Karl Ludwig. *Die Schluss-Acte der Wiener Ministerial-Conferenzen.* 2 vols. Berlin, 1860–1869.

Bernstorff, Augusta Louise Elizabeth Gräfin von. *Gräfin Elise von Bernstorff, geborene Gräfin von Dernath. Ein Bild aus der Zeit von 1789 bis 1836. Aus ihren Aufzeichnungen.* Edited by Elise von dem Busche-Kessell. 2 vols. Berlin, 1896.

Bibl, Viktor. *Metternich in neuer Beleuchtung: Sein geheimer Briefwechsel mit dem bayerischen Staatsminister Wrede: Nach unveröffentlichen Dokumenten aus den Archiven in Wien und München.* Vienna, 1928.

Chroust, Anton, ed. *Gesandtschaftsberichte aus München 1814–1848.* Abteilung I: *Die Berichte der französische Gesandten.* 6 vols. (Schriftenreihe zur bayerischen Landesgeschichte. Vols. 18, 19, 21–24.) Munich, 1935–1937.

———. *Gesandtschaftsberichte aus München 1814–1848.* Abteilung II: *Die Berichte der österreichischen Gesandten.* 4 vols. (Schriftenreihe zur bayerischen Landesgeschichte. Vols. 33, 36–38.) Munich, 1939–1942.

———. *Gesandtschaftsberichte aus München 1814–1848.* Abteilung III: *Die Berichte der preussischen Gesandten.* 5 vols. (Schriftenreihe zur bayerischen Landesgeschichte. Vols. 39–43.) Munich, 1949–1951.

Gentz, Friedrich von. *Briefe von und an Friedrich von Gentz.* Edited by Friedrich Carl Wittichen and Ernst Salzer. 3 vols. Munich, 1913.

———. *Tagebücher von Friedrich von Gentz (1829–1831).* Edited by August Fournier and Arnold Winkler. Vienna, 1920.

German Confederation. *Protokolle der deutschen Bundesversammlung.* Frankfurt am Main, 1815–1866.

Görsch, Reinhard, and Thomas Michael Mayer, eds., *Untersuchungsberichte zur republikanischen Bewegung in Hessen 1831–1834.* Frankfurt, 1982.

Huber, Ernst Rudolf. ed. *Dokumente zur deutschen Verfassungsgeschichte.* 3 vols. Stuttgart, 1961–1966.

Kübeck von Kübau, Carl Friedrich Freiherr. *Tagebücher des Carl Friedrich*

Freiherrn Kübeck von Kübau. Edited by Max Freiherr von Kübeck. 2 vols. Vienna, 1909.

Lebzeltern, Ludwig Graf von. *Les rapports diplomatique de Lebzeltern.* Edited by Grand Duc Nicolas Mikhailowitch. St. Petersburg, 1913.

Lerchenfeld, Maximilian Freiherr von. *Aus den Papieren des k.[öniglichen] b.[ayerischen] Staatsministers Maximilian Freiherrn von Lerchenfeld.* Edited by Maximilian Freiherr von Lerchenfeld. Nördlingen, 1887.

Metternich-Winneburg, Clemens Lothar Wenzel Fürst von. *Aus Metternichs nachgelassenen Papieren.* Edited by Prince Richard von Metternich. 8 vols. Vienna, 1880–1884.

Meyendorff, Peter Baron von. *Peter von Meyendorff: Ein russischer Diplomat an den Höfen von Berlin und Wien: Politischer und privater Briefwechsel, 1826–1863.* Edited by Otto Hoetsch. Berlin, 1923.

Oncken, Hermann, and F. E. M. Saemisch, eds. *Vorgeschichte und Begründung des deutschen Zollvereins 1815–1834: Akten der Staaten des Deutschen Bundes und der europäischen Mächte.* 3 vols. (Veröffentlichungen der Friedrich List Gesellschaft E. V., Vols. 8–10.) Berlin; 1934.

Prokesch von Osten, Anton Franz Graf. *Aus den Tagebücher des Grafen Prokesch von Osten 1830–1834.* Edited by Anton Graf Prokesch von Osten. Vienna, 1909.

Schiller, Herbert, ed. *Briefe an Cotta: Das Zeitalter der Restauration 1815–1832.* Stuttgart, 1927.

Schoeps, Hans-Joachim, ed. *Neue Quellen zur Geschichte Preussens im 19. Jahrhundert.* (Veröffentlichung der Gesellschaft für Geistesgeschichte.) Berlin, 1968.

Spielmann, C. "Regierungspräsident Karl von Ibell über die preussische Politik in den Jahren 1830–1831," *Annalen des Vereins für Nassauische Altertumskunde und Geschichtsforschung* 27 (1896): 61–95.

Ulmann, Heinrich, ed. *Denkwürdigkeiten aus dem Dienstleben des Hessen-Darmstädtischen Staatsministers Freiherrn du Thil 1803–1848.* (Deutsche Geschichtsquellen des 19. Jahrhunderts, Vol. 3) Osnabrück, 1967 [1921].

Weech, Friedrich Otto Aristides von. *Correspondenzen und Actenstücke zur Geschichte der Minister-Conferenzen in den Jahren 1819, 1820 und 1834.* Leipzig, 1865.

Welcker, Carl Theodor. *Wichtige Urkunden für den Rechtszustand der deutschen Nation.* Mannheim, 1844.

Secondary Sources

Aegidi, Ludwig Karl. *Aus dem Jahr 1819.* Hamburg, 1861.

Albrecht, Curt. *Die Triaspolitik des Frhr. [Freiherr] K.[arl] Aug.[ust] v. Wangenheim.* [Darstellungen aus der Württembergischen Geschichte, Vol. 12.] Stuttgart, 1914.

Allgemeine Deutsche Biographie. Published by the Historische Commission bei der Königlichen Akademie der Wissenschaften Munich. 56 vols. Leipzig, 1875–1912.

Andreas, Willy. *Der Aufbau des Staates im Zusammenhang der allgemeinen Politik.* (Vol. 1, *Geschichte der Badischen Verwaltungsorganisation und Verfassung in den Jahren 1802–1818*, published by Badische Historische Kommission.) Leipzig, 1913.

Arneth, Alfred Ritter von. *Johann Freiherr von Wessenberg: Ein österreichischer Staatsmann des neunzehnten Jahrhunderts.* 2 vols. Vienna, 1898.

Austensen, Roy. "Einheit oder Einigkeit? Another Look at Metternich's View of the German Dilemma," *German Studies Review* 6 (February 1983): 41–57.

Baack, Lawrence J. *Christian Bernstorff and Prussia: Diplomacy and Reform Conservatism, 1818–1832.* New Brunswick, N.J., 1980.

Baumann, Kurt, ed. *Das Hambacher Fest, 27. Mai 1832: Männer und Ideen.* Speyer, 1982 [1957].

Beer, Adolf. *Die Österreichische Handelspolitik im neunzehnten Jahrhundert.* Vienna, 1891.

Berdahl, Robert M. "New Thoughts on German Nationalism." *American Historical Review* 77 (February 1972): 65–80.

Bertier de Sauvigny, Guillaume de. *Metternich.* Paris, 1986.

———. *Metternich et son temps.* Paris, 1959.

Biedermann, Karl. *Fünfundzwanzig Jahre deutsche Geschichte.* 2 vols. Breslau, 1890.

Billinger, Robert D., Jr. "The Austro-Russian Struggle for Germany and the Carlsbad Decrees, 1815–1820." Masters thesis, University of North Carolina at Chapel Hill, 1968.

———. "The German Confederation: Metternich's School of Nationalism for the German Princes, 1815–1834." *Proceedings of the Consortium on Revolutionary Europe.* 2 vols. Athens, Ga., 1980, 1: 174–82.

———. "Metternich's Policy Toward the South German States, 1830–1834," Ph.D. diss., University of North Carolina at Chapel Hill, 1973.

———. "They Sing the Best Songs Badly: Metternich, Frederick William IV, and the German Confederation during the War Scare of 1840–41," *Deutscher Bund und deutsche Frage, 1815–1866* (Wiener Beiträge zur Geschichte der Neuzeit, vol. 16/17) Vienna, 1990.

———. "The War Scare of 1831 and the Prussian-South German Attempt to End Austrian Dominance in Germany," *Central European History* 9 (September 1976): 203–19.

Binder, Wilhelm. *Fürst Clemens von Metternich und sein Zeitalter: Ein geschichtlich-biographische Darstellung.* Ludwigsburg, 1836.

Böck, Hanns Helmut. *Karl Philipp Fürst von Wrede als politischer Berater König Ludwig I. von Bayern (1825–1838): Ein Beitrag zur Geschichte der Regierung König Ludwig I.* (Miscellanea Bavarica Monacensia, no. 8.) Munich, 1968.

Botzenhart, Manfred. *Metternichs Pariser Botschafterzeit.* (Neue Münstersche Beiträge zur Geschichtsforschung, Vol. 10.) Münster, 1967.

Branchert, Albert. "Österreich und die Anfänge der preussisch-deutschen Zollvereins." Ph.D. diss. University of Marburg, 1930.

Branig, Hans. *Fürst Wittgenstein: Ein preussischer Staatsmann der Restaurationszeit* (Veröffentlichungen aus den Archiven Preussischer Kulturbesitz, Band 17). Cologne, 1981.

Burg, Peter. "Der Bund des konstitutionellen Deutschland in der europäischen Mächtkonstellation nach den Plänen aus der Zeit der Revolutionen von 1830 und ihrer Folgewirkungen" (Paper presented to the Working Group on the Revolutions of 1830 at the International Historical Congress in Bucharest, 1980).

————. "Die französische Politik gegenüber Föderationen und Föderationsplänen deutscher Klein- und Mittelstaaten 1830–1833," in Raymond Poidevin and Heinz Otto Sieburg, eds., *Aspects des relations franco-allemandes 1830–1848* (Publications du centre de recherches relations internationales de l'université de Metz, no. 9.) Metz, 1978.

————. *Der Wiener Kongress; Der Deutsche Bund im europäischen Staatensystem.* Munich, 1984.

Büssem, Eberhard. *Die Karlsbader Beschlüsse von 1819.* Hildesheim, 1974.

Corti, Egon Caesar Conte. *Metternich und die Frauen.* 2 vols. Vienna, 1948–1949.

Dcsacovszky, Valeria. "Das Ministerium des Fürsten Ludwig von Öttingen-Wallerstein 1832–1837." Ph.D. diss., University of Munich, 1932.

Dehio, Ludwig. "Wittgenstein und das letzte Jahrzehnt Friedrich III." *Forschungen zur brandenburgischen und preussischen Geschichte* 35 (1923): 213–40.

Derndarsky, Michael. "Österreich und der Deutsche Bund 1815–1866," in *Österreich und die deutsche Frage im 19. und 20. Jahrhundert* (Wiener Beiträge zur Geschichte der Neuzeit, vol. 9) Munich, 1982.

Doeberl, M. "Bayern und die wirtschaftliche Einigung Deutschlands." *Abhandlungen der Königlich Bayerischen Akademie der Wissenschaften. Philosophisch-phililogische und historische Klasse,* vol. 29, pt. 2. Munich, 1915, 1–117.

————. *Entwicklungsgeschichte Bayerns.* 3 vols. Munich, 1908–1912.

Droysen, Johann Gustav. "Zur Geschichte der preussischen Politik in den Jahren 1830–1832." *Zeitschrift für preussischen Geschichte und Landeskunde* 11 (1874): 583–697. Also published in Droysen, *Abhandlungen zur neueren Geschichte.* Leipzig, 1876.

Eich, Ulrike. *Russland und Europa: Studien zur russischen Deutschlandspolitik in der Zeit des Wiener Kongress* (Passauer Historische Forschungen, Bd. I.) Cologne, 1986.

Eichstädt, Volkmar. *Die deutsche Publizistik von 1830: Ein Beitrag zur Entwicklungsgeschichte der konstitutionellen und nationalen Tendenzen.* (Historische Studien, no. 232.) Berlin, 1933.

Faber, Karl-Georg. *Die Rheinlande zwischen Restauration und Revolution: Probleme der rheinischen Geschichte von 1814 bis 1848 im Spiegel der Zeitgenössischen Publizistik.* Wiesbaden, 1966.

Gauer, Wilhelm. "Badischen Staatsräson und Frühliberalismus um die Juliwende: Regierung, Presse und öffentliche Meinung in Baden 1830–32: Ein Versuch." *Zeitschrift für Geschichte der Oberrheins* 84 (1932): 341–406.

Gerber, Harry. "Der Frankfurter Wachensturm von 3. April 1833. Neue Beiträge zu seinem Verlauf und seiner behördlichen Untersuchung." *Quellen und Darstellungen zur Geschichte der Burschenschaft und der deutschen Einheitsbewegung* 14 (1934): 171–212.

Glossy, Carl. *Literarische Geheimberichte aus dem Vormärz.* Vienna, 1912.

Gollwitzer, Heinz. *Ludwig I. von Bayern. Königtum in Vormärz: Eine politische Biographie.* Munich, 1986.

Grauer, Karl-Johannes. *Wilhelm I. König von Württemberg: Ein Bild seines Lebens und seiner Zeit.* Stuttgart, 1960.

Grube, Walter. *Der Stuttgarter Landtag 1457–1957.* Stuttgart, 1957.

Gruner, Wolf D. "Der Deutsche Bund—Modell für eine Zwischenlösung?" *Politik und Kultur* (Heft 5, 1982): 22–42.

————. *Die deutsche Frage: Ein Problem der europäischen Geschichte seit 1800.* Munich, 1985.

————. "Die Deutsche Politik Ludwig I," *Zeitschrift für bayerische Landesgeschichte* 49 (Heft 2, 1986): 449–507.

————. "Europa, Deutschland und die internationale Ordnung im 19. Jahrhundert," *Politik und Kultur* (Heft 2, 1984): 24–53.

————. "Europäischer Friede als Nationales Interesse. Die Rolle des Deutschen Bundes in der Britischen Politik 1814–1832," *Jahrbuch des Collegium Carolinum,* vol. 18. Munich, 1977.

Grunwald, Constantin Count de. *La vie de Metternich.* Paris, 1939.

Guichen, Eugène de. *La révolution de Juillet 1830 et l'Europe.* Paris, 1916.

Hahn, Hans-Werner. *Wirtschaftliche Integration im 19. Jahrhundert: Die hessischen Staaten und der Deutsche Zollverein* (Kritische Studien zur Geschichtswissenschaft, vol. 52.) Göttingen, 1982.

Hammer, Karl. *Die Französische Diplomatie der Restoration und Deutschland 1814–1830.* (Pariser Historische Studien, vol. 2.) Stuttgart, 1963.

Heer, Georg. *Geschichte der Deutschen Burschenschaft,* vol. 2: *Die Demogenzeit: Von den Karlsbader Beschlüssen bis zum Frankfurter Wachensturm (1820–1833).* (Quellen und Darstellungen zur Geschichte der Burschenschaft und der deutschen Einheitsbewegung, vol. 10.) Heidelberg, 1927.

Heigel, Karl Theodor. "Das Hambacher Fest von 27. Mai 1832." *Historische Zeitschrift* 111 (1913): 54–88.

Heilman, J. *Feldmarschall Fürst von Wrede.* Leipzig, 1881.

Hillebrand, Karl. *Geschichte Frankreichs von der Thronbesteigung Louis Philipp's bis zum Falle Napoleon's III.* 3 vols. Gotha, 1877–1898.

Hippel, Wolfgang von. *Freidrich Landolin Karl von Blittersdorff 1792–1861: Ein Beitrag zur badischen Landtags- und Bundespolitik im Vormärz.* (Veröffentlichungen der Kommission für Geschichtliche Landeskunde in Baden-Württemberg, Reihe B: Forschungen, vol. 38.) Stuttgart: 1967.

Hölzle, Erwin. "Der Deutsche Zollverein: Nationalpolitisches aus seiner Vorgeschichte." *Württembergische Jahrbücher für Statistik und Landeskunde,* 1932–1933. Edited by the Statistisches Landesamt. Stuttgart, 1935, 131–145.

Hörmann, Liselotte von. *Der bayerisch-badische Gebeitstreit (1825–1832).* (Historische Studien, no. 336.) Berlin, 1938.

Hoffmann, Kurt M. *Preussen und die Julimonarchie 1830–1834.* (Historische Studien, no. 288.) Berlin, 1936.

Huber, Ernst Rudolf. *Deutsche Verfassungsgeschichte seit 1789.* 7 vols. Stuttgart, 1957–1984.

Hubner, Gustav. *Kriegsgefahr über Europa (1830–1832): Im Urteil der Zeit und hundert Jahre später.* (Neue Deutsche Forschungen, Abteilung Neuere Geschichte, vol. 2.) Berlin, 1936.

Ilse, Leopold Fr. *Geschichte der deutschen Bundesversammlung insbesondere ihres Verhalten zu den deutschen National-Interessen.* 3 vols. Marburg, 1861–1862; reproduced by Verlag Dr. H. A. Gerstenberg, Hildesheim, 1972.

———. *Geschichte der politische Untersuchungen welche durch die neben der Bundesversammlung errichteten Commission, der Central-Untersuchungs-Commission zu Mainz und der Bundes-Central-Behörde zu Frankfurt in den Jahren 1819 bis 1827 und 1833 bis 1842 geführt sind.* Frankfurt a.M., 1860.

———. *Die Politik der beiden Grossmächte und der kurhessischen Verfassungsfrage vom Jahre 1830 bis 1860.* Berlin, 1861.

Kaltenborn, Carl von. *Geschichte der deutschen Bundesverhältnisse und Einheitsbestrebungen von 1806 bis 1850.* 2 vols. Berlin, 1852.

Kann, Robert A. "Metternich: A Reappraisal of his Impact on International Relations." *Journal of Modern History* 32 (December 1960): 333–39.

Kissinger, Henry A. *A World Restored: Metternich, Castlereagh and the Problems of Peace, 1812–1822.* Boston, 1957.

Kraehe, Enno E. *Metternich's German Policy.* 2 vols. Princeton, 1963–1983.

———. "Raison d'état et idéologie dans la politique Allemande de Metternich (1809–1820)." *Histoire moderne et contemporaine* 13 (July–Sept. 1966): 181–194.

Lang, Wilhelm. *Von und aus Schwaben.* 3 vols. Stuttgart, 1885–1886.

Lee, Lloyd. *The Politics of Harmony: Civil Service, Liberalism, and Social Reform in Baden, 1800–1850.* Newark, Del., 1980.

Leininger, Franz und H. Haupt. "Zur Geschichte des Frankfurter Attentats." *Quellen und Darstellungen zur Geschichte der Burschenschaft und der deutsche Einheitsbewegung* 5 (1920): 133–48.

Lutz, Heinrich. *Zwischen Habsburg und Preussen: Deutschland 1815–1866.* Berlin, 1985.

Nipperday, Thomas. *Deutsche Geschichte 1800–1866: Bürgerwelt und starker Staat.* Munich, 1983.

Palmer, Alan. *Metternich.* New York, 1972.

Petzold, A. "Die Zentral-Untersuchungs-Kommission in Mainz." *Quellen und Darstellungen zur Geschichte der Burschenschaft und der deutschen Einheitsbewegung* 5 (1920): 171–258.

Price, Arnold. *The Evolution of the Zollverein: A Study of the Ideas and Institutions Leading to German Economic Unification Between 1815 and 1833.* (University of Michigan Publications, History and Political Science, vol. 17.) Ann Arbor, 1949.

Quint, Wolfgang. *Souveränitätsbegriff und Souveränitätspolitik in Bayern. Von der Mitte des 17. bis zur ersten Hälfte des 19. Jahrhunderts.* (Schriften zur Verfassungsgeschichte, vol. 15.) Berlin, 1971.

Reinerman, Alan. *Austria and the Papacy in the Age of Metternich.* 2 vols. Washington, D.C., 1979–1989.

———. "Metternich and Reform: The Case of the Papal States, 1814–1848." *Journal of Modern History* 42 (December 1970): 524–48.

Reinöhl, Fritz. "Die österreichischen Informationsbüros des Vormärz, ihre Akten und Protokolle." *Archivalische Zeitschrift* 38 (1929): 261–88.

Richter, Franz. *Das Europäische Problem der preussischen Staatspolitik und die revolutionäre Krisis von 1830 bis 1832*. (Forschungen zur neueren und neuesten Geschichte, no. 2.) Leipzig, 1933.

Rieben, Hans. *Prinzipiengrundlage und Diplomatie in Metternichs Europapolitik 1815–1848*. (Berner Untersuchungen zur Allgemeinen Geschichte, no. 12.) Aarau, 1942.

Reig, Gisbert. "Die württembergischen Aussenpolitik und Diplomatie in der vormärzlichen Zeit." Ph.D. diss., University of Munich, 1954.

Sagnac, Philippe. "La Crise de l'occident et la question du rhin: Essai sur l'esprit public en France et en Allemagne (1830–1840)." *Revue des études napoleonienne* 16 (1919): 282–300.

Sauer, Paul. *Das württembergische Heer in der Zeit des Deutschen und des Norddeutschen Bund*. (Veröffenlichungen der Kommission für Geschichtliche Landeskunde in Baden-Württemberg, Reihe B: Forschungen, vol. 5.) Stuttgart, 1958.

Schiemann, Theodor. *Geschichte Russlands unter Kaiser Niklaus I*. 4 vols. Berlin, 1904–1919.

Schroeder, Paul W. *Metternich's Diplomacy at Its Zenith, 1820–1823*. Austin, 1962.

———. "Metternich Studies Since 1925." *Journal of Modern History* 33 (September 1961): 237–60.

Sheehan, James J. "What is German History? Reflections on the Role of the Nation in German History and Historiography." *Journal of Modern European History* 53 (March 1981): 1–23.

Spindler, Max. "Die Regierungszeit Ludwig I (1825–1848), *Bayerische Geschichte im 19. und 20. Jahrhundert, 1800–1970*, 2-pt. vol. (Munich, 1978) (Spec. ed. and unchanged reproduction of Max Spindler, ed., *Handbuch der bayerischen Geschichte*, Vol. 4: *Das neue Bayern, 1800–1970*, 2-pt. vol. Munich, 1974–1975.)

Srbik, Heinrich Ritter von. *Deutsche Einheit: Idee und Wirklichkeit von Heiligen Reich bis Königgrätz*. 4 vols. Munich, 1935.

———. *Metternich der Staatsmann und der Mensch*. 3 vols. Munich, 1925–1954.

———. Review of *Metternich in neuer Beleuchtung* by Viktor Bibl, *Mitteilungen des österreichischen Instituts für Geschichtsforschung* 42 (1927/28): 397–409.

Stern, Alfred. *Geschichte Europas seit den Verträgen von 1815 bis zum Frankfurter Frieden von 1871*. 10 vols. Berlin, 1913–1924.

Treitschke, Heinrich von. *Deutsche Geschichte im neunzehnten Jahrhundert*. 5 vols. Leipzig, 1879–1894.

———. "Preussen und das Bundeskriegswesen 1831." *Forschungen zur brandenburgischen und preussischen Geschichte* 2 (1889): 223–31. (Also in Appendix 20 in Treitschke, *Deutsche Geschichte*, 4: 740–45.)

Valentin, Veit. *Das Hambacher Nationalfest*. Berlin, 1932.

Veit-Brause, Irmline. "Die deutsch-französische Krise von 1840: Studien zur deutschen Einheitsbewegung." Ph.D. diss., Cologne, 1967.

Viereck, Peter. *Conservatism Revisited*. New York, 1949.

Wallenberg, Margaret Kruse. "The Revolutions of the 1830s and the Rise of German Nationalism." Ph.D. diss., Radcliffe College, 1962.

Webster, Charles K. *The Foreign Policy of Castlereagh, 1815–1822: Britain and the European Alliance*. London, 1934 [1925].

———. *The Foreign Policy of Palmerston, 1830–1841: Britain, the Liberal Movement and the Eastern Question*. 2 vols. New York, 1969.

Werner, George S. *Bavaria in the German Confederation, 1820–1848*. Rutherford, N.J., 1977.

Wertheimer, Eduard. "Erzherzog Karl und das Juli-Königtum." *Beilage zur Allgemeinen Zeitung* (Munich), nr. 126 (4 June 1902): 417–19.

Willis, Geoffrey Malden. *Ernst August, König von Hannover*. Hanover, 1961.

Winter, Alexander. *Karl Philipp Fürst von Wrede als Berater des Königs Max Joseph und der Kronprinzen Ludwig von Bayern (1813–1825)*. (Miscellanea Bavarica Monacensia, no. 7.) Munich, 1968.

Zuber, Karl-Heinz. *Der "Fürst Proletarier," Ludwig von Öttingen-Wallerstein (1791–1870)*. (Zeitschrift für Bayerische Landesgeschichte, Beiheft [Reihe B] nr. 10.) Munich, 1978.

Index